Luis de Molina's *De Iustitia et Iure*

Studies in the History of Christian Traditions

VOLUME 152

Luis de Molina's *De Iustitia et Iure*

Justice as Virtue in an Economic Context

By

Diego Alonso-Lasheras

BRILL

LEIDEN • BOSTON
2011

This book is printed on acid-free paper.

Library of Congress Cataloging-in-Publication Data

Alonso-Lasheras, Diego.
Luis de Molina's De iustitia et iure : justice as virtue in an economic context / by Diego Alonso-Lasheras.
p. cm. – (Studies in the history of Christian traditions ; v. 152)
Includes bibliographical references and index.
ISBN 978-90-04-20225-2 (hbk. : alk. paper)
1. Molina, Luis de, 1535-1600. De justitia et jure. 2. Economics–Religious aspects–Catholic Church. 3. Christian ethics–Catholic authors. 4. Thomas, Aquinas, Saint, 1225?-1274. Summa theologica. Secunda secundae. Quaestio 57-79. I. Title.

BX1749.T6M6533 2011
241'.6426–dc22

2011003307

ISSN 1573-5664
ISBN 978 90 04 20225 2

To my parents

In memoriam Andrés Alonso-Lasheras Smith

CONTENTS

ACKNOWLEDGEMENTS

This book developed out of my doctoral dissertation at Weston Jesuit School of Theology (Cambridge, Massachusetts) in 2007. Although an extremely lonesome task, writing a doctoral dissertation is always and also a communal task. The work that I present is clearly mine, especially in its shortcomings, but it would not have been possible without the help and the welcome presence of many people.

I thank the administration, the staff and the faculty of the Weston Jesuit School of Theology, especially Sr. Diane Dube, Ms. Terry Lima and Mr. Gus Garzon; they have been for me the 'kind face' of the school.

I thank all those who have helped me reading and correcting the dissertation, and the manuscript for this book: Fr. John Paris, S.J., Mr. Gus Garzon, Ms. Lucretia Yaghjian, Fr. Paul McCarty, S.J., James Hooks, S.J., Fr. Gerald Wehlan, S.J. and Fr. William Dingwall, OCSO.

I thank Fr. Thomas Massaro, S.J. for directing my dissertation. He accepted this role immediately without ever having met me. I thank Fr. James F. Keenan, S.J. and Fr. David Hollenbach, S.J. for accompanying the process as readers. I received from the three of them support, helpful insights and examples of solid scholarship.

I thank my Jesuit brothers for their support along the way: my former provincial Fr. Alfredo Verdoy, S.J. who allowed me to pursue studies in the USA; many friends in Spain, Italy and the USA for their moral support. They all showed me the universal face of the Society of Jesus. They have also taught me what St. Francis Xavier once said: "*Societas Iesu societas amoris*."

I also thank many other non Jesuit friends who have encouraged me with their support and care in the USA and in Spain. I especially want to mention the parishioners of St. Benedict's Parish in Sommerville, the St. John's Community, the inmates at Norfolk MCI and Nicolas Thicrry. They have all been a part of my experience of ministry and they have reminded me that my studies ought to be directed to the service of Christ and his Church.

I thank my brother Rafael and my sister-in-law Sara, my nieces Lucia and Victoria and my nephew Tomás for their love. I want to offer this work to the memory of my late nephew Andrés who died at the age of five months when I was writing the dissertation. May we all be one day reunited with him.

I especially thank my parents who have always loved me and supported me in all my endeavors; from them I have learnt the concern for social justice and the virtue of generosity. I dedicate this work to them. What I do and what I am, I owe it to them.

INTRODUCTION

In presenting a book on the moral theology of economic issues of a scholastic author such as Luis de Molina who lived, wrote and died more than 400 years ago, there are at least two questions that should be addressed from the beginning: why this author and how his work will be approached.

The discovery of the importance of Spanish scholastics for the history of economics is a rather recent one. The first work to discuss the significance of the topic is that of Marjorie Grice-Hutchinson, *The School of Salamanca*.[1] In this exploration of the monetary theory of the Spanish scholastics, she concluded that

> since the work of the School of Salamanca long continued to endure in other branches of law and theology, it seems at least possible that their monetary theory was also read and that it has played its part in the shaping of modern doctrine.[2]

Her work, though a short one, opened the way to further studies, and thereafter Luis de Molina has been taken into consideration by the historians of economics.[3] Francisco Gómez Camacho, S.J., in the wake of Grice-Hutchinson's earlier work, is perhaps the foremost figure who has dedicated himself to translating and popularizing Molina's works in the field of the history of economics.[4]

---

[1] "Yet Spanish economic literature, particularly of the sixteenth, seventeenth, and eighteenth centuries, is so extensive and interesting that it would take a whole series of monographs to do it justice." Marjorie Grice-Hutchinson, *The School of Salamanca; Readings in Spanish Monetary Theory, 1544–1605* (Oxford: Clarendon Press, 1952). ix.

[2] Ibid. 58.

[3] An account of the academic discussion can be found in the introduction to Marjorie Grice-Hutchinson, Laurence S. Moss, and Christopher K. Ryan, *Economic Thought in Spain: Selected Essays* (Brookfield, Vt.: E. Elgar, 1993). x–xv. An unpublished dissertation in Harvard's Widener library is: William Seavey Joyce, "The Economics of Luis de Molina: a Study in the Development of Scholastic Economics in the Sixteenth Century." (Harvard University, 1949).

[4] Francisco Gómez Camacho, "En torno a unos textos de Luis De Molina sobre la propiedad privada," *Revista española de teología* (1977). Francisco Gómez Camacho, "La 'estimación común' en la teoría molinista del precio justo," *Revista española de teología* (1978). Francisco Gómez Camacho, "Luis de Molina y la metodología de la ley natural," *Miscelánea Comillas* 43, no. 83 (1985). Francisco Gómez Camacho, *Orígenes del pensamiento económico en La Mancha: Luis de Molina, 1° Congreso de Historia*

In his encyclopedic *History of Economic Analysis*, Joseph A. Schumpeter states (in addressing the contribution of the scholastic doctors of the sixteenth and seventeenth centuries) that "it is with their system of moral theology and law that economics gained definite if not separate existence, and it is they who come nearer than does any other group to having been the 'founders' of scientific economics."[5] In his appreciation for the scholastic doctors he might have been influenced by Bernard Dempsey, S.J., who completed his doctorate at Harvard in 1940 working under Schumpeter.[6] Schumpeter wrote the prologue to Dempsey's book *Interest and Usury*, in which he surveys, along with contemporary interest theory, the contributions of Luis de Molina, Leonard Lessius and Juan de Lugo on the topic of usury.[7]

Schumpeter points out that in the scholastic tradition of natural law theory two concepts of natural law can be distinguished: the ethico-legal concept and the analytic concept. In describing the ethico-legal concepts, he points to Molina's development of the received doctrine.[8] What is most original is what he calls the analytic concept of natural law. Although he does not define it, he describes how it works. Schumpeter realizes how important circumstances are for Molina:

> [I]n order to find out what is naturally just in a particular case, it is first necessary to analyze these circumstances. The generalizations that we may derive by doing so can be called natural law in the analytic sense: the normative natural law presupposes an explanatory natural law.[9]

---

de Castilla-La Mancha, vol. VII (La Mancha: Junta de Comunidades de Castilla-La Mancha, 1988). Francisco Gómez Camacho, *Economía y filosofía moral: la formación del pensamiento económico europeo en la escolástica española*, (Madrid: Síntesis, 1998). Francisco Gómez Camacho, "Later Scholastic: Spanish Economic Thought," in *Ancient and Medieval Economic Ideas and Concepts of Social Justice*, ed. S. Todd Lowry and Barry Gordon (Leiden; New York: Brill, 1998). Francisco Gómez Camacho, "Introduction," in *Sourcebook in Late-Scholastic Monetary Theory. Contributions of Martin de Azpilicueta, Luis de Molina S.J. and Juan de Mariana, S.J.*, ed. Stephen J. Grabill (Lanham: Lexington Books, 2007).

[5] Joseph Alois Schumpeter and Elisabeth Boody Schumpeter, *History of Economic Analysis* (New York: Oxford University Press, 1954). 97. In a footnote just two pages earlier he says: "I am positive that [Lessius, Molina and de Lugo] must be included in any history of economics."

[6] Bernard William Dempsey, "A Comparative Study in Interest Theories" (Thesis (Ph.D.), Harvard University 1940).

[7] Bernard William Dempsey, *Interest and Usury*, (Washington D.C.: American Council on Public Affairs, 1943).

[8] Schumpeter and Schumpeter. 109.

[9] Ibid. 111–112.

In economic analysis Schumpeter describes the nature of the thing—the particular case analyzed—as the "social pattern involved, as viewed from a utilitarian Common Good or social expediency."[10] Drawing on Molina, Schumpeter helps to establish a bridge between ethics and economics, although he is basically interested in the economic theory of the scholastic doctors and not in their moral theology.[11]

Raymond de Roover, a scholar of economic history and the history of economic thought, dedicated some of his works to developing the points Schumpeter had introduced in summary fashion.[12] He valued *De Iustitia et Iure* as a great work of scholastic economics.[13] He especially takes into account Molina's doctrines on monopolies[14] and price theory.[15]

De Roover says that the scholastics did not have a general theory of economics, but he concedes that they had a philosophical one.[16] We would add that modern economists have been able to develop a general theory of economics through abstraction and mathematization, and also

---

[10] Ibid.

[11] "A modern economist may both analyze the phenomenon of price discrimination and pass a value judgment upon it. If he does the latter by calling it unjust, he is adopting a natural-law rule that does not differ, in this case, from that of the scholastics. If he approves of the Robinson-Patman Act, which forbids discrimination, he does what the scholastics would have done in their day by saying that this act is valid law because it conforms to an imperative of natural law. We may indeed call this, or any value judgment of any kind, unscientific or extrascientific. But there is no point in throwing out the analytic baby with the philosophic bath-water. And this is precisely what is being done by those who dismiss economics of the scholastic doctors or their laical successors merely by pointing to its associations with a system of moral and legal imperatives of natural laws in the analytic sense because of its association with a system of natural laws in the normative sense." Ibid. 111.

[12] Raymond Adrien de Roover, *Monopoly Theory Prior to Adam Smith: A Revision* (Cambridge, Mass.: Harvard University Press, 1951). Raymond Adrien de Roover, "The Scholastic Attitude toward Trade and Entrepeneurship." in *Business, Banking, and Economic Thought in Late Medieval and Early Modern Europe*, ed. Julius Kirschner (Chicago: University of Chicago Press, 1974). Raymond Adrien de Roover, *La pensé économique des scolastiques: doctrines et méthodes*, Conference Albert-Le-Grand 1970 (Montreal: Inst. d'Études Médiévales, 1971). Raymond Adrien de Roover, *L'évolution de la lettre de change, XIVe–XVIIIe siècles*, Affaires et Gens d'Affaires, 4 (Paris: A. Colin, 1953).

[13] de Roover, "The Scholastic Attitude toward Trade and Entrepeneurship." 275.

[14] Ibid. 280.

[15] "Luis Molina, toutefois, à la fin du XVIe siècle, déclare que la valeur et, pourtant, le prix dépendent des préférences des acheteurs; il cite en exemple les Africains qui affectionnent la verroterie à tel point qu'ils sont disposés à l'acheter à prix d'or. Par conséquent, toujours selon Molina, la valeur repose sur une évaluation qui est un processus mental dans lequel la psychologie de l'acheteur joue un rôle déterminant." de Roover, *La pensé économique des scolastiques, doctrines et méthodes*. 49.

[16] Ibid. 17–18.

by isolating economics from other social disciplines. This has also created distortions regarding the task of situating the role of the economy in the context of our lives and of placing economics within the matrix of the sciences. The scholastics did not propose a comprehensive theory of economics, but for its part modern economics fails in most cases to provide a consistent anthropology.

In *Economic Analysis before Adam Smith*, Barry Gordon dedicates the last chapters of his book to the scholastic doctors. According to Gordon, in "the hands of the Jesuit doctors of Spain in the latter half of the sixteenth century, *lucrum cessans* is established firmly as a common basis for the receipt of interest."[17] In addition, he considers that with Azpilicueta's innovation regarding the theory of money, "the clear relationship of the "value of money" to "purchasing power" was accepted, thanks to the support of men like Molina and Lessius."[18] For Molina this was not just a theoretical disquisition but a problematic current matter. He was aware that the sheer quantity of gold and silver coming from America was significantly driving up prices.[19]

A more recent account of scholastic economic thought is *Faith and Liberty* by Alejandro Chafuen,[20] a revision of his previous work *Christians for Freedom*.[21] This is a book of spirited apologetics that tries to "show the compatibility between the Catholic faith and the principles of the free economy."[22] The book is shallow in its analysis of scholastic natural law theory, and it fails to acknowledge the differences displayed by scholastic authors. These differences hold enormous practical consequences. In his analysis of the natural law, Chafuen uses Schumpeter's differentiation of the ethico-legal concept and the analytic concept as if

---

[17] Barry Gordon, *Economic Analysis before Adam Smith: Hesiod to Lessius* (London: Macmillan, 1975). 203.

[18] Ibid. 213–214.

[19] Marjorie Grice-Hutchinson, *Early Economic Thought in Spain, 1177–1740* (London; Boston: Allen & Unwin, 1978).

[20] Alejandro Antonio Chafuen, *Faith and Liberty: The Economic Thought of the Late Scholastics*, Studies in Ethics and Economics (Lanham, Md.: Lexington Books, 2003).

[21] Alejandro Antonio Chafuen, *Christians for Freedom: Late-Scholastic Economics* (San Francisco: Ignatius Press, 1986).

[22] Chafuen, *Faith and Liberty: The Economic Thought of the Late Scholastics*. 12. An illustration of the nature of the book is found in its concluding paragraph: "Private property is rooted in human freedom, which is founded in human nature, which, like any other nature, is created by God. Private property is the essential prerequisite for economic freedom. Many people are currently attempting to dry up its roots. It will take a new wave of Scholastic thought to save them, to return the plant of civilization to its natural fruitfulness." 60.

it were the author's own, failing to attribute the distinction to Schumpeter.[23] Another problem with the book is that it ignores the work of Francisco Gómez Camacho on the economic doctrines of the Spanish scholastics and especially of Luis de Molina. Camacho's analysis stresses the point that we cannot take the assertions of the scholastics and transplant them to our times in a facile way. This is precisely what Chafuen attempts to do. The most recent work on late-scholastic economics *The Salamanca School*,[24] follows in Chafuen's wake. It is also a good example of how it is impossible to read these authors from an economic point of view without taking into account that, first of all, they were theologians.

The studies of the last 40 years have helped to establish the importance of the scholastics in economic thought and particularly their influence on Adam Smith and modern economics.[25] Commentators like Chafuen attempt to exploit the scholastics to support their own argument. Chafuen specifically downplays both the subtleness of scholastic theology and how they could defend different and seemingly opposed plans of action without falling into relativism. In doing so, he neglects to recognize their signal achievements in the field of economic theory.

The importance given by historians of economic thought to Luis de Molina and his work *De Iustitia et Iure*, along with the undeniable importance of Molina for the history of Catholic theology,[26] is what led

---

[23] Ibid. 20.

[24] André Azevedo Alves and José Manuel Moreira, *The Salamanca School* (New York-London: Continuum, 2010).

[25] "In the case of Adam Smith, the ascendance which links him to scholasticism passes through his teacher, Francis Hutcheson, Samuel Pufendorf, and Hugo Grotius. Smith's library contained copies of both Grotius and Pufendorf. Moreover, there is evidence that Adam Smith read Grotius at the age of fifteen when he was a student at Glasgow College. At that time, his teacher was using as a textbook a translation of Pufendorf's *De Officio Hominis et Civis* by Gershom Carmichael (d. 1729), Hutcheson's predecessor in the chair of Moral Philosophy. In his lectures on political economy, as already stated, Hutcheson dealt with the subject in scholastic fashion as a branch of natural jurisprudence, particularly as 'a discussion of contracts.'" de Roover, "The Scholastic Attitude toward Trade and Entrepeneurship." 333.

[26] One of the more recent testimonies of the theological importance of Luis de Molina can be found in Bernard Quilliet, *L'acharnement théologique. Histoire de la grâce en Occident—IIIe-XXIe siècles* (Paris: Fayard, 2007). *De Concordia* has recently been translated into Spanish and published: Luis de Molina, *Concordia del libre arbitrio*, trad. Juan Antonio Hevia Echevarria, (Oviedo: Fundación Gustavo Bueno, 2007). For the political implications of Molina's doctrines see: Paolo Broggio, *La teologia e la politica. Controversie dottrinali, Curia romana e Monarchia spagnola tra Cinque e Seicento* (Firenze: Leo S. Olschki Editore, 2009).

me to study how economics and ethics interact in his work. There is, however, a second question to address: in what way will Molina's work be approached in this present book?

The term 'Catholic Social Teaching' refers to the magisterial teaching of the popes, and more recently the bishop's conferences on socio-economic topics, starting with the epoch-making encyclical *Rerum Novarum* (1891). The merit of the body of literature created by the highest magisterial authorities of the Catholic Church can hardly be exaggerated. Catholic Social Teaching, however, is a very recent phenomenon in the history of the Church. To explain that the genre made its debut in 1891 might lead the reader to believe that the Church did not concern itself with socio-economic matters until the very end of the nineteenth century. *Rerum Novarum* certainly marks a turning point in the history of this category of official church teaching, because it is the first time that the highest teaching authority of the Church involved itself in the timely issue of the labor movement that the industrial revolution had unleashed. Yet there are many examples of Catholic social doctrine preceding *Rerum Novarum*.

Many theologians of different times occupied themselves with the socio-economic problems they encountered. If we go back in time, the next great upheaval we find in world history with socioeconomic consequences before the industrial revolution is the unrest caused by the European exploration and colonization of the world, started by Portugal and soon followed by Spain. These two countries made their presence felt in the world in an unprecedented way. According to Marcel Bataillon, Spaniards "roamed over as much territory in the 70 years after 1492 as had been explored in the previous thousand years by other Europeans."[27] However important the feats of the explorers were, it was matched by the theoretical reflection of the men who taught in the Spanish and Portuguese universities of the time. John Mahoney affirms that "the sixteenth-century and later work of Spanish moralists particularly, on warfare, human and property rights, and international law, especially as European conquest and colonialism were developing, is of abiding importance."[28]

---

[27] Quoted in C.H. Carter, "The New World as a Factor in Interantional Relations 1492–1793," ed. Fredi Chiappelli, Michael J.B. Allen, and Robert Louis Benson, *First Images of America: The Impact of the New World on the Old* (Berkeley: University of California Press, 1976). 365.

[28] John Mahoney, *The Making of Moral Theology. A Study of the Roman Catholic Tradition*. (Oxford: Claredon Press, 1987). 33.

Alasdair MacIntyre in his book *Whose Justice? Which Rationality?* writes that:

> [w]hat Enlightenment made us for the most part blind to and what we now need to recover is, so I shall argue, a conception of rational enquiry as embodied in a tradition, a conception according to which the standards of rational justification themselves emerge from and are part of a history in which they are vindicated by the way in which they transcend the limitations of and provide remedies for the defects of their predecessors within the history of that tradition.[29]

McIntyre goes on to give an account of Aquinas' thought on justice and practical rationality, and how he was able to weave together the Augustinian and Aristotelian traditions. He then leaps forward to the Scottish Enlightenment. In doing so he skips over five centuries, centuries that are very important to the history of moral theology. These five hundred years roughly coincide with the centuries analyzed by the great historian of moral theology Louis Vereecke in his book *Da Guglielmo d'Ockham a sant'Alfonso de Liguori.*[30] These are the centuries that start with the great medieval synthesis and end with the consolidation of the manualist tradition. According to Vereecke, we are 'sons' of this period.[31]

The aim of the present book is to contribute to social moral theology. It will show how the tradition, starting with Aquinas, grew and concretized itself in the second half of the sixteenth century in relation specifically to what today we call the discipline of economics, and this will be done presenting Luis de Molina's *De Iustitia et Iure.*

Luis de Molina was one of the last comprehensive theologians, by which I mean one of the last theologians to conduct his work before moral theology broke off as a discipline from the rest of theology. Molina's death in 1600 coincides with the publication of the *Institutiones morales* of Azor, which is considered by many historians of moral theology to be the key date in establishing the field as a distinct area of theology.[32]

---

[29] Alasdair C. MacIntyre, *Whose Justice? Which Rationality?* (Notre Dame, Ind: University of Notre Dame Press, 1988). 7.

[30] Louis Vereecke, *Da Guglielmo d'Ockham a sant'Alfonso de Liguori. Saggi di storia della teologia morale moderna. 1300–1787* (Cisinello Balsamo: Edizioni Paoline, 1990).

[31] Ibid. 30–31.

[32] "La comparsa all'inizio dell XVII secolo, precisamente nel 1600, delle *Institutiones Morales* del gesuita spagnolo Giovanni Azor, segna in teologia morale l'avvento di un nuovo genere letterario. Separata ormai dalla filosofia viva, dal dogma e anche da una teologia morale speculativa, ed estranea alla spiritualità e alla mistica, questa Theologia moralis practica, modesto sussidio per il confessore, si darà l'impegnativo titolo di Theolgia moralis." Vereecke. 31–32. In his book *Time Past, Time Future* John A. Gallagher

Molina is most famous for his articulation of the relationship between grace and freedom. His book the *Concordia* has gained him a place in the history of theology. But Molina did not occupy himself merely in topics that fall, according to our contemporary division of theology, within the field of systematics. Molina was also concerned with moral issues, his *De Iustitia et Iure*, in which he addressed issues of justice relevant to his age, is his contribution to the field.

Molina's *De Iustitia et Iure* was originally conceived as a commentary on questions 57 to 79 in Aquinas' *Secunda Secundae* of the *Summa* which discuss the virtue of justice. The problems addressed in this massive work are related to the discipline known today as social ethics. Molina's final work was more far-reaching than a mere commentary on Aquinas' work, he dealt with justice and law in a more detailed way than Aquinas did, and discussed topics Thomas did not explore.[33]

This present book is not meant to focus on economic theory. It is necessary, however, to study the work of the scholastic doctors in this field because the economic point of view of their time was much different from that of today. One reason, of course, is that today's economic problems are particular to our age, but a more important reason is that they include in their analysis dimensions of humanity and human society not taken into consideration by modern economics. It is thus necessary to understand the scholastics' paradigm of economics and society in order to evaluate their notion of justice in an economic context.

Previous studies tend to offer accounts of Molina's doctrines on particular issues: law, natural law, economics, and economic ethics. They do not examine justice as a virtue in the frame of the *respublica* or commonwealth, or justice as a personal virtue (in this case a virtue of the tradesman or of the ruler) according to the common practice of the sixteenth century. To show Molina's mind at work it is necessary to take into account the frame of the tradition he inherited, historical factors such as the economic realities of his age, and his own personal genius.

---

also asserts the importance of the manuals in any adequate understanding of the history of moral theology. His book is a history of the whole manualist era. The first of the manuals is Azor's *Institutiones morales*. See John A. Gallager, *Time Past, Time Future* (Mahawh, NJ: Paulist Press, 1990).

[33] "hemos juzgado que sería util a la Iglesia y gratísimo a los teólogos, y aun necesario, que estas cuestiones se tratasen mucho más detenidamente y añadiendo otras que, sobre los contratos y otras cosas, el Angélico Doctor pasó por alto." Luis de Molina, *Los seis libros de la justicia y el derecho*, ed. Manuel Fraga Iribarne (Madrid: Impr. de J.L. Cosano, 1941). 123.

The goal of this book is to present Molina's moral theology on economic matters, at a time when economics and ethics still belonged to the same disciplinary matrix of moral philosophy. It discerns the pattern according to which bridges between economics and ethics are built. It also takes up matters of business ethics such as the character of the virtuous merchant, and investigates the political implication of how economic justice works out in the political body. The object of the investigation is not merely to undertake a historical examination of Molina's thought. We will go as far as to explore his basis of argumentation and his manner of reasoning with the certainty that, by going back to the tradition, we will be able to draw inspiration to deal with some of the problems of our time.

CHAPTER ONE

THE BIRTH OF A NEW WORLD: ECONOMICS AND THEOLOGY IN THE SIXTEENTH CENTURY

1. Introduction

In this chapter I will present the economic, scientific and theological contexts of the sixteenth century necessary to understand the work of Luis de Molina. The sixteenth century was, as I will show, a time of 'globalization', at least for the European mind. The European economy expanded to both the West and East Indies. Along with economic transformation, Europe saw the beginning of what was later called the Scientific Revolution. Theology did not stay behind these developments; it was actually part of them, restraining some tendencies, encouraging others.

We can say that Luis de Molina is a good example of a person in whom all these developments come together in a creative way. Hence, I will briefly present his life, and then I will present the general historical tendencies.

2. Luis de Molina

Luis de Molina emerges in the theological arena of the sixteenth century as a major figure. His works in systematic and moral theology were widely read and discussed. He also was a forerunner of economic theory, which he developed in his work *De Iustitia et Iure*. Molina embodied the theological, scientific and economic inquiries, developments and disputes of the late sixteenth century.

"In the life of Molina [...] there are few external deeds worthy of being remembered, as it happens with the life of many of those who teach, and far from public business and events, cross over from the solitude of his room to the crowd of the lecture room."[1] Johannes Rabeneck opens with

[1] "In vita Molinae, quam hic breviter enarrare intendimus, facta externa memoratu rara sunt, cum sicut multorum doctorum vita procul ab eventibus et a negotiis publicis

this remark in his biography—the best that currently exists—of Luis de Molina. Given the great controversies that Molina's work the *Concordia*[2] engendered, Rabeneck's assertion is an understatement.

Luis de Molina was born in September 1535 in Cuenca, Spain. He came from a family of hidalgos—the lower nobility. We know nothing of his childhood and primary education.[3] The little we do know is what he himself told the Jesuit Visitor Jerónimo Nadal in June or July 1561. He studied four years of grammar in his hometown. He then studied one year of law in Salamanca and six months in Alcalá.[4] What is unknown is why he interrupted his law studies and moved to Alcalá to take up theological studies.

It was in Alcalá on August 10, 1553 that Molina joined the Society of Jesus.[5] Molina was sent to Coimbra. During his second year as a novice Molina took classes at the university, where he studied philosophy for four years, from 1554 to 1558.[6] That last year he started his theological

---

intra cubiculi solitudinem et auditorii frequentiam transierit." Ioannes Rabeneck, "*De vita et scriptis Ludovici Molina*," *Archivium Storicum Societatis Iesu* (1950). 75.

[2] Luis de Molina, *Concordia Liberi Arbitrii Cvm Gratiae Donis: Divina Praescientia, Providentia, Praedestinatione, Et Reprobatione: Ad Nonnullos Primae Partis D. Thomae Articulos* (Olyssipone: Apud Antonium Riberium typographum Regium expensis Ioan-[n]is Hispani & Michaelis de Arenas bibliopolarum, 1588).

[3] "De su infancia y primera educación no tenemos cosa cierta." Alonso de Andrade, *Varones ilustres de la Compañía de Jesús* (Bilbao: 1891). 315. Quoted in Rabeneck. 79.

[4] "Habré estudiado doce años, quatro de grammática en Cuenca, uno de leies en Salamanca, y obra de seis meses de súmulas en Alcalá, todo esto antes de entrar en la Compañía." Gerónimo Nadal, *Epistolae P. Hieronumi Nadal Societatis Jesu, Ab Anno 1546 Ad 1577* (Matriti: Typis Augustini Avrial, 1898). 667.

[5] "El cual, considerando la santidad de aquellos religiosos, la paz con que moraban, el ejemplo con que procedían, el bien que hacían a todos y la alteza de su nuevo instituto, que era traer a Dios todo el mundo, poblar el cielo de almas, y en primero las suyas; obrando en su corazón la bondad divina, determinó de sacrificarse a Dios en esta nueva cruz de la Compañía, y, despreciando las esperanzas que tenía de valer en el mundo, seguir a Cristo desnudo, y no sólo crucificar su carne con todos sus apetitos, sino lo que (como dice San Jerónimo) es más difícil, sacrificar su voluntad, sujetándola al yugo de la obediencia." Andrade. 316.

[6] Historians have debated certain issues regarding Molina's philosophical studies, especially about whether he was a student of Pedro de Fonseca, called the Portuguese Aristotle, who disputed Molina's authorship of the idea of the *sciencia media*. It is a discussion not directly relevant to our research. For further information cfr: José de Oliveira Dias, "Ainda a controvertida paternidade da chamada ciência média," *Verbum* 11 (1951). 367–382. José de Oliveira Dias, "Em tôrno do duelo Fonseca-Molina. Uma argumentaçâo suicida," *Verbum* 11 (1954). 37–63. José de Oliveira Dias, "Fonseca e Molina. Os ultimos ecos dum litígio plurissecular," *Revista portuguesa de filosofia* II (1955). 64–67. Severiano Tavares, "A questáo Fonseca-Molina. Resposta a uma crítica," *Revista portuguesa de filosofia* II (1955). 78–88.

studies, which he pursued for three years. During his years in Coimbra he also taught philosophy.[7] He was ordained in 1561 or 1562 and then was sent to Evora to obtain a doctorate in theology, which he did not complete because he was sent back to Coimbra to teach philosophy.

In 1568 Molina was sent to Evora to teach theology. He lectured there until 1584. During all these years he commented on and glossed Aquinas' *Summa*. From September 1577 to July 1582 he lectured on IIª–IIae qq. 47–78, the questions dedicated to prudence and justice.[8] He dedicated a full five years of teaching to these 31 questions. It is by far the part of the *Summa* to which he dedicated the most time.[9] These lectures are the kernel of what was to become *De Iustitia et Iure*.

In 1584 Molina moved to Lisbon to work on the publication of his writings. Molina's project was a commentary on the entire Summa. Out of this vast project came the *Concordia liberii arbitri cum gratiae donis, divina praescientia, predestinatione et reprobatione*. The *Concordia* was the result of the commentary on some parts of questions 14, 19, 22 and 23 of the *Prima*, in which he tried to reconcile the problems of Divine Grace and human free will. Before publication, the controversy about the *Concordia* began.[10]

The dispute became a full theological war when in 1581 from Salamanca, Domingo Bañez tried to stop the publication of the book. The dispute was unending and was to last until well after Molina's death.[11] As Brodrick has noted, "[t]hat *Concordance* has caused more discord among theologians than anything published since the days of Arius."[12]

---

[7] "Estudié en Coimbra después de estar en la Compañía quatro años de artes, oiendo el último alguna teología. Después de esto, va en tres años que estudio teología, sustituyendo en artes alguna parte deste tiempo." Nadal. 667.

[8] Friedrich Stegmüller, *Geschichte des Molinismus* (Münster i. W.: Aschendorff, 1935). 6–7.

[9] On Iª–IIae qq. 1–76 he lectured from September 1568 to February 1570. On Iª qq. 1–74 he lectured from December of 1571 to July 1573. José Antonio de Aldama, "Luis de Molina: De Spe, II, qq. 17–22," *Archivo teológico granadino* I (1938).

[10] Manuscript copies of Molina's teachings were circulating. Although with time the work has come to be seen as the book that divided Jesuits from Dominicans, in the *De Auxilus* controversy, it was not so at the very beginning. Some Jesuits opposed the publication of the book, whereas Dominicans such as the General Inquisitor of Portugal approved it.

[11] A good account of these disputes in English can be found in James Brodrick, *Robert Bellarmine, Saint and Scholar* (Westminster, Md.: Newman Press, 1961). 189–216.

[12] James Brodrick, *The Progress of the Jesuits 1556–1579* (New York: Longmans, Green & Co., 1947). 132. Stegmüller holds a similar opinion when he says: "Kein Buch der neuren theologie hat wohl eine dramatischere Entstehungsgeschichte." Stegmüller. 1.

The book nevertheless received ecclesiastical approbation. It was first published in Lisbon in 1588.

In 1591 Molina returned to Spain where he was assigned to the Jesuit house in Cuenca, his hometown. There he continued the preparation of his writings for publication.[13] In 1593, the first volume of the *De Iustitia et Iure* was published. It was the evolution of the commentaries on the *Summa's* questions on justice, questions 57 to 80.[14]

Molina was forced out of his retirement in Cuenca. At what was then considered the advanced age of 65, Molina must have been in good health, as he was sent to Madrid in April 1600 to teach moral theology at the Imperial College. He had only been there six months when he died on 12 October 1600. Molina had begun his professional life as a theology professor who commented upon the *Summa*. He ended his life as a professor of moral theology, in the same year that Juan Azor published *Institutiones Morales*, the first manual of moral theology.[15]

3. The Birth of a New Economy

3.1. *The Shifting Center of Gravity*

According to Domenico Sella, "the most important event in the economic history of modern Europe is the discovery and colonization of the New World."[16] Many Europeans of the age realized the importance

[13] The first work to be published after the *Concordia* was his commentary on the first part of the *Summa*, of which his polemical book was originally but a section. Luis de Molina, *Commentaria in Primam Divi Thomae Partem: In Duos Tomos Divisa Adiectae Sunt Huic Secundae Editioni Eiusdem Autoris Disputationes, Ad Hanc Primam Partem D. Thomae Spectantes, Ex Libro Concordiae Liberi Arbitrij Cum Gratiae Donis, Excerptae* (Cuenca: Ex Officina Christiani Barnabae Typographi, 1592). Molina had become a 'hot' author. This work was reprinted in 1593 in Lyon and in 1594 in Venice.

[14] The twentieth century saw the publication of other parts of the vast project that had remained as manuscripts: Eduardo Moore, "Luis de Molina, S.J., De Caritate, Comentario a la II–II, qq 23–25," *Archivo teológico granadino* (1965). Eduardo Moore, "Luis de Molina, S.J., De Caritate, Comentario a la II–II, qq 26–29," *Archivo teológico granadino* (1966). Eduardo Moore, "Luis de Molina, S.J., De Fide, Comentario a la II–II, qq 1–16," *Archivo teológico granadino* (1976). Rafael Sánchez de Lamadrid, "Luis de Molina: De Bello, Comentario a la II–II, q. 40," *Archivo teológico granadino* (1939).

[15] Vereecke. 32. In his book *Time Past, Time Future*, John A. Gallager asserts the importance of the manuals in any adequate understanding of the history of moral theology. His book is a history of the whole manualist era. John A. Gallager, *Time Past, Time Future* (Mahawh, NJ: Paulist Press, 1990).

[16] Domenico Sella, "Las industrias europeas (1500–1700)," in *Historia económica de Europa*, ed. Carlo M. Cipolla (Barcelona: Ariel, 1979). 281.

of Columbus' voyages and their consequences. In his book for the use of merchants *Summa de tratos y contratos*, Tomás de Mercado, O.P., (1530?–1575) declared that "Andalusia and Portugal had passed, after the discovery of the Indies, from being the end of world to be the center of it."[17] The Iberian Peninsula, in fact, had been a peripheral part of Europe during the Middle Ages. The Portuguese exploration of the way to India around Africa, and the Spanish arrival in America entirely changed the European view of the world. It also changed the way Europe viewed itself. The center of gravity of economics, power, and culture on the continent started to shift from the Mediterranean to the Atlantic.[18] The way Europeans looked at the world, and the role of Europe in it, had entirely changed one century after Columbus's arrival in America in 1492 and Vasco da Gama's arrival in Calicut in 1498.

3.2. *Manufactures, Trade and the Curse of Gold*

One of the first consequences in Europe of the Spanish conquest of large areas of America was the arrival of remarkable quantities of gold. In the beginning the arrivals were not very large; they were just collections of gold in circulation in the newly conquered territories. Around the middle of the century, due to the exploitation of newly discovered mines and the improvement in the refining procedures, the quantities of precious metals shipped East through the Atlantic increased substantially.[19] Similarly, the Portuguese exploration of the coast of Africa brought gold to the

[17] Tomás de Mercado, *Summa de tratos y contratos* (Sevilla: Hernando Díaz, 1571). 17. Tomás de Mercado was born in Seville probably in 1530. He went to Mexico where he became a Dominican. He eventually became professor of theology and prior of the convent in the City of Mexico. He was sent to Salamanca to continue his studies. There he published his first version of the *Summa de tratos y contratos*. He later returned to Seville, where he republished the Summa, dedicated to the merchant's association. He died at sea while returning to Mexico in 1575.

[18] "El centro del nuevo Imperio ya no es Amberes, ni Italia, sino el océano Atlántico y la América minera cuyo peso mundial no hace sino crecer. Su centro ya no es Madrid, la nueva capital, que en 1561 sustituye a Valladolid, o Toledo sino Sevilla—incluso aunque ni el Rey Católico ni sus consejeros sean realmente conscientes de ello. Europa y el Mediterráneo, que les son tan familiares, siguen fascinándoles. Como siempre, los mayores acontecimientos no hacen, por así decir, ningún ruido: la faz del mundo se halla cambiada sin que realmente se hayan preocupado por ello." Fernand Braudel, *Carlos V y Felipe II* (Madrid: Alianza Editorial, 1999). 109–110.

[19] Between 1536 and 1540 four million of *pesos* of gold and silver were sent to Spain. Between 1576 and 1580 almost 30 millions crossed the Atlantic. For complete statistics of the arrival of precious metals see Pierre Vilar, *Oro y moneda en la historia. 1450–1920* (Barcelona: Ariel, 1969). 199.

European economy. According to Pierre Vilar, the arrival of large quantities of gold and silver was not mere chance, but the result of the European economy's quest for scarce precious metals.[20]

In its early stages, the arrival of silver and gold had a benign effect on the Spanish and Portuguese economies. The precious metals helped to increase demand for products that were shipped overseas. By the middle of the century, however, the amount of gold and silver grew to be greater than what the Iberian economies could accommodate. As a consequence, waves of inflation, which began in Andalusia and Portugal, spread throughout Europe, a situation defined by Earl J. Hamilton as a 'price revolution'.[21]

Because their capacity to adjust to price increases was limited, inflation began to affect people who lived on private incomes, leading to a redistribution of wealth. As an economic phenomenon, inflation and the resulting wealth redistribution was not new; history has always known times in which prices increase or decrease. What was new, however, was the speed with which this was happening. In the past, these phenomena occurred in ways that were difficult to observe and analyze. Now, however, they were taking place at a pace that made everyone aware of the situation, and this led moralists to begin to deal with them. The problem of a just price was not new to moral theologians. It had been discussed by many scholastic theologians during the Middle Ages. It usually referred to the price of basic staples and was tied to cases of speculation in times of scarcity. The novelty was the magnitude and rapidity of the price changes that affected all goods, acting as income redistributors,[22] which was a new aspect of the problem.[23]

The exploration of the world by Europeans not only resulted in the injection of large quantities of precious metals into the European economy. It also led to trade with the Indies, both East and West, which changed the practices of commerce. Large quantities of goods were

---

[20] "El descubrimiento de Colón no es, pues, una coincidencia 'extraeconómica'. Es el coronamiento de un proceso interno de la economía occidental en busca de oro y de especias, por razones coyunturales muy precisas, búsqueda cuyas vías mostró Portugal, pero que la España de 1492 y sus costas andaluzas estaban destinadas a ampliar." Ibid. 85.

[21] Earl J. Hamilton, *American Treasure and the Price Revolution in Spain, 1501–1650*, Harvard Economic Studies, V (New York: Octagon Books, 1965). 43.

[22] For a description of the process and the reflections of contemporaries see Vilar. 213–234.

[23] For the theological discussion regarding prices at the time, see Abelardo del Vigo, *Economía y ética en el siglo XVI* (Madrid: BAC, 2006). 568–650.

needed by the Portuguese for their trade. They needed goods in exchange for slaves and gold bought on the coasts of Africa, as well as spices and silks obtained in India, Indonesia, Japan and China. The Spanish colonization of America meant that large quantities of goods were shipped across the Atlantic to satisfy the demand for European products by the settlers and their descendants. At first, this trade included all kinds of goods, beginning with the basic staples that were common in Europe but unknown in Native American cultures. As Spanish society was reproduced in the colonies, imported goods were restricted to more sophisticated items such as wine, high quality textiles, weapons, books, paper, pottery and others.[24]

The inflationary problem caused by the large amounts of gold and silver arriving from America affected not only those who lived on fixed incomes, but the Spanish manufacturers as well, who had benefited in the beginning from the rise in prices. Spanish goods began to lose their competitiveness, and goods imported from other European countries began filling the holds of the ships crossing the Atlantic, which meant an increasing participation of foreign merchants in trade with the New World. Large colonies of Genovese and Flemish merchants settled in Seville. By 1575, much of what was shipped overseas was produced in the industrial centers of Europe, shipped to Seville, and then on to satisfy the demand in the New World. By the end of the century, Spanish manufacturers had lost ground to the French, English and Dutch. Seville became a trading post where goods that had been imported were re-exported across the Atlantic. By 1568 Jean Bodin, a noteworthy political thinker, was writing about the importance of American markets for French industries.[25] By the end of the sixteenth century moralists began to speak about the curse of gold ruining the realm.[26] The Cortes, the Spanish parliament, of 1586–1593 protested that Spain was serving as a mere bridge for the gold and silver arriving from America, which was leaving the country impoverished.[27]

[24] Sella. 283–284.
[25] Ibid. 284.
[26] Vilar. 230.
[27] "Con poder estar (nuestros reynos) los más ricos en el mundo oro y plata que en ellos ha entrado y entra de las Indias están los más pobres porque sólo sirven de puente para pasarlos a otros Reynos nuestros enemigos y de la Santa Fe Católica ..." quoted in Vilar. 231.

3.3. *New Financial Instruments: Companies, Bills of Exchange and Lending*

Trade had been growing and developing in Europe ever since the eleventh century, albeit with the occasional crisis. Along with trade, financial markets and financial instruments developed. In the sixteenth century new means of trade appeared, and previous restrictions on commercial opportunities and practices were lifted.

Since the Middle Ages merchants had formed associations to share in the risk of commercial shipping. The new trade with Asia and America required larger vessels and longer expeditions. This meant that shipping expeditions were more expensive and involved greater risk, and if successful proved more profitable. New modes of association were born. The medieval associations had been modes of maritime insurance. The new trade resulted in the emergence of well developed and stable companies.[28] The moral and economic problems of risk and profit, as well as the question of the price of goods, were thereby transformed.

As trade expanded geographically, in both type and quantity, the arrival of immense amounts of precious metals also affected the common people. The practice of barter and the payment of taxes through labor became less and less common. A monetarization of the economy occurred. As it was impractical to ship large quantities of minted gold and silver from one city to another, merchants needed more than just cash for their trade.

The use of exchange bills became a widespread practice because it allowed payments to be made in different cities. Tomás de Mercado described the common practices of discounting exchange bills, and discussed whether or not this constituted usury. He acknowledged that exchange bills, although not the same, were akin to usury. His chapter on exchange bills is quite extensive, because according to him this type of trade required special help to be understood, noting that exchange is "the art and trade most scrupulous and dangerous of all those that in good conscience can be practiced."[29] He distinguished two types of

---

[28] Hermann Kellenbez, "La técnica en la época de la revolución científica (1500–1700)," in *Historia económica de Europa*, ed. Carlo M. Cipolla (Barcelona: Ariel, 1979). 190. and Sella. 319.

[29] "Este arte y trato es en conciencia el más escrupuloso y peligroso de cuantos en conciencia se puede practicar por excluir aquellos que ya como manifiestamente ilícitos se condena como usurarios y salteadores." Mercado. Fourth book. De cambios. 5.

money exchange. The first type was money exchange from large currency to small currency, or vice versa, for the needs of trade; this was called *cambio menudo o manual*—petty or manual exchange. It presented no moral problem, and it was considered licit to obtain a moderate profit, of 3 to 5 percent, on account of the service that was rendered. Compared to the 35 % usually charged by usurious lenders, it was a small fee. The interest rate charged was determined by the public authority.[30]

The second type of money exchange was the *cambio real*—real exchange. For this the bills of exchange were used. An exchange bill would allow the payment of a certain amount of money at another time and location. For example, a Genovese merchant in Seville might hold his money in Genoa, and would therefore pay with an exchange bill, which was a promise to pay a certain amount of money at a certain date in Genoa. This happened, first of all, for practical reasons, but also because there were laws that prohibited taking gold and silver coin out of Spain. Real exchange did not present any moral problem in and of itself, and as important as it was for international trade, it was not considered problematic. The moral theologians of the time, however, were aware that the same currency did not have the same value in Antwerp, Seville, Naples or Genoa.[31] This price disparity prompted financial transactions which sought to wrest a profit from the difference in price. This was not the only problem moral theologians found in some uses of the real exchange. At a time when information circulated very slowly, and very few had access to accurate information, the practices of money changers, as described by Tomas de Mercado, sometimes resembled those of people profiting from privileged information. In addition to the reservation about a turning profit, which was not an apparent result of creation of wealth, there was the concern that privileged networks of information enriched merchants through exploitative arbitrage arrangements.

---

[30] Ibid. 6–10.

[31] One ducat was worth 11 reales in Seville, 13 reales in Rome and 6 reales in New Spain. One real was worth 34 maravedís in Seville, and 38 in Gran Canaria. The ducat was a gold coin of 3.52 grams that was officially worth 11 reales and 2 maravedís. The real was a silver coin of 3.11 grams that was officially worth 34 maravedís. Luís Correa Lima, *Teologia de Mercado. Uma visao da economia mundial no tempo em que os economistas eram teologos*. (Bauru, Sao Paulo: Editora da Universidade do Sagrado Coracao, 2001). 101.

The Medina trade fair was called a forge of bills, for the large number of bills produced. Although it was the most important fair of the time in Spain, to which merchants from Lisbon, Seville, Burgos, Barcelona, Flanders and Florence came, almost no currency was seen at the fair. Everything was paid for through bills.[32] The fairs acted as clearing systems. In Medina, where more than 2000 merchants congregated, only around 15 bankers did the clearing.[33] Because bills did not go from one city to another instantly—it took some time for a bill to travel from Seville to Antwerp—, bills posed a problem because they were often being used not for the real exchange of goods, but for lending by keeping bills circulating from city to city for the necessary amount of time. This practice became known as the *cambio seco*—dry exchange because it was sterile—in which no real need for exchange was being served, but credit was being granted.[34] This third type of exchange was highly problematic for moral theologians for they saw in it a way of circumventing the prohibition of usury.

Some theologians were more sympathetic to the cause of merchants than was papal authority. They tried to find a legitimate rationale for the charging of interest. The reason for the prohibition on taking more money than what had been originally given in a loan was that money was considered to be sterile, and that the passing of time did not make money produce fruit. Having someone else's money did not render the same service that having his house or working tools did.[35] This meant that there were no internal reasons for the act of lending that would allow for charging interest; therefore an external reason for the act of lending had to be found. These extrinsic reasons to charge interest were known as the *titulus extrinsecus*.

3.4. *A Pious Merchant Class*

New financial mechanisms created new moral problems that merchants wished to resolve. The problems with both trade and new economic

[32] "A estas ferias van de todas las naciones, de Lisboa, de Sevilla, de Burgos, de Barcelona, de Flandes y Florencia, o a pagar seguros, o a tomar cambios, o a darlos, y finalmente es una fragua de cedulas, que casi no se vee blanca, sino todas letras." Mercado. Fourth book. De Cambios 15.

[33] Geoffrey Parker, "El surgimiento de las finanzas modernas en Europa (1500–1700)," in *Historia económica de Europa*, ed. Carlo M. Cipolla (Barcelona: Ariel, 1979). 425.

[34] Ibid. 422–421. The practice is also mentioned in Lima. 73.

[35] Thomas Aquinas, IIª–IIae q. 78 a. 1 co.

practices were not just the domain of friars, priest and confessors. The immense body of literature produced in the sixteenth century about matters related to trade[36] arose from pastoral practice, not out of mere intellectual curiosity, for sixteenth century merchants cared about their eternal salvation.

Today, we know about the pious life of Gonzalo de la Palma, a merchant of Toledo, who formed a 'company' first with others, and afterward with his sons. He was a wealthy merchant, but an opponent of quick profits and trade with the Indies. His son Luis de la Palma S.J.,[37] one of his four sons to become a priest, tells us how his father "never allowed his sons to freight ships or to confide his property to the sea. He was even more opposed to stowing other people's goods. He thought it unjust to earn money through a neighbor's risk."[38] When new types of contracts or trade arose, he would consult with learned men, although well aware that learned men could easily be fooled if all the information was not given to them.[39] The merchant of Toledo was a pious Christian who donated large amounts of money to works of charity. He helped the imprisoned. He helped prostitutes to redeem themselves and, especially, favored the confraternity of the Mother of God that took care of the poor. In addition, he supported many other Toledo fraternities to which he belonged. There is a wealth of similar examples, such as Rodrigo de Dueñas, an important merchant of Medina, or Antonio Acosta, father of another famous Jesuit, José de Acosta S.J.[40]

---

[36] See Eduardo Moore, *La moral en el siglo XVI y primera mitad del XVII* (Granada: 1956). Julio Caro Baroja, *Las formas complejas de la vida religiosa: religión, sociedad y carácter en la España de los siglos XVI Y XVII* (Madrid: Akal, 1978). 389–414. Francisco Gómez Camacho, "Later Scholastic: Spanish Economic Thought."

[37] Luis de la Palma (1559–1641) was a renonwed spiritual writer. His *Historia de la Sagrada Pasión* saw many editions and translations. He also fulfilled many leadership roles in the Society of Jesus.

[38] "Nunca consintió a sus hijos—asociados con él—que cargasen navíos y fiasen su hacienda al mar. Aún era más enemigo de la embarcación de mercancías fiadas. Que le parecía injusto pretender ganar con riesgo del prójimo." Caro Baroja. 377–378.

[39] Many merchants consulted theologians. Father Diego Lainez S.J., theologian in the council of Trent and later second general of the Society of Jesus was consulted by the merchants of Genoa. Fr. Robert Bellarmine S.J. later cardinal was consulted by the merchants of Antwerp. Lima. 27. Caro Baroja points to the fact that many priests of the time belonged to merchant families. Caro Baroja. 416–428.

[40] Caro Baroja. 363–414. José de Acosta (1540–1600) was a missionary, theologian and Americanist. Four of his brothers were also Jesuits. He was sent to Peru, where he served as provincial. He wrote extensively about the new lands. He went on to assume various leadership roles in the order.

Marjorie Grice-Hutchinson, pointing out the importance of the Spanish Scholastics for the history of economic thought, relates in her groundbreaking *The School of Salamanca*:

> From about 1540 onwards there appeared a whole crop of handbooks, written mostly by learned friars, which paint a vivid picture of the business life of the times. Their authors vie with one another in offering the merchant the perfect guide for the salvation of his soul, though one writer's injunction to his readers that they were "not to twist a rule of iron into one of lead" suggests that their teaching was often followed in the letter rather than the spirit. These little books reflect, in a simplified form comprehensible to the layman, the more elaborate body of doctrine that was in the process of evolution at the universities.[41]

From the beginning of the century, economic practices were evolving. Some of them presented moral dilemmas to pious merchants, others did not find an accommodation in the traditional teachings of theologians. Yet, the evolution of economic practices paved the way for an evolution of traditional moral doctrines.[42]

3.5. *The Economic Consequences of Imperial Destiny*

It was not just trade that had transformed the economic system. All over Europe the new monarchies were increasing public spending, and this problem became especially acute in Spain. We have noted that the Iberian Peninsula had been, for most of the Middle Ages, a mere side-show in European politics, with the king of France, the Emperor and the pope as the main players. It was not only the New World that contributed to making Spain and Portugal central players in Europe's economy and political life. In 1518 the young Charles I of Spain, grandson of Isabella and Ferdinand, was elected to the Imperial throne—since he was also the grandson of Maximilian of Habsburg and Mary of Burgundy—and then married his cousin Isabella of Portugal. Through this young man four important kingdoms came together: Castille, Aragon with its Italian possessions, Austria and Burgundy, which included Flanders. Additionally Cortés conquered the Aztec Empire in Mexico in 1521 and Pizarro, the Inca Empire, in Peru in 1532, making Charles the most powerful man of his time. However, he led a life of endless battles against France and the German Protestant princes, and fought fiercely against

---

[41] Marjorie Grice-Hutchinson, *The School of Salamanca; Readings in Spanish Monetary Theory, 1544–1605*. 4.

[42] Vereecke. 361.

the Ottoman Empire of Suleiman II the Magnificent. Although a devout Catholic, he even quarreled with the Pope. His troops sacked Rome in 1527.

Castille—the kingdom that Charles inherited from his maternal grandmother Isabella—was to foot the bill for most of this fighting and in doing so would ruin itself.[43] The Indies' gold not only fuelled trade, it also supported war in an unprecedented way. For the first time in Europe since the times of the Roman Empire, large mercenary armies were being recruited, equipped and moved across Europe. The gold arrived in Seville where it was minted, but with most of the soldiers stationed in Milan, Flanders and Germany, large quantities of money had to be delivered to pay for the hired troops. According to Geoffrey Parker, "Between 1561 and 1610 Spain, by far the country with the largest overseas expenditures, sent 280 million Dutch florins to the Low Countries, especially in bills of exchange."[44] This was a sign of the impact of war on the royal budget, and indicates how politics was affecting economics and the financial system.

Yet if this dawning modern era was bringing about new economic, political and moral problems, it was also bringing about novel approaches to these problems. The sixteenth century saw great social and political change, which was accompanied by a change in the ways of learning.

---

[43] Grice-Hutchinson notes how although the internal problems of Spain were grave they might have found solution "had it not been for the heaviest of all the drags that hampered Castilian progress—Spain's close political links with Europe, and her involvement in the wars in which the Habsburgs were committed." Marjorie Grice-Hutchinson, *Early Economic Thought in Spain, 1177–1740*. 92.

[44] Parker. 439. Translation is mine. For the importance of war and the new regular armies in industrial production see. Walter Minchinton, "Tipos y estructura de la demanda (1500–1700)," in *Historia económica de Europa*, ed. Carlo M. Cipolla (Barcelona: Ariel, 1979). 68–139. In page 90 he states that: "El elemento más gravoso, aunque intermitente, que ejemplifica el cambio de escala y de carácter del gasto público, apareció con la institucionalización de la guerra. [...] La guerra, que había sido un fenómeno casual y espasmódico, aumentó de escala y de complejidad. De ese modo se expansionó su demanda sobre los recursos sobre alimentos y equipo. Se establecieron ejércitos y armadas permanentes, aumentó el número de hombres en armas y aumentaron sus necesidades de equipo. Se construyeron fortificaciones, cuarteles y arsenales, aumentó el tamaño de los barcos de guerra y se requirieron uniformes, armas y suministros a una escala hasta entonces sin precedentes. Desde el siglo XVI se hicieron intentos para que las dotaciones de armas fueran estándar; en el siglo siguiente apareció el suministro y alojamiento. Fue el gobierno español el primero en desarrollar un sistema para proporcionar a las tropas comida y alojamiento a través de funcionarios del gobierno, furrieles o servís, en lugar de dejar a cada soldado en particular la resolución de esas cuestiones. Además la guerra constituyó un estímulo para el progreso de la técnica."

What was to be called the Scientific Revolution was underway. The ways of theology were also changing. In the next three sections we shall see how these changes affected moral theology.

4. A New Science for a New World

The Age of Discoveries, as the sixteenth century has been called, was not just an age of geographical conquest. While Europeans were scattering around the world, an internal movement was taking place on the continent. The Aristotelian paradigm of science was beginning to break up.[45] The exploration and exploitation of other parts of the world were changing the European world view, and not just geographically. Technological developments made exploration of the world possible, and in addition these same technological developments were helping from within to change the ways of learning. This section will sketch some elements of what has been called the Scientific Revolution in as much as they affect our research.

Howard Margolis points to the year 1600, the year Molina died, as a key year around which many notable scientific discoveries were made.[46] Although the Scientific Revolution prolonged itself far beyond 1600, its agitation was at work during the sixteenth century. In those years scholasticism was the stronghold of the normal science, whether physics, theology or biology. Nonetheless, the Aristotelian paradigm was encountering significant challenges. The scholastics sought to respond to those challenges and in doing so their own system was modified. Thomas S. Kuhn, in *The Structure of Scientific Revolutions*, refers to crisis science, as opposed to normal science, as "the proliferation of competing articulations, the willingness to try anything, the expression of explicit discontent, the recourse to philosophy and to debate over fundamentals."[47]

---

[45] I am dependent for this analysis on Thomas Kuhn, *The Structure of Scientific Revolutions*, 2nd ed. (Chicago: University of Chicago Press, 1970). A paradigm is "an exemplary solution to a preeminent research problem with two characteristics: it is sufficiently unprecedented to attract the members of other schools, and it is sufficiently open-ended to leave enough interesting problems for further scientific work." Paul Hoyningen-Huene, "Kuhn, Thomas Samuel," in *Routledge Encyclopedia of Philosophy*, ed. Craig Edward (London: Routledge, 1998). 316. Dependent on the concept of paradigm are the concepts of normal science, crisis science, and incommensurability.

[46] Howard Margolis, *It Started with Copernicus. How Turning the World inside out Led to the Scientific Revolution* (New York: McGraw-Hill, 2002). 3–7.

[47] Kuhn, *The Structure of Scientific Revolutions*. 91.

Although Kuhn is referring to the natural sciences, this description is also applicable to the theological panorama of the sixteenth century.

4.1. *Mariners, Conquistadors and Missionaries and the Importance of Doing*

An example of the challenges that the new discoveries were bringing to science, both the natural sciences and to theology, can be found in the reports of the explorers. The arrival of Europeans in new lands was challenging established knowledge. What mariners, conquistadors and settlers—men who had little, if any, studies—were reporting on, challenged the authority of the old masters: both the Greek philosophers and the Fathers of the Church.[48] Additionally, missionaries reported extraordinary things. A major example of how these reports affected intellectual discussion is José de Acosta's *Historia natural y moral de las Indias* (1590). In his book, Acosta, a learned Jesuit, reports that the New World is populated with "animals of number and aspect never before known, of which neither the Greek, nor the Latin, or any other people of this part of the world have memory."[49] Acosta's book had great impact. It was translated into German, French, English, Italian and Dutch. It was at the center of the debate that shook European culture from the middle of the sixteenth century onward.

The reports of the explorers, whether mariners, conquistadors or missionaries, led to questions that had no easy answers. From non-relativistic or skeptical positions some of the religious men of the time who were in touch with the new lands—directly or through missionaries, merchants or conquistadors—came to understand that what was being discovered challenged the normal science.[50]

4.2. *The Importance of Doing*

The development of technology was not, however, merely providing new and extraordinary data. It was also changing the way in which scientific data was obtained. In the Aristotelian system—the paradigm of Western thought—, the most perfect way of life was the theoretical one. This notion had been Christianized and consequently understood as

---

48 Paolo Rossi, *La nascita della scienza moderna in Europa* (Roma: Laterza, 1997). 75

49 "animali di numero e aspetto mai conosciuto, dei quali non hanno memoria né greci, ne latini, de alcun altro popolo del mondo de aca." Quoted in Ibid. 76.

50 Caro Baroja. 269.

the contemplative life. The most emblematically perfect life in Medieval Europe was the life of the Carthusians. This perfection not only applied to a religious perfection; it was also applicable to a perfection regarding how to acquire knowledge. It was in the quiet of the cloister that knowledge was considered to be better attained. The sixteenth century saw a revision of this view regarding perfection.

The active life was already being praised in the fifteenth century. Many Renaissance artists were experts in mechanical arts. Lorenzo Ghiberti was expert in metal working, Leonardo da Vinci was expert in military engineering, and Albert Dürer was a fine geometrician. Some of them published books on these mechanical arts. Active pursuits of practical nature, therefore, began to be viewed as acceptable sources of knowledge.

Margolis states that "printing, artillery and clocks were creating a new world in Europe at the same time that explorers were discovering the New World across the sea."[51] The important consequences of these advancements in technology were also transforming the way men expert in mechanics saw themselves and the way the larger society viewed at what had been until then looked upon as manual labor. This was an epistemological transformation. Paolo Rossi points out that

> A defense of the mechanical arts against the charge of indignity, actually implicated giving up a thousand-years-old image of what the science ought to be, it implicated the end of a distinction of the essence between knowing and doing.[52]

In his *De Tradendis Disciplinis* (1531) Juan Luis Vives[53] invited learned European people to pay attention to practical problems such as mechanics, agriculture or navigation. He recommended that these learned people go to workshops and farms to learn from artisans.[54]

The development of machines also affected learning in another way. Through a machine a person is somehow exhibiting mastery over nature, and is able to determine the way nature works. According to Mauro Dorato the mechanization of the sixteenth century also caused a transformation in the idea of what nature was. The Scientific Revolution

[51] Margolis. 79. In their time, Tommaso di Campanella and Francis Bacon also emphasized the importance of these three technological achievements in the changes that were taking place. Rossi. 55.

[52] Rossi. 16. This certainly affected the work of moral theologians.

[53] Juan Luis Vives (1492–1540) was a Spanish humanist, friend of Erasmus and Thomas Moore.

[54] Rossi. 37.

necessitated passing from a paradigm of ideal forms to a paradigm of reliable laws. Of course, the notion of laws of nature existed prior to the Scientific Revolution. The natural law tradition in ethics attests to that. In the natural law tradition the laws were prescriptive. The notion of laws of nature which the Scientific Revolution proposed was different; in the new paradigm the laws of nature were descriptive. This move was largely brought about by the role of technology in transforming the dominant metaphor regarding nature; since machines reproduced nature, so nature could be understood as a machine. Dorato declares that

> the possibility of reproducing the functioning of parts of the natural world through the construction of machines was an essential factor in the long process leading to the formulation of a notion of "law of nature" that was completely descriptive, and therefore lacking in normative elements.[55]

Machines would eventually provide a metaphor for understanding nature. Nature was similar to a large mechanism and the way it worked was as rigid as the cogs of a machine. The transformation of the idea of nature greatly affected theology; of this we will say more when we deal with theology in the sixteenth century.

4.3. *The Impact of the Movable Type*

One of the major technical inventions that led to the transformation of the world was the movable type. In 1456 Hans Gutenberg printed the Bible in Mainz. By 1480 there were printing presses in 110 European cities, rising to 286 by 1500. In Venice, Lyons, Antwerp and Leipzig printing became an important industry.[56]

It was not long before editions of classical works became available to an unprecedented degree. Additionally, the sixteenth century also saw the publication of critical editions of Antiquity's classics.

[55] Mauro Dorato, *The Software of the Universe: An Introduction to the History and Philosophy of the Laws of Nature*, Ashgate New Critical Thinking in Philosophy and Index. (Aldershot, England; Burlington, VT: Ashgate, 2005). 2. Dorato further develops this when he says "What I would like to emphasize now is that the tight link between the way we conceive nature and the way we understand its regularities has established, since the beginning of human intellectual history, a profound conceptual network connecting *descriptive* and *prescriptive* elements, in such a way that "law" is what necessarily presupposes a *will* that *plans*, *orders*, and *governs*." 4. I work under this assumption, and I will try to prove that the transformation of the idea of law in the natural sciences that are descriptive, actually affected the idea of natural law in ethics, which are prescriptive.

[56] Of which 50 in Italy, 30 in Germany, 8 in the Netherlands and in Spain, 5 in Belgium and Switzerland, 4 in England. Rossi. 56.

Books became more readily available than they had ever been. Furthermore, with the great increase in learned and well read people in Europe in the sixteenth century the circles of learning and knowledge were greatly enlarged. This transformed the ways knowledge and learning were approached. Luther's idea of the self-interpretation of the Bible would have made little sense in the eras preceding the printing press, when very few people had direct access to the Bible. This book, as almost any other book, was rarely a personal possession, but rather a communal one. After the invention of the printing press, owning a Bible was affordable and self-interpretation of the Bible became materially possible.

The importance of the printing press resides not only in the impact that easily available books exerted on society, but on how the press transformed the ways of scientific progress. In the sixteenth century, communication and diffusion of knowledge became a value. This change first took place among engineers and those involved in the production of machines. The new science was conceived as antagonistic to the knowledge of monks, scholastics, humanists and university professors. The battle was largely fought with books as key weapons. The new scientific community was created through communication among the practitioners of the new science, but also through the publication of books.[57] Theological wars were also fought through the mediums of books. The most important example of this was the Protestant Reformation.

4.4. *Coping with Change and the Changing Paradigm of Science*

Tyco Brahe is an example of how contemporaries sought to deal with the new scientific developments. In his 1588 *Astronomiae instauratae mechanica*, Brahe proposed a new geometric astronomy to replace that of Ptolemy and to meet the challenges of Copernicus' astronomy. Brahe was an acute observer of the heavens, so impressive that his first observations

---

[57] Rossi. 17–34. Also Hermann Kellenbenz considers very important the impact of books; "La imprenta y los resultados de la imprenta son lo primero que nos viene a la cabeza cuando nos preguntamos qué adelantos técnicos se hicieron en Europa entre el siglo XV y el principio del XVI. La imprenta permitió que la circulación de información sobre nuevos descubrimientos técnicos fuera mucho más fácil que en los tiempos en que todo había de escribirse a mano. Nadie podía prever las consecuencias de ello, qué alcance había de tener o lo grande que había de ser su efecto sobre la civilización occidental." Kellenbenz. 143.

earned him an island and a castle, a gift of the king of Denmark. In his castle of Uraniborg ('the heavenly castle'), he built instruments to observe the heavens. His observation of comets led him to the dismissal of the traditional belief that stars and the planets were set on solid spheres.[58] Tyconian astronomy, nonetheless, tried to save part of the old astronomy and to reconcile it with these new discoveries. He tried to cope with 'the Copernican absurdity' and the 'Ptolemaic redundancies.'[59] This meant that in Brahe's astronomy the planets rotated around the Sun, but—to save the conviction that the earth was the centre of the Universe—the Sun itself rotated around the Earth. Margolis remarks that Brahe's system provided an alternative that "left the Earth where philosophers and theologians and anyone with common sense knew it should be" and at the same time "provided a manifest cause for … why the simple motion of the Sun is necessarily involved in the motion of all five planets."[60]

For Tyco Brahe the theological aspect of his quest was essential. Connections between his concept of the laws of nature and divine will can be traced in his work. Dorato points out that Brahe is the only sixteenth-century astronomer who clearly formulated "the thesis of the divine origins of natural law in his *De Disclipinis Mathematicis* (1574), when he writes that 'the wondrous and perpetual laws of the celestial motion, so diverse and yet so harmonious, prove the existence of God.'"[61]

The new discoveries, and the accompanying theories that they gave rise to, penetrated slowly into the academic world. It was nonetheless affected by them. The new scientific theories were challenging the traditional idea that the Earth was the center of the universe, and that human beings stood in the center of it all. These scientific theories had theological impact. The theology of the time also struggled, as in Brahe's case, to reconcile the old and the new.[62] All of this resulted in a paradigm shift, which began to take place in the second half of the sixteenth century. The exploration of nature with new technological developments changed the

58 Rossi. 91–94.
59 Margolis. 45.
60 Ibid. 47.
61 Dorato. 19.
62 Margolis points out the fact that "The Tyconic compromise … provided a refuge for people who could not believe Copernicus but also no longer felt confortable with Ptolemy. After the Church condemned Copernicanism, the Tychonic choice became the only option open to loyal Catholics." Margolis. 195.

prevalent notions regarding what nature was. For the natural sciences, the laws of nature started to shift from prescriptive to merely descriptive. Nature still taught, but in other ways.[63]

Experimentation and experience slowly won a respect that had until then been reserved for philosophical speculation. Doing became a respectable mode of knowledge. The minute description of phenomena entered the intellectual realm that had previously speculated about the four causes of the Aristotelian system.[64] In order to understand the theological works of the second half of the sixteenth century, we must take this paradigm shift into account. Moral theology was also affected by this shift. There were, however, changes brought about from within. We shall survey the theological panorama in the next section.

5. Moral Theology in Sixteenth-Century Spain and Portugal

According to Vereecke, "Moral Theology in the sixteenth century was Spanish."[65] The arrival of Columbus to the island of Guahani, on October 12th 1492 opened for Spain such a wide range of moral dilemmas that moral theology flourished in response to these new challenges. America represented a theological challenge,[66] because it was a radically new world. During the Middle Ages, Christianity had known the problems of confrontation with Islam. America presented radically different problems. The native populations of the Indies did not threaten Europe as

[63] In his letter to Madama Chistine of Lorena of 1612 Galileo said: "there is a great difference between commanding a mathematician or a philosopher and directing a merchant or a lawyer, and that the demonstrated conclusions about the things of nature and of heavens cannot be changed with the same ease as opinions about what is lawful or not in a contract, rent or exchange." A.C. Crombie, *Science, Art, and Nature in Medieval and Modern Thought* (London; Rio Grande, Ohio: Hambledon Press, 1996). 356.

[64] Carlo M. Cipolla, "Introducción," in *Historia económica de Europa*, ed. Carlo M. Cipolla (Barcelona: Ariel, 1979). 8.

[65] "Nel secolo XVI la teologia morale è spagnola." Vereecke. 40.

[66] For a detail account of how this worked Lewis Hanke, "The Theological Significance of the Discovery of America," ed. Fredi Chiappelli, Michael J.B. Allen, and Robert Louis Benson, *First Images of America: The Impact of the New World on the Old* (Berkeley: University of California Press, 1976). 363–374. In page 365 he states that "Spaniards were not only in the forefront of those who explored the vast reaches of the New World ... but they were pioneers too in tackling the theoretical and theological issues involved." Also John Mahoney considers very important the theological reflection on social ethics of Spanish moral theologians of the sixteenth century. Mahoney. 33.

Islam did.[67] The natives of the Indies seemed open to conversion, which was not the case with Islam. The rules that had helped Christianity in relating to Islam were of no use in dealing with this New World, leading Spanish theologians to pose questions about what was happening in America.[68] In doing so they transformed the frames of moral theology.

5.1. *Francisco de Vitoria and Aquinas' Return*

The first recorded person to protest the behavior of colonizers in the newly conquered lands was Fray Francisco de Montesinos, O.P., who in the advent of 1511 began a homily saying: "Tell me; by what right or justice do you hold these Indians in such a cruel and horrible servitude?"[69] Montesinos was part of the first contingent of Dominicans to go to the New World. They had arrived at La Española encouraged by the Master General of the order Thomas de Vio, O.P., known as Cajetan. They came from the Dominican Convent of San Esteban in Salamanca. Montesinos was eventually expelled from La Española because of the content of his preaching, and he returned to Spain. San Esteban's Convent, however, became the center in which Dominican missionaries where formed before being sent to the New World. It is by more than mere chance that some years later Francisco de Vitoria would live in that same convent during his years as professor in Salamanca.

Vitoria is certainly the man who most contributed to making the sixteenth century a Spanish century in moral theology. He studied in Paris from 1509 to 1522. As a student of Peter Crockaert he collaborated

---

[67] In 1453 Constantinople, the capital of the Byzantine empire had fallen to the Turks. The Turkish menace was a constant preoccupation in Europe during the sixteenth century. In 1526 they had conquered Hungary and in 1529 they besieged Vienna.

[68] Although we will deal with this more extensively later, we can give an example of the theological impact of America in Molina's work: "Atque cum nostris saeculis inventa fuerit quarta orbis ars, longe major quam tres aliae antea cognitae, ad quam nostris saeculis praedicatio Evangelii est delata, nec dumque in tota ea parte Evangelium sit promulgandtum, quin et navigationibus varia loca alia indies reperiantur, ad quae Evangelium numquam fuit delatum, ad interioraque earum nondum in multis earum Evangeliis praedicatiio devenerit, constat sane usque ad hanc diem eam praedicationem in universo orbe, quam Christus antecessuram consummationem saeculi praedixit, nondum esse complete factam." V. 64. 5, 226.

[69] Bartolomé de las Casas, *History of the Indies III*. 4–5. quoted in Roland G. Musto, *Catholic Peacemakers. A Documentary History*, vol. II. From the Renaissance to the Twentieth Century, Part I (New York and London: Garland Publishing, 1996). 90.

in the edition of the *Secunda Secundae* of Aquinas' *Summa*. Vitoria became a part of the Thomistic renaissance of the sixteenth century,[70] especially because in 1526 the chair of Prime of theology at the University of Salamanca became vacant, and he was elected to the chair with a large majority.[71] Although he never published anything in his lifetime, Vitoria's presence in Salamanca was to prove very fruitful.

At the beginning of the sixteenth century, theology was still taught in accordance with the *Sentences* of Peter Lombard. In Paris, some professors, among them Peter Crockaert, had started to teach theology in accordance with Aquinas' *Summa*. In Salamanca, Vitoria also began to teach according to the order of the *Summa*.[72] Until the sixteenth century, Thomism had been a theological school confined to the Order of Preachers. During the sixteenth century both Dominicans and Jesuit theologians defended Aquinas' system. Although giving different interpretations to them, they favored the teaching of Aquinas in their writings. Aquinas became the most popular theologian in the Catholic Church.

The appropriation of Aquinas was, however, accomplished in a free way, and consequently resulted in a transformation of theology.[73] In his exposition of Aquinas, Vitoria certainly privileged the *Secunda Pars*.[74] Although he wrote a commentary on it, it was not published until the twentieth century, and so the text was not influential in his time. Vitoria's most influential literary works were his *Relectiones*, which were first published after his death in Lyons in 1557. The *relectiones* were lectures that every professor holding a chair was to give once a year. Vitoria's *Relectiones* privileged moral theology by tackling the ethical issues of his time, and in doing so Vitoria contributed to the clarification of issues regarding the competences of political and ecclesiastical

70 Vereecke. 538.

71 In those days professors were appointed to chairs through a balanced voting arrangement in which all the students had a vote. But, depending on their seniority, they were granted more or fewer ballots. Francisco de Vitoria, *Obras*, ed. Teofílo Urdanoz (Madrid: BAC, 1960). 18–22.

72 Part of the prohibition was due to the practical fact that there were many more commentaries on Peter the Lombard Sentences than on Aquinas' *Summa*.

73 For Gómez Camacho Vitoria, Soto and Cano belonged to an open-minded scholasticism. He does not include Domingo Bañez in this group. He suggests that this open minded scholasticism was followed by many Jesuits. Gómez Camacho, *Economía y filosofía moral: La formación del pensamiento económico europeo en la escolástica española*. 35.

74 From 1531 to 1538 he lectured on the entire Summa. Of these seven years he dedicated four to the Secunda Pars. Vitoria, *Obras*. 77.

power. He also laid the foundations of international law.[75] We can certainly identify in Vitoria a certain preference for moral theology.[76]

A quest for order and method deeply influenced moral theology. It would eventually result in the separation of moral theology from the rest of theology. This change happened slowly but steadily during the sixteenth century.[77] Vereecke points to Juan Azor's *Institutiones Morales*—the first of the manuals—of 1600 as the date of this separation.[78] This separation had been anticipated in Aquinas' order that grouped all ethical issues in the *Secunda Secundae*.[79]

Azor's systematization signalled the change from a moral theology of virtue to a moral theology of obligations. The Decalogue became the underlying outline for the teaching of moral theology. Virtues were considered important, but, subordinated to the Ten Commandments, which appeared as obligations.[80] This legalistic slant had been growing during the sixteenth century, fostered by the influence of nominalism.

New moral theology genres had already appeared in the sixteenth century. The advent of one such genre may be dated at 1553 when Domingo de Soto published the first treatise *De Iustitia et Iure*,[81] an exposition on problems related to justice. Although it was grounded in Aquinas' treatment of the virtue of justice, it departed from it in many ways. We shall see more of the new genres in the next chapter.

---

[75] In *De Potestate Civile* (1528), *De Potestate Ecclesiae* (1532 and 1533), and *De Potestate Papae et Concilii* (1534), he discussed the issues of ecclesiology but also of church and state relations. His *De matrimonio* (1530) dealt with the important political issue of the annulment of Henry VIII's marriage to Catherine of Aragon, aunt of Charles V. In *De Indiis* (1539) he approached the issue of the lawfulness of Spanish conquest in America. In *De Iure Belli* (1539) he discussed the law of war and in it along with the previous one he laid the foundation of what was to become international law. Ibid. 82.

[76] Raúl González Fabre, *Justicia en el mercado. Fundamentación de la ética del mercado según Francisco de Vitoria* (Caracas: CONICIT-UCAB, 1998). 50.

[77] Moore. 76.

[78] Vereecke. 31.

[79] Ibid. 33.

[80] E. Moore E.L. Lisson, J.T. Bretske, "Teología: V. Moral," in *Diccionario Histórico de la Compañía de Jesús. Biográfico—Temático*, ed. Charles E. O'Neill S.J. and Joaquín María Domínguez S.J. (Roma-Madrid: Institutum Historicum S.J.-Universidad Pontificia Comillas, 2001). 3741.

[81] "Con anterioridad a Soto, los doctores escolásticos habían tratado los temas económicos en sus comentarios a la *Summa* de santo Tomás. Domingo de Soto fue el primero en escribir un tratado moral *De Iustitia et Iure* como obra independiente. A partir de Soto se escribieron tratados *De Iustitia et Iure* por los mejores doctores escolásticos, Molina, Lugo, Lessio, etc., y en ellos se expone el mejor pensamiento económico de su tiempo." Gómez Camacho. *Economia y filosofia moral: La formación del pensamiento económico europeo en la escolástica española*. 38.

These transformations were influenced, not solely by Aquinas' revival but also by the way Aquinas' works were used.[82] If we say that there was a free appropriation of Aquinas, it is because the use of his works in the sixteenth century was broadly influenced by nominalism. A theological or philosophical purist might be horrified by this mixture of Aquinas and nominalism, but it actually proved to be extremely fruitful. Nominalist moral theology had traditionally dedicated great attention to social and economic problems. Its combination with Thomistic approaches gave it a more universal and permanent grounding.[83] The result was a concrete approach to contemporary ethical problems, and a theological framework that exhibited greater sensitivity to context than Aquinas had achieved.

5.2. *Nominalism and its Fruits in Ethics*

The discussion about universals was one of the major debates of the Middle Ages. It revolved around the interpretation of Aristotle's *Metaphysics*. The label nominalism referred to a variety of philosophical and theological themes that loosely clustered together.[84] The thinkers who were first identified as nominalists were all influenced by William of Ockham.[85] In Ockham's own interpretation of orthodox Aristotelism, everything that exists is particular. For Claude Panaccio "the core of Ockham's system lies in the idea that only individuals exist and that universals are nothing but signs, written or spoken."[86] However, this did not necessarily constitute relativism, for Ockham insisted that the way these signs were formed in the mind conformed to certain rules and these were not the result of pure whim. Still, universals had no existence outside the human mind. For Ockham the existence of universals in the way Aquinas and many other realists defended it was incompatible with God's omnipotence.

Ockham never systematically collected his views on ethics, but he wrote about ethical issues in the *Sentences*, the *Quodlibeta Septem* and the *Quaestiones Variae*. For Ockham, ethics encompassed two separate parts.

---

[82] Not only theological texts such as those of Aquinas were freely appropriated. The same could be said about the way in which the late scholastics used Roman law. de Roover, *La pensè èconomique des scolastiques: doctrines et mèthodes*. 22.

[83] Andrés Martín. 461.

[84] Claude Panaccio, "William of Ockham," in *Routledge Encyclopedia of Philosophy*, ed. Craig Edward (London: Routledge, 1998). 734.

[85] Frederick Copleston S.J., *A History of Philosophy*, vol. V. Modern Philosophy: The British Philosophers (Garden City, NY: Image Books, 1964).

[86] Panaccio. 734.

The first part was positive moral science, that is, the knowledge about the legal obligations we are subject to. This knowledge in turn is divided into knowledge about human laws and knowledge about divine laws. The second part of ethics, according to Ockham, was non-positive moral science. Panaccio describes it as "directive knowledge about human action (or praxis) insofar as it is based on natural reason or experience".[87] We have identified here three elements of Ockham's ethics that would characterize nominalist ethics: reason, experience and the importance of law. These elements would come to influence the ways of moral reasoning of the Spanish Scholastics.[88]

Nominalist ethics had a legalistic slant, and law became a preferred topic.[89] They also relied on the notion of *recta ratio* (right reason), a central idea for Ockham. In this, as in many other things, Ockham was dependent on Scotus.[90] *Recta ratio* is the rational and well-informed use of prudence and moral conscience. Nonetheless, it is more than natural reason. It involves the use of any relevant truth available to the agent. This enhances not only the importance of experience, but also brings Christian revelation into moral reasoning.[91] This is what makes it possible for nominalist ethics to hold a high regard for reason in its moral methodology, and to hold, at the same time, that the ultimate foundation for a moral command is God's loving and wise will.[92]

The tendency of nominalist ethics to favor experience, and the importance it gave to the concrete, fostered a great deal of research on social and economic issues.[93] At the beginning of the sixteenth century nominalism had, to its credit, produced a well-developed body of literature on social and economic problems. The most important nominalist of the sixteenth century, and arguably the last of the great Medieval nominalists,

---

[87] Ibid. 744.

[88] Gómez Camacho, *Economía y filosofía moral: La formación del pensamiento económico europeo en la escolástica española*. 78–84.

[89] James F. Keenan, "The Casuistry of John Mair, Nominalist Professor of Paris," in *The Context of Casuistry*, ed. James F. Keenan and Thomas A. Shannon (Washington, D.C.: Georgetown University Press, 1995). 95.

[90] Thomas A. Shannon, "Method in Ethics: A Scotistic Contribution," in *The Context of Casuistry*, ed. James F. Keenan and Thomas A. Shannon (Washington, D.C.: Georgetown University Press, 1995). 3–24.

[91] Panaccio. 744.

[92] Marilyn Mc Cord Adams, "The Structure of Ockham's Moral Theory," in *The Context of Casuistry*, ed. James F. Keenan and Thomas A. Shannon (Washington, D.C.: Georgetown University Press, 1995). 43.

[93] "Los nominalistas Oyta, Oresme, Buridano y Gersón escriben buenos tratados sobre los contratos en la época gremial, siglos XIV y XV." Andrés Martín. 466.

was John Mair. Vitoria, who coincided with Mair in Paris, was influenced by him.[94] In referring to Mair's writings, Keenan notes that "a comparison of the scholastic writings of earlier figures like Thomas Aquinas with John Mair demonstrates how much Mair invoked ordinary figures involved in ordinary affairs." He further points out that the "images of Socrates the restaurateur, fair-goer, or clever investor cannot be found in the high scholasticism of the thirteenth century."[95] The greater importance given to experience is clear in the writings of the Scottish professor in Paris.

Nominalism, in the sixteenth century, was considered the modern way. Nominalists were also called the *moderni*, the modern ones. When, at the beginning of the sixteenth century, Spanish theologians had to confront the moral issues resulting from the exploration and conquest of the Indies, as well as those arising from the developing patterns of trade, they found in the writings of nominalist theologians and philosophers a wider base from which to explore the new problems than was available in Thomistic literature.[96] Vitoria acknowledged that "the modern authors have started to elaborate in their subject matter, because they did not find any other place in which to deal with it in an easier way."[97] Nominalism offered sound analysis, and was a respected school of thought. Thomists were willing to accept from Mair and other nominalist authors what they found of interest. Thomism and nominalism were opposing theological systems, but they were not necessarily inimical.[98]

---

[94] For Mair's influence on Vitoria see Ricardo García Villoslada, *La Universidad de Paris durante los estudios de Francisco de Vitoria (1507–1522)* (Rome: apud aedes Universitatis Gregorianae, 1938). 127–164.

[95] Keenan, "The Casuistry of John Mair, Nominalist Professor of Paris." 93. Actually when Molina acknowledged that he had consulted the master of the mint in Cuenca, Mair acknowledges in his commentary on the *Sentences* that what he knows about the exchange contract that Spanish merchants practice in Antwerp is through the information he obtained from friars who went to Antwerp every year. Vereecke. 348.

[96] Mair is the first known theologian to refer to the New World in a published book as a moral theology problem. He says "Hispanii tales invenerunt in mare atlantico an iuste regnum ab eis abstulerunt quod rex eorum prius habebat vel quamcumque aliam policiam?" John Major, *In Secundum Librum Sententiarum* (Paris: 1519). d. 44, q. 3. In Vitoria, *Obras*. 51.

[97] Francisco de Vitoria. *Comentario a la II–II q. 63 a. 1*. quoted in Andrés Martín. 461.

[98] "Se la teologia de Martin Lutero può essere compressa soltanto partendo di posizioni nominalistiche, sembra che anche la morale del secolo XVI debba essere analizzata alla luce dei principi di Guglielmo d'Ockam. Il pensiero di costui non comprende soltanto una nuova metodologia, un rigoroso sistema di logica, una teologia dogmatica polemica verso il tomismo, ma anche una nuova morale che caratterizzarà l'evoluzione dei teologi e dei moralisti ben oltre gli inizi del XVI secolo." Vereecke. 34.

Aquinas' system is of course very different from nominalism. Nonetheless, the way of progression articulated in the *Summa* allows a Thomistic view to incorporate many nominalist elements. Aquinas in the *Summa* leaves every article open for further inquiry. Bonnie Kent compares Thomas with a "host laboring to produce congenial, fruitful conversation among guests deeply at odds with each other. Like all good hosts, he conceals how hard he must work to ensure that conflicts are defused and the party goes well."[99] This characteristic of Aquinas' method of research, integrating new questions in the theological framework, was continued in the Spanish Scholastics, when they confronted a wide variety of new problems. This meant that the various theological treatises of the sixteenth century from professed Thomistic authors included the discussion of many previous theologians. The most relevant authorities would be discussed, even if they were from a rival school, before giving the author's own personal solution. This led some twentieth-century Thomists to conclude that the teaching of Aquinas was not always a correct one, and that Aquinas's doctrines were, to say the least, wrongly interpreted.[100]

The use of Aquinas in the sixteenth century constituted a free use of the Angelic Doctor's writings. In the same way that Aquinas did not hesitate to blend Aristotle's philosophical views with various strands of the Christian tradition, the theologians of the sixteenth century were eager to integrate Aquinas with nominalism without compunction. This was especially true of Jesuits.[101] This attitude might also have been influenced by the fact that at the time theological inquiry was understood, not so much as a personal and individual inquiry, but as a communal task.[102] This communal task was animated by controversy. We shall see now how

[99] Bonnie Kent, "Habits and Virtues," in *The Ethics of Aquinas*, ed. Stephen J. Pope (Washington D.C.: Georgetown University Press, 2002). 116.

[100] Vicente Beltrán de Heredia, "La enseñanza de santo Tomás en la Compañía de Jesús durante el primer siglo de su existencia. La legislación," *La Ciencia Tomista* XII (1915), and Vicente Beltrán de Heredia, "La enseñanza de santo Tomás en la Compañía de Jesús durante el primer siglo de su existencia. La práctica," *La Ciencia Tomista* XII (1915).

[101] Wilhelm Weber, *Wirschaftsethik am Vorabend des Liberalismus: Höhepunkt und Abschluss der Scholastischen Wirtschaftsbetrachtung durch Ludwig Molina, S.J. (1535–1600)* (Münster: Aschendorffsche Verlagsbuchhandlung, 1959), 22. In 1586 the first version of the *Ratio Studiorum* was published. According to Weber it was ill received in Spain and Portugal because it established that a close adherence to Aquinas should be pursued in theological studies.

[102] Gómez Camacho, *Economía y filosofía moral: La formación del pensamiento económico europeo en la escolástica española*. 83–84.

controversy and the epistemology of the Spanish Scholastics affected theological develpoment, and how it led to another of the theological fruits of the time, namely Probabilism.

5.3. *Probabilism: Different Kinds of Knowledge and Recta Ratio*

5.3.1. *Science, Faith, Opinion, Doubt and Scruples*

The epistemology of the Spanish Scholastics is a key to understanding the theological discussions of the time.[103] According to Gómez Camacho, "there was some skepticism among the nominalists about the possibility of knowledge of an order in the world that human reason could discover." If universals were creations of mind then "the relationship between abstract concepts (*universales*) and individual concepts (*singulares*) was one of the controversial subjects dividing nominalists and followers of St. Thomas."[104] Gómez Camacho discovers in Martín de Azpilicueta's *Manual de Confesores* a summary of the epistemology of the Spanish Scholastics that blends Thomistic with nominalist views. Martín de Azpilicueta, known as *Doctor Navarrus*, was considered a major theologian in the sixteenth century.[105] His epistemological taxonomy is a major example of the typology of knowledge with which a moral theologian of the time would have worked.[106]

The final section of Navarrus's *Manual* offered some rules to assist confessors. These rules distinguished five types of knowledge: science, faith, opinion, doubt and scruples. The first, science, is "the knowledge we possess from what one sees. This includes not only what one hears, tastes or smells, but also what we see with our soul through syllogism or scientific reason, that is through intuitive reason, taken from the senses or without them."[107] Second is faith, "the knowledge with which we

[103] Miriam Turrini, *La coscienza e le leggi: morale e diritto nei testi per la confessione della prima età moderna*, Annali dell'Istituto Storico Italo Germanico. Monografia; 13 (Bologna: Societa editrice Il Mulino, 1991). 148–170.

[104] Gómez Camacho, "Later Scholastic: Spanish Economic Thought." 506.

[105] Martin de Azpilicueta was born in Navarre. He studied at the University of Alcalá with Dr. Miranda, a disciple of Mair in Paris. He said that to be a good confessor one had to be not only a theologian but also well versed in civil and canon law. He was actually a professor of canon law. He taught in Toulose and Cahors in France, in Salamanca and in Coimbra in Portugal. He died in Rome where he had been sent by Phillip II to take part in the legal process for heresy against Cardinal Carranza.

[106] Both Gómez Camacho and Turrini agree on this. Gómez Camacho, "Later Scholastic: Spanish Economic Thought." 507. Turrini. 143–188.

[107] "Scientia é il conoscimiento con che si giudica quel che si vede. Per vedere intendiamo ancora il toccare, udire, gustare et odorare che sono i cinque sensi esteriori, et ancho

judge something with certainty without seeing it."[108] Third, opinion is the "knowledge with which we judge something that we do not see to be in a certain way, but not firmly, with a fear that the contrary might be true."[109] Doubt is "knowledge of two contrary things without judging which is true."[110] Last, scruple is "the knowledge of something that represents an appearance against what one knows by science, believes by faith, thinks by opinion or doubts."[111] The first four types of knowledge were incompatible; anyone could fall, according to different situations, into each one of them.

Our search is influenced by this distinction, since it was opinion that ultimately moved moral actions. Science and faith could provide firm knowledge of facts and principles, but never a firm knowledge of the concrete action that we might be obliged to take. Moral action was ultimately based on opinion. Opinion, however, did not mean whim. Principles and facts intervened in any given decision, and they were not the result of whim. Opinion meant that moral action was never the result of a 'necessary' deduction, but was rather the result of the use of the *recta ratio*,[112] which, as we have seen, encompassed the use of prudence.[113]

According to Gómez Camacho, there are five characteristics of the way in which the Spanish Scholastics employed *recta ratio*. *Recta ratio* is for them a reason that is fallible, practical, situated, controversial

---

(sic) la vista dell'anima, o sia per sillogismo, o ragione scientifica, che fa sapere, o sia per notitia intuitiva mentale, raccolta della sensitiva, o senza quella." Martín de Azpilcueta, *Manuale de'confessori et penitenti* (In Vinetia: Appresso Gabriel Giolito di Ferrari). 893. I have only been able to consult the Italian translation of Azpilicueta's manual.

[108] "Fede è il conoscimento, con che fermamente giudichiamo esser così quello che non vediamo." Ibid.

[109] "Opinione è conocimiento, con che giudichiamo alcuna cosa che non vediamo esser cosí, pero non fermamente, con timore, che il contrario sia vero." Ibid.

[110] "Dubbio è conoscimento di due cose contrarie, senza giudicare, che alcuna di quelle sia veritá." Ibid.

[111] "Scrupulo è conoscimento di alcuna cosa, che rappresenta alcuna apparientia contra chello, che si sa, crede, pensa o dubbita, senza sapere giudicare il contrario." Ibid.

[112] Gómez Camacho, *Economía y filosofía moral: La formación del pensamiento económico europeo en la escolástica española*. 66–68.

[113] A normal theological reason of the time to act in a certain way would be the concept of *communis doctorum sententia* or *consentit Doctores communiter*. This concept is directly related to the paradigm of uncertainty and of probability. We cannot be completely sure in many cases, but that does not leave us at the mercy of pure relativism or of pure personal opinion. There exists a common opinion of those who know about the topic, and that is a first milestone in order to make a decision in the concrete.

and paradigmatic.[114] First, *Recta ratio* is a fallible reason. Nature is our teacher; however this does not guarantee infallibility.

Secondly, *Recta ratio* is also a practical reason, and this is so in two senses. It is practical not only because it refers to action, but also because it takes into account circumstances of time and place.[115] This is, as we shall see later, what favored the development of casuistry in the sixteenth century.

Thirdly, *recta ratio* was also a situated reason: different situations called for different moral decisions. The change of circumstances was something that *recta ratio* could not ignore. This was not sheer relativism. The importance of the situation, that is time, place, and circumstances, did not mean a relativistic approach. It meant that reality was actually being taken into account. That is why there is a taste for the analysis of particular cases, something that shows the nominalist influence in their thought.

Fourthly, *recta ratio* was controversial because controversy was the only way to combat, refine or refute unfounded opinions. Decisions were made by opinion, but this, as I have already noted, did not constitute a descent into relativism. Opinions were discussed, reasons for them were offered, and rational grounds for action were debated. This actually led to the development of moral theology and embryonic economics.[116]

Lastly, *recta ratio* was paradigmatic, as the term is employed by Thomas Kuhn. This actually means that to understand their moral reasoning, their disciplinary matrix has to be taken into account. From Antiquity to the ius-naturalistic philosophers of the seventeenth and eighteenth centuries, the term natural law had been used, and it is still used today in the Catholic tradition. We have, however, to keep in mind that although the term remained unaltered, the actual content of what it was being referred to changed.[117] Care must be employed in order not to confuse

---

[114] Gómez Camacho, *Economía y filosofía moral: La formación del pensamiento económico europeo en la escolástica española*. 79–84.

[115] Ibid. 82.

[116] That is why Gómez Camacho underlines the importance of controversy in scholastic epistemology. Controversy is the way the *Summa* is organized; it is the way *De Iustitia et Iure* is organized too. Actually this led *De Iustitia et Iure* treatises to detail economic practices, and that is what has attracted the attention of historians of economics to them.

[117] For example, according to Isidore of Seville, *ius naturalis* refered to what was right for humankind because of its animal condition (matrimony, the urge to mate and the raising of the offspring). *Ius gentium* refered to that right thing, which arising from the nature of things, pertained to humankind as part of its spiritual, social nature—

the same words when they are referring to different objects. Sometimes the difference is not great, sometimes it is of some importance. In the development of Catholic moral theology there is continuity, but not a perfect continuity. In the sixteenth century—and I believe this is not a characteristic exclusive to this age—concepts are being transformed to adapt to the new times.[118]

The different types of knowledge, coupled with the characteristic idea of *recta ratio*, contributed to the widespread quotation of the opinion of authorities in any book on moral theology. In the same way that Aquinas quoted the theological position of other authors in order to discuss them, opinions—that is knowledge that was neither firm nor clear but judicative, the result of *recta ratio*—were quoted. This practice actually led to the development of Probabilism.

5.3.2. *Probabilism*

Probabilism was an invention of the sixteenth century to deal with the perennial problem of moral uncertainty.[119] Probabilism was formulated by Bartolomé de Medina, O.P.[120] in his *Expositiones in Primam Secundae Divi Thomae* when he said, "it seems to me that if an opinion is probable, then one is permitted to follow that opinion, even if the opposite is more probable."[121] The meaning of the Latin *probabilis* is one of those cases in which we see how the meaning of words changes with time. *Probabilis* could mean "approved by acknowledged authorities," which in moral theology became known as external probability. *Probabilis*, however, could also mean "something that was well argued for." It was

for example, the immunity of ambassadors. In Spanish Scholasticism this was clearly different: *ius naturalis* refered to morality, and did not refer exclusively or primarily to what humanity shares with other animals. For the scholastics of the sixteenth century, with Vitoria as the main architect, *ius gentium* designated an international law that had the aim of protecting a common morality.

[118] Rossi warns against this false continuity drawing from Gaston Bachelard, *La formazione dello spirito scientifico* (Milano: Cortina 1995). Rossi. 4.

[119] Thomas Deman, "Probabilisme," in *Dictionaire de Théologie Catholique, XII*, ed. Eugène Mangeot Alfred Vacant, Emile Amann (Paris: Librairie Letonzey et Ané, 1936). 466. Martin W.F. Stone points to nominalist theologian Jean Gerson as a medieval forerunner of Probabilism in his quest to soothe scrupulous consciences. Martin W.F. Stone, "Scrupulosity and Conscience: Probabilism in Early Modern Scholastic Ethics," in *Contexts of Conscience in Early Modern Europe, 1500–1700*, ed. Edward Vallance and Harald Braun (Houndmills, Basingstoke, Hampshire; New York: Palgrave Macmillan, 2004). 3–6.

[120] A student of Vitoria, Medina succeeded Cano in the Chair of Prime at Salamanca.

[121] I take the translation offered in Stone. 7.

a position with substantial reason in its favor. This became known in ethical debate as internal probability.[122] With time, probabilism in moral theology would fall into a game of merely quoting authorities. But in the beginning, moral probability also referred to a well argued case in which *recta ratio* was used to prove the advisability of a certain course of action. Although coined by a Dominican, probabilism would become associated with the Society of Jesus, and Francisco Suarez, S.J. and Gabriel Vázquez, S.J. would provide the classic formulation of probabilism.[123]

New times were certainly bringing about new ethical challenges, and new solutions were being proposed for these difficulties, and probabilism was one of the major new solutions. The problems of trade are directly related to the appearance of probabilism. The new mercantile practices of the time were causing much anxiety both to merchants and to moral theologians. A large part of casuistry was oriented to assessing new contracts.[124] The confessional and the university chair had become well acquainted with the new problems. Medina published his commentary on *Prima Secundae* in 1577. Two years later, in 1579, he published *Breve instrucción de cómo se ha de administrar el sacramento de la penitencia*. In this work we can find a summary version of his doctrine of Probabilism. According to Medina, in cases in which a confessor is in doubt (where there is some reasonable measure of probability on both sides), the confessor could grant absolution even against his own opinion. He offers an example, referring to business practices:

> The confessor has the opinion that he who has lent some money should take nothing in exchange for the profit he is giving up, because of the loan. On the other hand the penitent following the contrary opinion, which is probable, received something as *lucrum cessans*. In this case, I hold that the confessor can, and is even obliged to absolve the penitent. The reason is that the penitent is not sinning in receiving that quantity, for it was licit for him, and for all, to follow the probable opinion.[125]

---

[122] Ibid. 10. In classical Latin *probabilis* meant "probable, credible, not impossible or acceptable, worthy of approval, good." *Cassel's Latin Dictionary*, (New York: Wiley Publishing, 1977). In Scholastic Latin it also meant "clear, conclusive." *Lexicon Latinitatis Medii Aevi, Praesertim Ad Res Ecclesiasticas Investigandas Pertinens*, (Thurnholti: Typographi Brepols Editores Pontificii, 1975).

[123] Stone. 10–16.

[124] The chapters of Vereecke's book that refer to the sixteenth century abound with topics related to economic problems, showing the importance of economic issues in the moral theology of the time.

[125] "en los casos dudosos que por una parte y por otra son probables, y tienen haz y envés, puede el confesor, aunque sea contra la opinión que tiene él, absolver al penitente.

Confessors and practitioners of moral theology found themselves perplexed and divided about the moral rectitude of many new business practices such as slave trade, money exchange and the obligation of canon and civil law in particular cases. The proliferation of books, and contrary opinions, did not help, but actually introduced a greater degree of doubt and perplexity. Simultaneously they found themselves in need of finding a practical solution to determine whether or not to grant absolution. As Stone suggests, Probabilism was an "important component in the ongoing and quite sincere attempts made by some early moral thinkers to confront the recalcitrant nature of many episodes of human moral experience, in a world they believed to be characterized by contingency and human sinfulness".[126] In doing so, the confessors were becoming somewhat like the merchants with whom they dealt. They were weighing, measuring and assessing opinions and sins, as merchants did with their businesses, while trying to find a solution for singular cases.[127]

6. The Problems of Divine Grace

6.1. *The Theological Controversies regarding Grace*

In his monumental study *Surnaturel*, Henry de Lubac explained how the idea of pure nature was born out of medieval speculations about the *potentia Dei absoluta*, an idea dear to the nominalists. It was Cajetan, followed by others, who afforded entry into Thomistic thought, to the concept of supernatural, as opposed and complementary to pure nature. According to de Lubac this was a very particular, and inaccurate, interpretation of Aquinas.[128] However, of interest to our study is this key point: what was once closely knit together in the concept of nature was

---

Pongo un exemplo. Tiene el confessor por opinión que el que presta no puede llevar cosa alguna por lo que dexa de ganar, por razón del empréstito, y por otra parte el penitente siguiendo la opinión contraria, que es probable, recibió algo por el lucro cessante. En este caso, digo que puede el confessor, y aun está obligado a absolver al penitente. Y la razón es, porque tal penitente no peca en recibir aquella cantidad, pues le era lícito y a todos lo es seguir la opinión probable." Bartolomé de Medina, *Breve instrucción de cómo se ha de administrar el sacramento de la penitencia*, (Salamanca 1579). Book I, Chapter 1, pp. 19–20. Quoted in Caro Baroja. 391–392.

[126] Stone. 3.

[127] Caro Baroja. 390.

[128] Henri de Lubac, *Surnaturel. Études Historiques* (Paris: Éditions Montaigne, 1956). 105–106.

being separated in the sixteenth century. Therefore, the ties of grace and nature were being dissolved, and as the ideas of pure nature and the supernatural were being developed, the resulting views on grace were also influencing moral theology.

The separation of the natural from the supernatural was a dangerous ethical move. As Phillip J. Donelly S.J. notes:

> If there were no other end to regulate our lives by enforcing strict moral obligations except the supernatural of whose existence we obtain knowledge from revelation, we would have to conclude that, before the Christian era, and even now, outside the pale of Christianity, man lived and still lives without any perceptible moral law; in this hypothesis, there would not be strictly speaking, any natural law.[129]

The order of Aquinas' *Summa* had prepared the separation of moral theology from the rest of theology, for this order grouped together, within a separate section, all the topics of moral theology. If this order of exposition had prepared the separation, the developments in the natural sciences pushed for the move. It was not by chance that when nature began to be desacrilized by scientists, theologians began to make the distinction between natural and supernatural. This is so because certain attributes presupposed in the common concept of nature were being challenged by the natural sciences.[130] To save the theological truth, theologians reshaped the theological concept of nature.

If, on the other hand, theologians of the time were being repelled from the natural sciences with a concept of nature that could scarcely admit God as part of it, on the other side tendencies within theological circles sought to separate nature and grace.[131] The most extreme case was Luther, for whom human nature offered no practical guidance for morality, because with the Fall reason had been entirely corrupted.

The Christian doctrines of human free will and divine grace had been controversial topics since Augustine's times. In the sixteenth century, however, the discussion about grace again became a point of polemical

---

[129] Phillip J. Donnelly, "Discussions on the Supernatural Order," *Theological Studies* IX, no. 2 (1948). 222.

[130] "La natura di cui parlano i moderni é radicalmente diversa dalla natura di cui parlano i filisofi medievali. Nella natura dei moderni non si dá (come nella tradizione) una distinzione di essenza fra corpi naturali e corpi artificiali." Rossi. xvi.

[131] Queralt emphasizes the care that Molina took, and this could be extended to other theologians of the time, to hold together both ends of the problem. Antonio Queralt, "El fin último natural en Luis de Molina," *Estudios eclesiásticos* 34 (1960).

interest. It was one of the main issues over which the Reformers and the Catholic Church clashed. For Luther the question of grace was the issue—the article by which the Church stood or fell. This is evident in the first Protestant creeds.[132] But even within the Catholic Church, the topic proved controversial. Trent's decree on justification—the council's masterpiece—had avoided any pronouncements on questions disputed by the schools. This meant that the field was open to theological discussion. This open-endedness produced nearly open warfare among the theological schools. The question of grace and free will had caused an intense discussion in Louvain around the person and writings of Michel Baius.[133] The Jesuit Leonard Lessius, who also wrote an important *De Iustitia et Iure*, played a major role in the controversy challenging Baius' doctrines. When Luis de Molina published *Concordia* in 1588, the epicenter of the discussion moved to Spain where religious orders aligned on one side or the other.[134] In the seventeenth century the epicenter of the discussion would move to France. The clash between Jansenists and the Jesuits prompted Blaise Pascal to write his famous *Provincial Letters* that brought casuistry into disrepute. We can see that free will and divine grace appear paired with moral theology in Lessius, Molina and Pascal. By no means did this happen by mere chance.[135]

Although they appear far apart on the theological map of the twenty-first century, the topics of grace and moral theology are intimately intertwined. In the *Summa* "God is the exterior principle that moves us toward the good, instructing us by the law and helping us through grace."[136]

[132] Art. II. 5 of the Articles of Smalcald.

[133] The controversy regarding Michel Baius had begun in 1563, just after he returned from Trent where he had served as theologian of the King of Spain.

[134] An overview of this development appears in Luis de Molina, *On Divine Foreknowledge: Part IV of Concordia*, ed. Alfred J. Freddoso, trans. Alfred J. Freddoso (Ithaca: Cornell University Press, 1988). 1–80.

[135] An overview of the three controversies from the perspective of the doctrine of justification can be found in Alister E. McGrath, *Iustitia Dei. A History of the Christian Doctrine of Justification*, 3rd ed. (Cambridge: Cambridge university Press, 2005). 344–357. It is also very illustrative Quilliet. 336–358. Grice-Hutchinson also observes a link between the doctrines of grace and monetary theory. Grice-Hutchinson, *The School of Salamanca; Readings in Spanish Monetary Theory, 1544–1605*. 46.

[136] "Principium autem exterius movens ad bonum est Deus, qui et nos instruit per legem, et iuvat per gratiam. Unde primo, de lege; secundo, de gratia dicendum est." Ia–IIae q. 90 pr.

6.2. *The Political Dimension of Divine Grace*

There is another way in which the problems of grace of the time affected moral theology. The end of the Middle Ages saw a great transformation of political structures and European states began moving towards political absolutism. In political absolutism the kings considered themselves kings by the grace of God. Politically this meant that the law had no exception and was universal in extent. This had not been the dominant conception of law in the Middle Ages.[137] Nor was it the conception of law imagined when talking about natural law.

Developing the history of how our contemporary idea of the law of nature appeared, Dorato points out that "the cultural and social grounds necessary to the emergence of the notion of natural law [he is using natural law as it pertains to the natural sciences, not as the idea present in the tradition of moral philosophy and theology] were formed as a result of the combined action of two factors which have only been fully realized in modern times." The first of the factors is the mathematization and mechanization of divine laws, which we saw when discussing how mechanization affected the Scientific Revolution. The second factor was "the emergence of absolutist political regimes, which overthrew previous feudal systems." These new political systems were "a condition necessary to the emergence of natural law [remember he is referring to the laws of nature] as something that has no exception and is universal."[138] In Spanish Scholasticism the mechanical idea of society had not yet caught on. Society was imagined through the metaphor of the body. This organic metaphor made of the idea of law a particular one.[139] Law for the Spanish Scholastics was not procedural. It was a matter of history. It was something that united.[140] It was drawn from experience. Natural law was

---

[137] Harold Joseph Berman, "Law and Revolution: The Formation of the Western Legal Tradition," (Cambridge, Mass.: Harvard University Press, 1983). 1–45.

[138] Dorato. 11.

[139] "Se podrá decir que este organicismo igualitario refleja perfectamente el proceso histórico en que los doctores españoles viven, un momento en el que está desapareciendo la estructura de la sociedad feudal, pero aun no se ha impuesto la visión individualista liberal. Por eso la contribución de los miembros de la sociedad al bien común y a la unidad social no se interpreta en términos mecanicistas, sino en los que se derivan de la metáfora biológica del cuerpo; pero un cuerpo en el que los miembros son las personas que pueden cambiar su situación social subiendo o bajando en la escala social." Gómez Camacho, *Economía y filosofía moral: La formación del pensamiento económico europeo en la escolástica española*. 107.

[140] "The presence of a sense of the wholeness of life with all other aspects of life, a sense that legal institutions and legal processes as well as legal norms and legal decisions are

that which was observed to remain unchanged among all people. Later philosophers and theologians might have given a metaphysical foundation to it, but there was an epistemological precedent for this move. In ancient times and in the Middle Ages people realized that there were certain patterns of behavior that seem to be invariant across cultures. They called this natural law. From a Christian point of view they realized that this was related to Creation, which makes everyone equal before God. In this creation God not only maintained everything in place from the beginning, but God also exercised an ongoing Providence. Moreover, men had access to that Providence. For the Spanish Scholastics, natural law was, in fact, a form of self-directed providence.[141] Natural law was the mode by which God instructed humanity and was intimately interwoven with the history of salvation and with the biblical narrative. Natural law was not a postulate of practical reason. It was, according to theologians, one of the ways to participate in God's divine providence. We shall see more of this in the next section.

7. The *Concordia*

Molina's most famous book is the *Concordia*. It is arguably one of the most famous books ever written by a Jesuit, and also one of the most polemical. In it, Molina tried to reconcile the Christian doctrines of human free will and divine grace. The purpose of this section is to show how Molina's position on grace and free will influenced his fundamental moral theology. I will set out now the content of the *Concordia* in as much as it influences the approach to moral theology. In the last two chapters, I will explain how this doctrine influences his views on justice.

---

all integrated in the harmony of the universe. Law, like art and myth and religion, and like language itself, was for the peoples of Europe, in the early stages of their history, not primarily a matter of making and applying rules in order to determine guilt and fix judgment, not an instrument to separate people from one another on the basis of principles, but rather a matter of holding people together, a matter of reconciliation." Berman. 78.

[141] "Que la voz de la ley natural se expresara en términos de probabilidad y no de necesidad marcará una diferencia esencial entre el modo de concebir la naturaleza los doctores españoles y el modo de concebir el pensamiento científica posterior. Esa diferencia descansa en la aceptación o rechazo del Principio de Uniformidad de la Naturaleza, del que ya los escolásticos del siglo XIV se habían ocupado en sus discusiones metodológicas." Gómez Camacho, *Economía y filosofía moral: La formación del pensamiento económico europeo en la escolástica española*. 68.

7.1. *The Theological Problem: The Common Ground of Bañezians and Molinists*

For Christianity God is Creator, Omniscient, Redeemer and Provident. The world is not just created by God, but is also guided by him to its perfection. This assertion is not overly problematic as long as it refers to non-humans. The problem arises when we take into account creatures that have free will—humans and angels. Then the assertion brings up the question of human action (we will not take into account the problem of the angels), responsibility in history and the problem of evil. If God guides history, is there any room for free human action?

Luther and Erasmus had publicly debated over this question between 1524 and 1526. In the Catholic field it remained clear that the world and human history were neither the result of anarchy of causes nor of a necessary and deterministic order so strict that it left no room for human freedom. Free will was the topic of the sixteenth and seventeenth centuries. What had to be reconciled was God's Omniscience and Providence with human free will.[142] This was not an easy task.

The question raised the problem of causality in the world. Molina observed that "the medieval Aristotelians maintain [...] that all creatures have genuine causal power, too—though [...] in order for them to exercise this power God must also act to produce the relevant effect."[143] This invoked the idea of God's general concurrence (*concursus generalis*), the idea that God was ultimately the first cause of everything. This meant that, albeit ultimately everything finds its cause in God, in a particular case the cause of an effect should be traced to the secondary cause, not to God's general concurrence.[144] If this is so, then what it was next required was an explanation of the way human freedom acted in history. Here is where Bañezians and Molinists disagreed. The problem

---

[142] Marcelino Ocaña García, *Luis de Molina (1535–1600)*, 1. ed., Biblioteca Filosífica. Colección Filósofos y Textos (Madrid: Ediciones del Orto, 1995). 14–16.

[143] Molina, *On Divine Foreknowledge: Part IV of the Concordia*. 17.

[144] "Medieval writers frequently appeal to the sun's causal influence on terrestrial events in order to illuminate this point. By providing heat and light the sun causally contributes to animal reproduction on earth. But this causal influence is general, since it has to be channeled or rendered particular by further causes. So, for instance, the sun is a general cause in the production of, say, this calf, since its causal contribution has to be channeled toward the production of a calf (as opposed to, say, a duckling) by further, particular, causes (a cow and a bull). Likewise, God's general causal influence is required in order for secondary causes to bring about any effects whatever anywhere in the created world. But God's causal influence as the primary and maximal universal cause must be particularized and channeled toward given effects by secondary causes." Ibid. 17.

arose from the interpretation of Thomas Aquinas's *Summa* Ia q. 14 a. 13.[145] What had to be explained was how God, being perfectly provident, had "comprehensive knowledge of what will happen in the created order."[146]

7.2. *Molinism*

7.2.1. *Indeterminism*

For Molina the only way to avoid falling into some variety of determinism was to state that "God's general concurrence is an action of God directly on the effect and not in the secondary agents themselves, whereas the Thomistic opponents take God's general concurrence to be a divine action directly on the secondary agents ("premoving" them) and through them on the effect."[147] This was applied to the doctrine of grace.

When God wanted an effect to take place, he would grant his grace to a person in order to obtain it. If the effect occurred, we could talk of efficacious grace, but if the effect did not occur we could not say that God's general concurrence was not there, because he had granted his grace. Molina would say that there was an inefficacious grace, but still sufficient grace. God merely permitted the unwanted effect to take place by granting his sufficient grace to the agent. God's general concurrence acted, according to Molina, in the effect, not in the agent. God acted as a cause, but not moving the agent, rather by granting his causation power to the effect. By asserting this, Molina was enhancing the role of human free will. It was this very free will that was rendering grace efficacious or inefficacious, because God acted in the effect and not in the agent.[148] This was what the Bañezians contested. They labeled Molina a Pelagian because they saw his approach as leaving God's causation power and,

---

[145] "In fact, both Bañezianism and Molinism are probably best regarded as alternative attempts to compensate for what many Catholic thinkers, especially in light of the Reformer's influential writings on these very matters, took to be a lacuna or at least a lack of explicitness in St. Thomas's work." Ibid. 8.

[146] Ibid. 4.

[147] Ibid. 18.

[148] "Bañezians hold that efficacious concurrence is intrinsically or essentially efficacious with respect to the intended effect and that merely sufficient concurrence is intrinsically inefficacious with respect to such an effect. Molina contends to the contrary that God's general concurrence is in itself neither efficacious nor inefficacious, but is instead an intrinsically 'neutral' causal influence that is rendered efficacious or inefficacious extrinsically by the relevant secondary causes. As we will see, this disagreement has an immediate and profound impact on the analysis of free choice and of causal indeterminism in general." Ibid. 18.

therefore, divine grace in the hands of the creature. Bañezians thought that what occurred, occurred because God had exercised his causation power on the agent, premoving him.

Human freedom with respect to an object resulted, in the Molinist account, as some kind of indeterminism with respect to it. Freddoso points out that "Molina sees clearly that if God's actions were the only actual source of contingency, then the world would for all practical purposes be thoroughly deterministic."[149] By granting this indetermination to human freedom, Molina was allowing another source of contingency in the world beyond God's will. God's general concourse could cause, or not cause, something according to the free undetermined will of the human person. Freedom amounted to indetermination and to contingency because what was determined was necessary and not contingent.[150]

In proposing this view, Molina was granting great importance to the contingent and to the will of the agent. Although based in Thomism, the world order that resulted from this approach was no longer the perfect architecture of Thomas in which Creation was an elaborate staging to give glory to God. In Molina's account the agent almost seem to control God's power of causation. This is what upset the Bañezians. This metaphysical doctrine was accompanied by an epistemological one.

7.2.2. Triplex est sciencia in Deo[151]

To be able to explain the way general concourse occurred, Molina had to address the problem of divine foreknowledge. If God was to lend his general concourse he must know what the agent was going to decide in order to be able to lend it. But how could he do so to a free, and therefore non determined, action. To be able to explain this, Molina distinguished three types of knowledge in God that correlate to different states of affairs. This threefold knowledge in God was a novelty. The professor from Evora became famous for his resulting theory of the middle science (*scientia media*).

[149] Ibid. 20.

[150] "For Molina, then, to be free with respect to a given object (that is, a state of affairs) is to have a faculty, namely, a will or intellective appetite, by virtue of which one is capable of choosing indeterministically with respect to that object. In paradigmatic instances the agent has three options: (i) to elicit an act of willing an object, (ii) to elicit an act of dissenting from or rejecting the object, or (iii) to refrain from either willing or dissenting. So every free action involves a free choice, which are typically issues forth in a 'commanded' (as opposed to 'elicited') act—most often, in free human action, a basic bodily movement." Ibid. 25.

[151] V. 57. 3, p. 199, it explicitly makes reference to *Concordia* I, q. 14, a. 13.

It was common scholastic doctrine that there exist in God two types of knowledge: natural knowledge and free knowledge. Natural knowledge was the knowledge God had as Creator, as the Artisan of the universe. This knowledge allowed him to know how things would work out because he had created them and knew the nature of things. It was the knowledge of how things worked in the world without the intervention of any will. Natural knowledge was the knowledge of all the possible future contingents, and a prevolitional knowledge.[152]

At the same time there was God's free knowledge by which he knew about future contingents that depended not on the nature of created things, but on God's free will. This was a postvolitional knowledge, a knowledge dependent in the exercise of will. What Molina did was to come up with a third category, middle knowledge, by which God knew the conditional future contingents. They were conditional because they did not happen because of the nature of things—as was the case of free knowledge—but they might not necessarily have happened—as was the case of natural knowledge. They were not actual future contingent, but conditional future contingents. God could know these because he had super-comprehension, meaning that God is "able to have epistemic certitude regarding states of affairs that do not (at least yet) have metaphysical certitude." Only God had super-comprehension, creatures did not, because "future contingents can be known infallibly and with certitude only by a cognitively perfect being."[153]

Through his middle knowledge God knew conditional future contingents, but only he, not the creature, could know that. Bañezians did not question the assertion that God knew conditional future contingents. For them "God knows conditional future contingents in the same way He knows absolute future contingents, namely, through His decreeing that they obtain."[154] For Molina such decreeing did not take place. It

[152] "Notice that God's natural knowledge includes a comprehensive grasp of all the active and passive causal powers creatures might have and exercise, since such causal powers are ultimately rooted in their natures. What's more, by His natural knowledge God knows all the possible spatial and temporal arrangements of creaturely agents and patients and hence knows all the ways in which they might causally interact with one another. And by His natural knowledge He also knows prevolitionally (i) what would result from any possible causal interaction in which all the relevant created causes act deterministically and (ii) what might result from any possible causal interaction in which some created cause acts indeterministically." Molina, *On Divine Foreknowledge: Part IV of the Concordia*, 12.

[153] Ibid. 52.

[154] Ibid. 51.

was somehow the creature who decreed, and God who granted his general concourse to the effect. Bañezians questioned super-comprehension and middle knowledge. The metaphysical, as well as the epistemological doctrine certainly introduced a novelty, and this novelty had profound impact on the way moral reasoning functioned in the scholastic mindset.

7.3. *Consequences for Moral Theology*

We have already mentioned the importance granted to the actions of the creature in Molinism. In itself it is a big step. Besides this, the middle knowledge seemed to create a blind spot in the creature's participation within the Divine Mind. Middle science was, as I have said, only possible to God. The human being could participate in God's mind, but only in the natural and in the free sciences. This participation was the basis for the entire natural law theory, one of the pillars of Catholic moral theology. Molina had opened a metaphysical and epistemological gate for the uncertainty with which he and his contemporaries were dealing.[155] This was affected by the change in *Weltanschauung*. A new scientific paradigm was being forged, but also a new paradigm in moral theology. In this time of uncertainty, one could at most aspire to a certain probability of the goodness of its actions. Because the conditional future contingents were only known to God, there were situations in which the best the rational creature could do was to try to use his rationality to find the correct thing to do, but without the warranty of participating in God's mind. There was no recourse to the authority concept of participation in God's mind. This was a metaphysical and epistemological support for probabilism. Probabilism as a moral doctrine found in the *Concordia* a strong philosophical and theological ground.

Now that we have stated this metaphysical and epistemological frame that affects all of Molina's theological work, we shall turn to *De Iustitia et Iure*, and investigate Molina's fundamental moral theology.

---

[155] Diez-Alegría points out how the middle science does not appear in the manuscript of 1568 but it comes up in the final printed version of the *De Iustitia et Iure*. It is a sign that Molina thought it relevant for his moral reasoning. José María Díez-Alegría, *El desarrollo de la doctrina de la ley natural en Luís de Molina y en los maestros de la universidad de Evora de 1565 a 1591. Estudio histórico y textos inéditos* (Barcelonna: 1951). 57.

CHAPTER TWO

MOLINA'S FUNDAMENTAL MORAL THEOLOGY

1. Introduction

This chapter presents Molina's theological framework in two sections. The first section explains the genesis of the book *De Iustitia et Iure*. In doing so it helps understand the way in which Molina's moral reasoning progresses, a way that is neither that of Aquinas, with which we are more familiarized, nor that of our times, but a middle development between both. The book is neither medieval, nor modern. The genesis of the book explains its structure, the way in which a *disputatio*—the basic unit of argumentation—was developed, and the particularities of this genre in moral theology.

The second section, much longer than the first, is an account of Molina's fundamental moral theology. It contains his explanations on law—natural and positive—and others aspects of Molina's fundamental moral theology not explicitly discussed in the work, but present in it.

2. *De Iustitia et Iure*

2.1. *Genesis of the Book: Teaching Methods and New Literary Genres*

Molina's work is the result of his teaching experience in Coimbra and especially in Evora, and the result of a vast project. Molina had been allowed to abandon teaching in order to prepare his works for publication. Of his vast project only a small part was published during his lifetime: the *Concordia*, the commentary on the *Prima* and the three initial volumes of *De Iustitia et Iure* that contained the first two treatises. The final volume that contained the last three treatises was published shortly after his death. The first volume of *De Iustitia et Iure* was published in Cuenca in 1593. The second and third volumes were published in 1597 and 1600. The rest of the work was prepared for publication after Molina's death and published in Antwerp in 1609. Partial or complete editions of the work appeared during the seventeenth century in Venice, Mainz, Cologne and Lyons. The last complete edition of the book is that of Cologne of 1733.[1]

Since *De Iustitia et Iure* is the result of his lectures, it is therefore important to understand the teaching methods of the time. This will enable us to understand the genesis of this book, what it says and the way it proceeds.

During the Middle Ages and through the sixteenth century, teaching began with the *lectio*. The teacher would literarilly read from a book to his students. The reading was interspersed with comments of the professor that the students usually wrote down. A book was usually the subject matter of a course. To give a course was *legere librum*.[2] The *lectio* was just the beginning of the process. The reading and the professor's commentary upon it raised *quaestiones*. How was the text or a comment about it to be understood? These questions resulted in discussions. Hence comes the term *disputatio*.[3]

The disputation was a long established way of teaching, widely used in European universities. It was at the University of Paris that disputations, as all other methods of active learning, were most developed in the sixteenth century. The ensemble of pedagogical methods used in Paris was called the *modus parisiensis*. The first Jesuits studied in Paris, and cherished their education there. When in 1548 the first Jesuit school was established in Messina, it explicitly adopted this *modus parisiensis* as a pedagogical model. So successful was the practice of applying these methods of higher education to all stages of education that those disputations and all type of students' competitions became a veritable hallmark of Jesuit education.[4] When the final version of the *Ratio Studiorum* was published in 1599, the disputation, along with the *lectio* and the *repetitio*, was a key pedagogical instrument.[5]

---

[1] For a detailed table of editions see: Beatriz Eugenia Sosa Morato, *La noción de derecho en "Los seis libros de la justicia y el derecho" de Luis De Molina* (Pamplona: Ediciones Universidad de Navarra, 1985). 323.

[2] In his letter to Acquaviva, Molina says: "Aora a diez y nueve años se me ordenó leiese un curso de artes [...] Poco después de aver leido este curso [...] A catorze años que leo theulogía en Evora." Stegmüller. 550–551.

[3] Gabriel Codina Mir, *Aux sources de la pédagogie des jésuites, Le "modus parisiensis."* (Roma: Institutum Historicum S.I., 1968). 109–118.

[4] John W. O'Malley, *The First Jesuits* (Cambridge: Harvard University Press, 2002). 217. Codina Mir. 329.

[5] "Disputations are to be scheduled once a week when there are only a few in the

In a disputation a student would be given a theological thesis to defend, and time to prepare its defense. This happened usually once a week, but it would take place also on special occasions such as the feast of an important saint or the visit to the school of an important person. A student would defend a theological thesis. He would face two or three opponents who would argue against the theological thesis he was defending. Before beginning the rules of "fair play" were read. This academic event was presided over by a regent, the professor of theology, and sometimes even by the prefect or the rector, depending on the occasion. The students had been well trained in rhetoric and various modes of arguing were employed. Sometimes authorities, Scripture, Councils or approved doctors, were quoted against the theological thesis. Facts could be adduced or logical syllogisms developed. The disputation could assume many shapes; it depended on the topic and the disputants. It was an exercise in rhetoric, as well as an exercise in theology or philosophy. Important to our study is the fact that disputations had different forms and that they tended to explore the topic in multiple ways.[6] Unlike the manuals that would soon appear, disputations do not intend to repeat what was common doctrine about a certain topic, but to exercise the theological mind of the contestants and, when later written, that of the reader.[7]

All these methods of teaching (*lectio*, *dictatio*, *repetitio* and *disputatio*) are reflected in *De Iustitia et Iure*, but especially the disputation. The book is divided into five treatises and each treatise is divided into disputations. More about the structure and method of the book will be said in the next section. We will now continue with other factors that stand at the genesis of the book.

The *De Legibus* and *De Iustitia et Iure* treatises are the most important body of theological and juridical literature of the Spanish Golden

academy, twice a week when there are many members. They should be scheduled on the weekly holiday or on both the weekly holiday and on Sunday. One student, generally a philosopher, should defend a thesis for an hour on Sunday afternoon, while two object. On the recreation day, two or three are to defend theses for two hours, one a theology student, the others, students of philosophy while as many or more will offer objections." *The Jesuit Ratio Studiorum of 1599*, ed. Farrell S.J., Allan P., trans. Farrell S.J., Allan P. (Washington D.C.: Conference of Major Superior of Jesuits, 1970). 107.

[6] "On pourra définir cette méthode comme une activité inlassable, un exercice et une pratique constante, une sorte d'incessante gymnastique de l'esprit qui met en œuvre dans le processus d'éducation toutes les ressources et toutes les facultés de la personne humaine." Codina Mir. 109.

[7] For a further description of what a disputation was see rule 18 of the Professors of the Higher Faculties in the Ratio Studiorum. *The Jesuit Ratio Studiorum of 1599*. 28.

Age.[8] As we have seen, Domingo de Soto was the first theologian to publish a *De Iustitia et Iure* treatise in 1553 in Salamanca. He said he was moved to write such a book because of the way in which usury and greed were practiced in the contracts and agreements of his time.[9] But neither greed nor usury were new to Soto's times. What made treatises on justice and law thrive was the fact that new circumstances were requiring new intellectual means to address the current social problems. Both speculative scholastic theology and the more practical *summae confessorum* were not well suited for the new times. A new literary genre was born out of necessity. There were many new problems: the justness of the Spanish conquest, the new problems around slavery that appeared with the colonization of America and the Portuguese slave trade, the new problems of trade driven partly by the sheer amount of gold and silver arriving from the Americas, the problem of the validity of the institutions of the newly discovered lands, and the applicability of European institutions to the New World. It was not a situation merely of new circumstances that could be easily integrated in the classical scholastic intellectual frame. The new issues were breaking the old framework apart.

We find these new topics, which Aquinas had never broached, being discussed by theologians as best they could. They were employing the classical resources, but they were also reaching out to new ones as they realized that the traditional methodologies were not enough. But this starts to burst the bounds of the normal learning of the time.[10] This is what led Molina to say in his letter to Aquaviva that he had realized that the treatment of Aquinas and other theologians was too brief. Theolo-

---

[8] Luis de Molina, *La teoría del justo precio*, ed. Francisco Gómez Camacho (Madrid: Editora Nacional, 1981). 14. He is quoting Avelino Folgado, "Los tratados *De Legibus* y *De Iustita et Iure* en los autores españoles del siglo XVI y primera mitad del XVII," *La Ciudad de Dios* CLXXII (1959). 275.

[9] "Con anterioridad a Soto, los doctores escolásticos habían tratado los temas económicos en sus comentarios a la *Summa* de santo Tomás. Domingo de Soto fue el primero en escribir un tratado moral *De Iustitia et Iure* como obra independiente. A partir de Soto se escribieron tratados *De Iustitia et Iure* por los mejores doctores escolásticos, Molina, Lugo, Lessio, etc., y en ellos se expone el mejor pensamiento económico de su tiempo. La razón por la que Soto se decidió a escribir su tratado de la forma que lo hizo nos la da a conocer él mismo: los pactos y acuerdos en los que la usura y la avaricia se practican con frecuencia en la sociedad de su tiempo." Gómez Camacho, *Economía y filosofía moral: La formación del pensamiento económico europeo en la escolástica española*. 38.

[10] Gómez Camacho insists on the idea of a change in paradigm in the sense of Thomas Kuhn in the time of the second scholastic that affects the way economics are conceived. Ibid. 11–13.

gians were quieting consciences for lack of knowledge on moral questions. That led him to drop the previous reliance upon Aquinas' order and to write five treatises on justice that would include all that Aquinas had said and much more.[11]

Aquinas starts his questions on justice by defining what justice is and delineating its parts. This takes five questions. He then moves to the vices that inhibit the practice of justice, which takes 15 questions. The longest part of the discussion is the last part: 43 questions dedicated to the virtues related to justice, such as religion, piety, observance and epikeia. Molina would take only the first five questions and he will then move away from the Thomist order. New times were requiring new literary genres and intellectual categories to solve new problems.

2.2. *Structure and Method*

2.2.1. *Structure of the Book*

De Iustita et Iure is divided in five treatises of unequal length. Each treatise is divided into disputations. The first book *De iustitia in genere* is dedicated to defining justice and defining its various types. It held only 13 disputations on justice and right in general and their parts, as well as on injustice. Here is where Molina follows Aquinas more closely. At the beginning of his questions regarding justice, the *Summa* dedicates questions 57 to 62 of the *Secunda Secundae* to justice, right, injustice and judgment.[12]

The second treatise *De iustitia commutativa*, devoted to commutative justice, is by far the longest.[13] And although this is where Molina departs from closely following Aquinas, it still adheres to the Thomist order. In II^{a}–IIae q. 63 vices are addressed, that is, specific problematic issues concerning justice. Times had greatly changed, and Molina did not

[11] "Despues pareciendome que estava por los theologos y principalmente por Santo Thomas muy cortamente tratada la materia de iustitia, y que estavan con razon desacreditados los theologos para cosa de govierno, y que en muchas cosas preguntados se hallavan atados y con poca luz para responder, y cobardes para acometer negocios de servicio de Dios, y dalles salida y de embaracer conscientias, por tener corta notitia en cosas morales, maxime en la materia de iustitia (como confieso averme a mi acontecido diversas vezes en missiones y fuera dellas) determiné dexar a Santo Thomas desde la q. 62 hasta el principio de la materia de religione, que serán como quinze quaestiones, y hazer cinco tratados de iustitia, en que díxese todo lo que Santo Thomas dixo en aquellas quaestiones y mucho mas que él no tocó." Stegmüller. 552.

[12] To see the summary: II^{a}–IIae, q. 57. proemium.

[13] Molina himself says in the prologue to *De Iustita et Iure*: "... secundus ... qui vastissimus est."

address the same topics that Aquinas did. He started with the theory of rights and discussed dominion. He then went on to discuss specific problematic issues.

The discussion about dominion and its different forms occupies an important part of the work, and took Molina deeply into juridical questions. Dominion for the scholastics was not just about property. The problem of dominion was the problem of the origins of society and the legitimacy of its most important institutions: family, private property and political power. They differentiated within dominion *dominium paternum*, *dominium privatum* and *dominium iurisdictionis*.[14] The second treatise discusses issues of civil law that fall under the field of dominion and the different forms it might take. It is in this treatise that we find the specific economic topics that we will analyze in chapter four. Usury is dealt with in the 303rd to the 335th disputations, just price in the 346th to the 364th disputations, money exchange in disputations 396 to 410.

The third treatise refers to criminal law; the fourth to honor, fame and other spiritual goods. The fifth treatise *De iudicio et executione per publicas potestates* deals with procedural law and the theory of law. In the prologue Molina talked about a sixth treatise on distributive justice, but it was never completed. It is in the first and fifth treatises that we find what we might call the fundamental moral theology of Molina. The specific issues are found in the other sections.

The book is difficult to read. The only divisions are treatises and disputations. In the first treatise there are only 13 disputations, so this does not present a problem. But in the rest of the treatises, and especially the second, the sequence of topics is not always clear. Also the length of the disputations is very variable. While some are just a page or two. Others are much longer. We shall see the different reasons for this in the next section.

2.2.2. *Structure of a Disputation*

The pedagogical practice of the disputation not only resulted in naming the divisions of every treatise. This type of dialectical exercise affected the internal structure of written theological discussion, which followed a progression similar to that of oral disputations.

[14] We will approach the problems regarding the concept of *dominium* in the third chapter.

In the Cologne edition[15] at the beginning of every disputation there is an outline of what will be argued in the disputation. Some outlines have just a few points. Others are very long. Molina followed the scholastic method, but the structure of a disputation was not as clear as that of Aquinas' questions in the *Summa*. There are several reasons for this.

A first cause is a rhetorical one. A disputation is a rhetorical exercise, not a philosophical or theological one, although the content might be theological or philosophical. In a disputation different rhetorical structures could be used, and this is reflected in *De Iustitia et Iure*.

Some of the disputations perfectly reproduce the structure of a question of the *Summa*. In those cases we find first the false solutions with the arguments for them, then Molina's own solution proving it with reasons and authorities. Finally he answers the difficulties and refutes the false solutions first proposed. This is the inherited structure that serves as a template behind each disputation.[16] The disputation on private property is a good example of how the method of argumentation of the *Summa* underlies the text.[17] In other cases the structure is not so clear.

Other disputations, though, are more juridical exposition about points of law. In these cases the structure of the disputation looks more like a juridical disputation of the time. In that era legal reasoning began by

---

[15] This work uses of the Cologne edition. Luis de Molina, *De justitia et jure: opera omnia, tractatibus quinque, tomisque totidem comprensa* (Coloniae Allobrogum: Sumptibus fratrum de Tournes, 1759).

We shall quote through the Cologne edition because it is the most followed way. Gómez Camacho, de Roover and Noonan follow this edition when quoting. In the Cologne edition every disputation is preceded by a table of contents of the disputation. Every entry of this table of contents in preceded by an Arabic numeral, the numeral then reappears in the margin of the body of the disputation marking the sections of it. Every page of the edition contains two columns of text and is numbered. The first full edition from Venice follows a different pattern of numeration that makes it less practical for quotation. In our way of quoting we will place first the number of the treatise in Roman numerals, then the number of the disputation in Arabic numerals, then the number of the entry of the table of contents. Finally we shall put the page number from which the quotation was taken in the Cologne edition. I.e. for entry 4 of disputation 35 of the fifth treatise we shall write: V. 35. 4. and then the page number.

[16] We find annotations in the margins of the disputation that help to follow the structure, such as: *dubium, responseo, conclusio, exceptio, ad probationes in contrario, primum, secundum, refellitur*. They echo the *Summa*, but also the rhetoric of practical exercises. This is a parallel of Aquinas' very precise and technical words—*Ad primum, Praeterea, Sed contra, Respondeo, Ad primum, Ad secundum, Ad tertium*, etc.—that act as the backbone of a *quaestio*, and guide the reader through it. These annotations are in the margins. They do not shape the text that is becoming independent of the traditional classical structure.

[17] II. 20. pp. 54–58.

explaining the terms of the definition, and discussing them.[18] It next proceeded to offering arguments of advisability, arguments of opportunity, of justice or of logic. There was an entire conceptual structure that helped subsume the particular case. The third and last resource in legal reasoning in this age was that of quoting different authorities.

Other disputations particularly gather data relevant for the moral reasoning. The disputation on the Empire has a long historical preface on the origins of it.[19] Other disputations are filled with data that Molina himself has gathered, sometimes from talking to people. The disputation on slavery is a good example of how scholastic theology, juridical knowledge and empirical data come together, and start to reshape the ways of moral reasoning.

2.2.3. *The Ways of Moral Reasoning*

The topic of slavery is treated in disputations 32 to 40. In disputation 32 Molina has concluded that slavery was against natural law because it went against the first constitution of things, how things had been in the beginning, but that it became licit when circumstances changed and *ius gentium* introduced it. I will discuss at length the importance of circumstances in the section about *ius naturale*. In disputation 33 he discussed the legal titles for slavery. In disputation 34 he narrates where and how the Portuguese acquired their slaves. He proved his knowledge of how the slave trade was conducted, knowledge he had acquired from other Jesuits who had been in those places, but also from going to the docks of Lisbon and talking to the slave merchants themselves.[20] It is a valuable first-hand account.

It is in disputation 35 that Molina discussed what should be thought of the Portuguese slave trade. He first referred himself to the positive law that had been exposed in the preceding disputation about the just title to have *dominium* over slaves. The most important title was the *ius belli*. Slaves were captive enemies who had been spared death. This law did

---

[18] Francisco Carpintero Benitez, "En torno al método de los juristas medievales," *Anuario de Historia del Derecho Español* LII (1982). 625–629.

[19] II. 24. pp. 66–67.

[20] Example of the accounts of received from Jesuits is "... quae relatione accepimus partim ab aliis, et praecipue a nostris, qui inibi commorantur ..." II. 34. 11. p. 94. There are similar references in II. 35. 17. p. 104, II. 34. 20. p. 97. An example of an account received from merchants: "Denique quantum intelligere potui ex mercatoribus, qui eiusmodi mancipia in Aethyopia emunt, eaque inde huc asportant (cum quibus locutus sum, quique nihil eorum, quae retuli, diffitentur) illi nihil aliud curant in hac negotiatione, quam suum lucrum et commodum." II. 34. 6. pp. 92–93.

not apply among Christians, but could be used by Christians fighting against non Christians. Slavery could also be the result of some grave crimes. Molina, however, noted that moral principles, especially if they are universal in nature, are less useful and effective. He felt, therefore, compelled to define the question. He did so in five theses which he argued using the juridical mode of reasoning. In the second thesis, for example, he discussed whether it was licit to buy a slave that had been enslaved by the legitimate authority because of a 'sufficient' crime. He discussed each term within the thesis. He then went on to try to prove each part of the thesis using different types of reasoning. For the first part of the thesis, he acknowledged, that it would be legitimate to buy such a slave, if the 'sufficient' crime was one for which the same penalty would have been used in Portugal. For the second part of the thesis Molina considers self-evident according to natural reason that the person enslaved cannot be punished to slavery because of the crimes of others. He established a criterion that would help a merchant to act when there was uncertainty, when he warned that the merchant should not buy a slave if he had the suspicion that the person had been 'unjustly' enslaved. He used the criteria of harmony with the natural law, probability and legal presumption to help act in those cases. Molina accepted the institution of slavery in itself, but on account of how the slave trade was conducted—and the dubious titles of property over the slaves—the final conclusion of this disputation in five theses was that "this type of negotiation seems to me most likely a mortal sin."[21]

This way of reasoning shows that Molina knew the complexity of commercial dealing, but he also knew that this action was related to salvation. He carefully analyzed the different degrees of certainty. The way of reasoning resembled the theory and method of today's economic decisions. One receives the impression the author realized that the classical *Summa* was not fully adequate for the purpose of moral theology, and therefore he started exploring other ways of reasoning. At the same time he respectd and cared about the teachings of Aquinas, even when he disagreed with him.

[21] "Mihi longe verisimilius est, negotiationem hanc emenrium eiusmodi mancipia ab infidelibus illis in locis, eaque inde asportantium, iniustam, iniquamque esse, omnesque qui illam exercent, lethaliter peccare, esseque in statu damnatione aeternae, nisi quem invincibilis ignorantia excuset, in qua neminem eorum esse affirmare auderem." II. 35. 16. p. 103.

We find empirical data in Molina, as in most of the authors of the treatises *De Iustitia et Iure* or *De Legibus*. This is why Molina has attracted the attention of historians of economics, particularly the fact that in his writings we can find detailed accounts of economic practices of the time. But this also has theological implications. Moral theology can not limit itself to abstract principles; it needs to apply them, and in order to do so it is important to know what the order of reality is. We shall see examples of it when we get to the analysis of usury, just price and money exchange. This way of proceeding in moral theology might be traced to Molina's own fundamental moral theology.

3. Fundamental Moral Theology

We will now examine Molina's fundamental moral theology. Although today the term 'fundamental moral theology' is common, there is no such heading in *De Iustitiae et Iure*. But in the text we find many elements that belong in what we generally group today under the heading fundamental moral theology. Molina's longest section on these topics is on the law. It includes the problem of natural law (*ius naturale* and *lex naturalis*), the use of the Bible in moral reasoning (*de lege veteris* and *de lege nova*) and the ecclesiastical context of our moral decisions (*lex positiva ecclessiastica*). Seldom did Molina talk in his books about his Jesuit identity,[22] but this undoubtedly influenced and shaped his moral theology. I will dedicate a brief section to exploring how his spirituality shaped his moral reasoning. The last section on his writings on matters of fundamental moral theology will develop his kinship to casuistry.

Any Christian moral theology springs from reflection on the revealed God. Although many times unacknowledged, there is an initial reliance upon the Bible and what we find there regarding the relationship with God and neighbor. I shall start by investigating Molina's use of the Bible in his moral reasoning.

3.1. *Use of the Bible*

In 1516 Erasmus wrote his *Paraclesis*, the preface to his Greek and Latin edition of the New Testament he wrote against scholastic theology. He said that he wished that

---

[22] Some examples of where he does so can be found in: II. 34. 14. p. 95; V. 46. 9. p. 154.

> just as Paul wrote that the law of Moses was not full of glory compared with the Gospel succeeding it, so may all Christians hold the Gospels and the Letters of the Apostles as so holy that in comparison with them these other writings [he was referring to the writings of Albert the Great, Aquinas, Ockham and other Scholastics] do not seem holy.[23]

In writing this he was giving voice to a common criticism of scholastic theology: that it was complicated, detached from the Bible and of not much use for the Christian life.

Scholastic theology declined at the end of the fourteen and fifteen centuries because it was drawn toward subtle problems detached from the Bible and the life of the Church.[24] Humanism, with its appreciation of fine literature helped in the revival of Biblical studies in the sixteenth century. The newly founded Society of Jesus participated in this renewal of biblical scholarship.[25]

The rebirth of biblical studies can be considered one of the sources of the rebirth of scholastic theology in the sixteenth century. Nourished by Scripture, theology blossomed again. Although for a humanist like Erasmus it would have seemed insufficient, a work like *De Iustitia et iure* is influenced by this turn to Scripture. The first signal of this is the biblical index we find in each volume of the work.[26] The fifth volume, the one on law, has the longest biblical index. This is so because the discussion about the law was in scholastic theology the theological *locus* where the relevance of the Bible was discussed. We find two terms of great importance *lex vetus* and *lex nova*. Eighteen disputations are dedicated to the Old and to the New Laws, which make up more

---

[23] Desiderius Erasmus. *Opera omnia*, vol. 4 (London: Gregg, 1962). 143.

[24] In Spain the Bible was nevertheless widely read in the fifteen century. "De mayor interés es la proliferación de traducciones de origen y directriz tanto judía como cristiana, fenómeno español curioso y, al parecer, único, por su extensión, en la Europa del cuatrocientos. [...] La lectura de la Biblia en lengua vernácula era frecuente en el siglo XV, no sólo en las sinagogas y entre los conversos, sino también en no pocos conventos y entre los seglares. Fray José de Sigüenza aporta datos del biblismo entre los jerónimos del siglo XV. Sólo así se explica el crecido número de traducciones y de glosas. La evolución del lenguaje y el deseo de hacer accesible su lectura llevó a una cierta libertad en la traducción, que se añadía a una teoría, común por entonces, sobre la misión del traductor. De ahí la frescura y lozanía lingüística de estas biblias romanceadas. Por aquí les acechó el peligro de corrupción e impropiedad." Andrés Martín. I. 318–322.

[25] "La Compañía de Jesús se abrazó con los estudios bíblicos: Juan Maldonado (1534–1583), Francisco de Ribera († 1595) Juan Bautista Villalpando († 1608), Francisco de Toledo († 1596), Martín del Río († 1668)." Ibid. II. 635.

[26] I. pp. 594–596; II. p. 866; III. p. 606; IV. pp. 509–512; V. pp. 257–267.

that half of the *De legibus*.[27] It is a clear sign that this was an important topic and that the Bible was taken seriously.

In these eighteen disputations Molina begins arguing against the Manicheans that the Old Testament is good and God-given. He showed a great command of the Scripture, and, although he used it many times for proof-testing, he went beyond that usage on many occasions. He particularly relied on Pauline texts, the ones considered Pauline at his time,[28] and within Paul he relied on Romans most of all. From here he went on to show the obligation of the Old Law for Israel and how suitable was the law and the way in which it was granted. He then set out the different types of precepts within the Old Law: *moralia, ceremonialia et iudicialia*.[29] This was going to permit him to articulate the way in which the Old Testament was morally normative. We will see in the section about the natural law that the precepts of the Decalogue coincide with the first principles of the natural law. He then developed the dispensability of the precepts of the Decalogue. This we will discuss in detail in the section on the natural law.

The use of *lex nova* and *lex vetus* to refers to the Gospel and to the Old Testament affords a legalistic slant to the way the Bible is used in moral theology. The terminology, though, was not coined by the scholastics, but was made acceptable by the extensive use on the part of the Church Fathers.

Although the term *lex* is translated into modern languages as law, it does not have in Molina's use the legalistic connotation it might have for us. *Lex* could well mean something like "way of life". This, of course, needed to be expressed by a set of rules. But Molina was well aware that this set of rules did not exhaust the way of life. They indicated the way and help to explain it. He acknowledged that in the New Law the merits and passion of Christ by far exceed the aid of the natural and the written laws.[30] He also knew that the law can be harmful if deprived from grace.[31] He recommended that legislators make laws that are not

[27] V. 50–67. pp. 164–230.

[28] He quotes extensively Hebrews. Cajetan had held that Hebrews was neither from Paul nor canonical. This opinion had been held by some Protestants. Trent had included it in the canon, without discussing its authorship. Molina discusses the issue and takes it as being from Paul.

[29] This division is taken from Aquinas I^{a}–IIae q. 99.

[30] "Praeterrea in nova lege, persoluto iam pretio nostrae redemptionis, longe maiora auxilia gratiae dantur meritis et passione Christi iam exhibitis, quam quodam tempore legis naturae et scriptae conferrentur ..." and he summarizes the parable of the eleventh hour—Mt 20: 1–16—to illustrate this. V. 50. 6. p. 170.

[31] "In eis enim et in similibus aliis testimoniis solum intendit, legem solam sine gratia

difficult to observe. He went further in recommending that legislators should reduce the number of laws because they constitute a great burden on people. He is referring to both civil and canon law, but he considers this reduction of laws especially expedient in ecclesiastical censures.[32]

Molina was fully aware that the law, in the biblical sense was instruction, something already acknowledged by Aquinas.[33] This might be the reason why he widely used wisdom literature, which was rarely used by theologians of his time. He also discusses the different ways in which the term law was used in Scripture: the law of our organs that we share with the animals, the law of sin, the law of rain and waters. He considered all these uses metaphorical. The only strictly proper use of the term law is that of rational creatures.[34]

Besides its broad understanding of the term law, Molina's theology shows other influences of solid biblical scholarship. Scholastic theology did not know the historico-critical methods, but it had developed hermeneutical tools and had progressed far beyond a mere literal interpretation of Scripture. Medieval hermeneutics had distinguished four senses in the Scriptures: literal, allegoric, moral and anagogical.[35]

---

per Christum, nihil omnino prodesse, sed potius esse occasionem maioris mali ac maiori ruinae spiritualis hominibus ex ipsorum prava inclinatione ..." V. 50. 10. p. 173.

[32] "Attendere vero legislatores debent, non solum num singulae leges, quas codunt, servatu non sit difficiles, sed etiam num omnes simul quae ab ipsis conduntur, et quae a suis antecessoribus sunt conditae, servari ad modum difficile possint, iugum legum non admodum difficile sibi subditis imponant. Atque fortasse expediret non parum, multas ex iuris civilis et canonici leges abrogari, ut iugum humanarum legum temporis progressu a variis legum latoribus mirum in modum multiplicatum, hominumque cervicibus impositum, redderetur leviur, legumque cuatodia ac subditorum obedientia esset exactior, nec ex tanta legum multiplicitate periculum immineret animarum. Inter alia autem fortasse expediret, censuras omnes Ecclesiasticas ad longe minorem numerum ae methodum redigi, multas ex illis abrogando." V. 66. 6. p. 230.

[33] "Consequenter considerandum est de principiis exterioribus actuum. [...] Principium autem exterius movens ad bonum est Deus, qui et nos instruit per legem, et iuvat per gratiam." Iª–IIae q. 90.

[34] "Porro eiusmodi vires ac me ia, a particularibus legibus Dei aeternis derivata, quipus criaturas mente minime praeditas Deus in earum fines dirige, et per quas easdem suas leges quoad id eternas exequutioni mandate, non per propietatem, sed per simmilitudinem legis dicuntur, [...] cum tamen leges creatures libero praeditis arbitrio a Deo inditae aut aliter illis traditae ac promulgatae, quas in suis operibus liberis sequi teneantur, propriissiime legume, a sempiterna Dei lege derivatarum, rationem habeant." V. 46. 19. p. 150.

[35] These four senses were summed up in a couplet by Nicholas of Lyra (1270–1349): "Littera gesta docet, quid credas allegoria, moralis agas, quo tendas anagogia." Werner G. Jeanrond, *Theological Hermeneutics. Development and Significance* (New York: Crossroad, 1991). 26–30.

Humanism tried to fight the excesses of allegorical interpretation, and went back to the literal sense under the premise that the literal sense was the base for the other senses. Molina, of course, used the moral sense, but he often referred to the literal when taking into account the stories told in the Bible. In this case Scripture became not a code of law, from which to draw a maxim that might apply to the case considered, but a model of identification, as he did with Abraham.[36] When articulating the relationship between the Old and the New Testaments, he relied on patristic theology that found in the Old Testament allegories and types of what becomes full in Christ.[37] He occasionally referred to the spiritual meaning of the Scripture. He considered that some of the judicial precepts of the Old Testament have, in addition to the literal sense, a spiritual meaning from which the Church can profit, especially when they are in harmony with the New Law.[38]

Finally Molina introduced Scripture in his moral reasoning through the category of counsels. This was a category commonly used at the time to refer to the vowed religious life of poverty, chastity and obedience as a life of evangelical counsels given by Christ.[39] But evangelical counsels did not exhaust the counsels that could be found in Scripture. Counsels were

---

[36] "Discendentibus vero temporis progressu hominibus a Deo per idolatria, [...] creccentibusque peccatis, ac ignorantia circa naturalem ac divinam legem, coepit Deus deligeresibi populum in Abrahamo, cui iterum Messiam mundi redemptorem de semine illius providit, atque in Isaac et Jacob, cuius soboli Moysis tempore legem scriptam tradidit, relicto adhuc reliquo orbis in priori illo statu legis naturae, in quo salvari poterant, adimplendo supernaturalis praecepta, quae, ut diximus supra, status ille comprehendebat." V. 46. 13. p. 145. Other examples can be found in V. 46. 15. p. 148 and V. 50. 5. p. 169.

[37] Molina found that in Baruch 2:35 lies hidden the New Law. "Quamvis congruentiae quaedam redid possint, ut scilicet a minus perfecto ad id, quo perfectum est, deveniretur, et ut mundus experientia tot saeculorum suae misseriae melius intelligeret, quam necessaria illi esset gratia Christi, gratantiusque tanta beneficia acciperet, ut ad adventum Messiae legemque gratiae melius suscipenda, variis praeviis figures ac prophetiis mundus disponetur" V. 64. 2. p. 225.

[38] "Quia vero iudicalia veteris legis praecepta praecipue ad regimen illius reipublicae, etiam ut saecularis erat, fuerunt a Deo lata prout status eius legis ac temporis effagitabat, tamen aliquibus eorum aliquid aliud in sensu spirituali voluerit significari, nihil sane prohibited, aliqua horum vel in ecclesia Christiana a summis Pontificubus, vel in republicis saecularibus statui ac servari" V. 63. 2. p. 224. He also refers to the spiritual sense in other places like V. 50. 5. p. 168 and V. 64. 5. p. 227.

[39] He addresses this in V. 67. 2. p. 230 and he gives examples of other counsels that do not refer to religious life such as "ad vitandam hypo crisim, inanem gloriam, rectam habendamque intentionem, ad amplectendam crucem, vitamque Dei amore contemnendam, ad aeternum supplicium vitandum".

not precepts, but they help to better and more accurately attain a certain end.[40] They could be found also in the Old Testament. Molina gave Ex 22: 24 and 25 as an example of counsels.[41] These clearly have nothing to do with vowed religious life. He was basing his reasoning here, as he acknowledges, on the authority of Aquinas and Jerome.[42] We will see more of the importance of counsels when we address the problems of usury.

Although the Bible was important for Molina's work, it was for Molina not sufficient for the resolution of the moral problems posed in his era. He even considered the writings of Aquinas, whom he used as a starting point for his moral analysis, insufficient and too brief on such issues as the law of contracts. The methodology of the natural law had long been established in scholastic theology. Molina took up the task of further developing it to solve new problems.

3.2. *Molina's Conception of Natural Law*

3.2.1. De Legibus et Constitutionibus

A key preliminary question regarding natural law is to what extent it is a legitimate or even a necessary source for moral theology. For Molina and all theologians in the scholastic tradition, the Bible was a necessary but not a sufficient source for solving moral questions. Here we examine its supplementation with reflections on natural law.

The problem of the sources in moral theology, of how to find what is normative, was approached in the scholastic theology of the sixteenth century in the treatises about the law. Molina's treatment of definition and types of law is found at the end of *De Iustitia et Iure*, in disputations 46 to 73 of the fifth, and last, treatise of his work. It appears as an independent section of the fifth treatise, under the heading *De Legibus et Constitutionibus*.[43]

---

[40] "consilia in ea permisceri ad eundem finem melius obtinendum, atque ad exactiorem ac meliorem observationem legum ad eundem finem in ea laturum, non parum conducentia." V. 46. 29. p. 154.

[41] "If you lend money to one of your poor neighbors among my people, you shall not act like an extortioner toward him by demanding interest from him." in V. 63. 9. p. 188. "If you take your neighbor's cloak as a pledge, you shall return it to him before sunset" in V. 46. 29. p. 154.

[42] Ia–IIae q. 99 a. 5 and St. Jerome's prologue to his commentary on Mark.

[43] This title, already used by Cicero for one of his works, would become common and would soon develop as a standard one for works treating ethics, whether theological or

The section follows a structure very similar to that of Aquinas, altering somewhat the order of the types of law. It discusses first the law in general, and in doing so it includes there the discussion of eternal law, and then proceeds to discuss natural law, the Old Law, the New Law and human law.[44] In dealing with the law, he had to discuss new problems that had arisen since Aquinas' time. The most important was the nature of the natural law that William of Ockham had raised when asserting that God could dispense of all the precepts of the Decalogue.

In this section we will concentrate on natural law, its relationship with the eternal law, that is briefly elaborated, and to human law, because of the importance it holds for matters of justice. Although we have already addressed the Old and the New Law in the section on the use of Scripture, we shall also refer to them when treating natural law on the question of whether or not the Decalogue belonged to natural law. If it does, the question arises on whether the precepts of the Decalogue were dispensable or not. This discussion deeply influences our understanding of what natural law is.

3.2.2. *The Theological Nature of Natural Law*

Although for us the concept of natural law smacks of philosophy and rationalism, this was not the case for the scholastics.[45] Natural law was a

---

philosophical. This section is the result of the development of Molina's teaching in Evora on I^{a}–IIae, qq. 98–108 in 1570. This part was published posthumously and because of this some questions have arisen regarding the literary authenticity of the work that was given to the press after Molina's death. José María Díez-Alegría S.J. studied the copies of the notes of his lectures on the Old Law and concluded that the section *De Legibus et Constitutionibus* was a refined version of his classes. The manuscript was almost ready for publication when he died, and as such, it was handed over for printing, although it was not a perfectly finished work, and it retained, because of this, some degree of vagueness. Díez-Alegría. 46–62.

[44] The only difference from Aquinas' classification is that it places human law between natural law and the Old Law. This type of division was quite common at the time. Johannes Consobrinus and Francesco Medici, *Tractatus P[Er] Utilimus De Iusticia [Com]Mutatiua* (Imp[re]ssus vero Parisii: [Louis Martineau], 1483). 4. Domingo de Soto, *Libri Decem De Iustitia Et Iure* (Lugduni: Apud heredes Iacobi Iuntae). books I and II.

[45] "Another line of development, with which we are not concerned in this study, was pursued through the works of Grotius and Pufendorf, and arose from exploring the implications for natural law not so much of God's absolute power but of the speculative possibility of there not being a God. It was this line of thought which was to result in what Oskar Köhler describes as 'the detheologization of natural law' to become 'at once the foundation of the tolerant state as well coming an absolute concept as the *primum principium* of political and social life'." Mahoney. 81.

theological problem.[46] There were, of course, different ways of conceiving natural law, and how it played in moral life.[47]

There are a number of reasons why natural law was considered a theological topic. The first one is that, although it is a concept that can be traced to the Greek and Roman philosophical traditions, the existence of natural law was considered to be affirmed in Scripture. Saint Paul's letter to the Romans was the text most widely cited, and Romans was, after Luther, a text every good theologian was eager to address.[48]

The second reason to consider natural law a theological matter is that it was dependent—in different ways according to different conceptions—on eternal law.[49] For Aquinas, whose teachings were always in the background for Molina even if he did not always follow him, natural law was a participation in eternal law, this is the way God exercises his providence for the world. Not only that, natural law according to the *Summa*

---

[46] Jean Porter makes a similar point referring to the early scholastics: "The concept of nature was a theological and not a merely philosophical notion for them [the early scholastics], thanks to the extensive work on the theological significance of the natural world that began early in the twelfth century [...] The doctrine of the natural law was valuable to theologians and jurists in this period because it offered a generally acceptable framework for adjudicating these competing claims, by providing a theological interpretation of the most fundamental principles of human action." Jean Porter, *Natural and Divine Law. Reclaiming the Tradition for Christian Ethics*, Series in Ethics (Grand Rapids, Michigan: Saint Paul University, 1999). 17. The period of her study goes up to the death of both Aquinas and Bonaventure in 1274. Obviously the study does not examine Ockham, whose position reshapes the discussion. In that sense what I say here is a step in a similar direction but taking into account that 300 years have gone by between Aquinas' death and Molina's work.

[47] Aquinas, Duns Scotus and Ockham all discussed natural law but their views on it were radically different.

[48] Psalm 4 and Job 38 also contained biblical grounding for natural law. "Tertio, eadem lex naturalis dicitur, quoniam naturaliter est indita mentibus nostris et angelorum, iuxta illud Psali 4 ubi cum Regius propheta illam multorum interrogationnem retulisset: *Qui ostendi nobis bona?* ipse respondet: *Signarum* (hoc est, inditum ac impressum) *est super nos lumen vultus tui Domine*, quo scilicet naturaliter illud agnoscimus. Et illud Pauli at Romani 2 ... Atque iuxta illud Job 38: *Quis posuit in visceribus hominis sapientiam?* Illi nempe inditam, tam quoad speculabilia quoad moralia." V. 47. 2. p. 157. The citation of Psalm 4, Rm 2 and Jb 38 were common ones to prove the existence of natural law by scriptural means.

[49] "Inter varias leges, quas supra ex illucusque dictis facile distingui posse diximus, primo loco hucusque distinximus legem Dei aeternam ac incommutabilem, ex qua caeterae derivantur. Secundo autem loc distinguitur lex naturalis, ad finem naturalem humanae felicitates moralis ac speculativae ordinate. Quid autem ea sit, a legeque Dei aeterna derivari, atque de iure divino naturalei eam esse, satis ex supra dictis patet." V. 46. 20. pp. 150–151.

was a kind of participation in divine providence.[50] A similar doctrine is repeated by Molina when he says that eternal law provides for all things and governs all things. It pertains to eternal law to steer all things to their ends, and to provide for those ends to that which exists in God.[51]

The third rationale for holding that natural law was a theological problem was the fact that natural law was actually a problem of biblical interpretation. This accounts for a great part of the development of the discussion about the nature of natural law in the late Middle Ages. In the Old Testament we find many cases in which a commandment is transgressed. The problem arises when some of these transgressions are performed by the agent under divine command, or when, although not done explicitly under divine command, these transgressions are somehow depicted in the narrative as licit, just and honest. As long as the commandment can be classified as morally indifferent, the case was somewhat easy to solve. It was just a case of divine positive law that, dependent only on divine will, God could override.

A greater problem arose when the broken commandment was thought to pertain to natural law. This raised the problem of the dispensability of natural law. Was a commandment of natural law dispensable and, if so, under what circumstances? What did this mean about the nature of natural law? Two classic examples discussed were the marriage of the sons of Adam with their sisters, which was incest, and the despoiling of the Egyptians by the fleeing Israelites, which was robbery.[52] It certainly looked as if the circumstances made the act right. But by that token, would it then be correct to say that circumstances change natural law? Or perhaps that God might change his mind according to circumstances? The scholastics were aware of the problem of the universality of the natural law, but also of the fact that there were sometimes cases that appeared to be exceptions to it. The way of explaining this was a theological problem, not just because it was in the field of moral theology, but because it was a statement about God's mind, knowledge and providence—which worked through eternal law—of which natural law was a participation by the human creature. The problems about knowledge of God and about divine providence, which Molina had developed in the *Concordia*, were

[50] Iª–IIae q. 91 a. 2 co.

[51] "Deinde eadem lege aeterna Deus cunctis rebus providit et cuncta gubernat, ratioque dirigendi res omnes in suos fines, eisque ad eosdem fines providendi in Deo existens, ad legem De iaeternam pertinet." V. 46. 16. p. 148.

[52] Gn 4: 17 and Ex 12: 36.

not just problems about divine grace. As we have already set out, the theological stance one assumed regarding these questions also affected one's view on how God intervened in history and the place of humanity in it. This proceeded largely through reflection on natural law. What made natural law binding was a major topic of dispute.[53]

There is a fourth reason why natural law was a theological topic. According to Molina, natural law existed from the beginning, even before the Fall, but it became more important after the Fall. Natural law existed as the only means of justification before the gift of the written law to the Jewish people and till the coming of Christ for the Gentiles. Natural law was part of God's plan of salvation.[54] Actually when he discussed the problem of whether the just of the Old Testament were really adopted children of God, or merely in figure or type, he stated that some say that through natural law they were actually made children of God.[55] This fourth reason was more than a mere discussion of some primal time or of what was the order of things before the coming of Christ. The issue became a highly topical question with the Spanish arrival in America. The salvation of the people in the Indies was a hot topic. Clearly enough, before the preaching of the Gospel, they could have not been saved by baptism, whether *vere aut voti*. This meant that they could only be held accountable for natural law, not for the law of Christ.[56] With this development natural law re-acquired importance.

Having shown the theological status—and political impact—of natural law, we have to set out Molina's account of it. But before we do so it is necessary to recall an essential distinction of scholastic theology: the distinction between *ius* and *lex*.

---

[53] Molina summarizes the history of the discussion in V. 57. pp. 198–204, a disputation with the title: "Utrum in praeceptis decalogi divina saltem potentia locum habeat dispensatio." He sets out the positions of Ockham, Scotus, and Major. He discusses them and positions himself with Aquinas, but in doing so he has to develop the views of Aquinas because the Angelic Doctor wrote before the other three. In V. 46. 14. p. 146 he also discusses Jean Gerson's opinion that the natural law "non posse vere et propie dici legem divinam."

[54] "Legem novam non fuisse tradendam statim a principio mundi ... sed tot saeculis praecedere debuisse legem naturae, et post eam lege scriptam, ac tandem haec alia, ad tempuus legis gratiae attinentia, Dei misericordia fuisse sequenda ..." V. 64. 2. p. 225.

[55] "Est tanem proculdubio affirmandum, iustos veteris testamentis ac legis naturae vere ac proprie fuisse filios Dei adoptivos." V. 65. 3. p. 227.

[56] Francisco de Vitoria in *De Indis* argues that war can be made on the Indian nations when they commit *iniuriae*, but not when they commit *peccatae*. With this distinction natural law becomes politically important. Francisco de Vitoria, *Relectio De Indis.*, ed. L. Pereña y J.M. Pérez Prendes (Madrid: CSIC, 1967). 63.

3.2.3. Ius *and* Lex

Up to this point we have indiscriminately talked about natural law, but in scholastic theology there is a distinction of great importance.[57] It is the distinction between *ius* and *lex*. *Ius* is a very rich word in Latin. It can mean law, but it can also mean right, duty, justice, oath, that what is just as well as that what is binding. *Lex* can mean law, statue, principle, condition. *Ius* in its moral meaning is that which is right, but to assert the reason why that is right there is always the *lex*. According to Aquinas the *lex* is imposed upon others in the mode of a ruler or a measure. It is that which measures the right thing.[58] But to some extent it is first *ius*—the right thing—that exists, and then the *lex*—the rule that measures it. It is important to remember this because for Molina what is *de iure naturale* can and does change, but at the same time he affirms that the *lex naturalis* does not change.[59] To understand this we have to see how Molina defines nature, how he defines the *ius naturale* and how he proposes the *lex naturalis*. These differentiations are especially important to our study because *ius* is the object of the virtue of justice which we are studying.[60] But before doing so we shall say a word about law in general according to Molina.

Molina and the scholastics often discuss whether the law is one or multiple; in scholastic vocabulary *lex* is understood in different ways. Molina asks whether the term *lex* refer to a single law given by a legitimate authority, or whether it refers to a collection of laws.[61] And he accepts that both uses are legitimate.[62] When saying *lex*, he might be referring to a single precept, but also to a collection of them. The context indicates

---

[57] We will still refer to natural law; when doing so we will refer to it as a tradition of thought that includes the differentiation between *lex* and *ius* we present in this section.

[58] Iª–IIae q. 90 a. 1 co.

[59] "Evenit etiam saepe in moralibus, ut id, quod sub certis circumstantiis est de iure naturali, deficiente aliqua earum, aut superveniente circumstantia alia, definatn esse de iure naturali, et interdum, ut id non efficere, vel ut efficere contrarium, sit de iure naturali." V. 49. 3. p. 162. Further down he says "legem naturalem mutationem seu variationem non suscipere." V. 49. 4. p. 162. Although Molina does not quote him, this is what Aquinas says in IIª–IIae q. 57 a. 2 ad. 2.

[60] "Unde manifestum est quod ius est obiectum iustitiae." IIª–IIae q. 57 a. 1 co.

[61] The same distinction can be used in English. When we say "I study law" or "the law of the land", we are referring to an entire system. When we say "there is no law against it", we are referring to a single piece of legislation.

[62] "Uno, pro quacunque singulari lege lata ab eo, qui ad id potestatem habet, iuxta ea quae supra explicata sunt. Altero vero modo, pro collectione multarum legum, quae ad unum finem ordinantur, vel naturaler felicitatis naturaler cuiusque." V. 46. 23. 152. But also Iª–IIae, q. 91, a. 5, and Soto, *Libri Decem De Iustitia Et Iure*. I, q. 4, a. 2.

whether it is one or the other. When it is used collectively, it is because what collects them is the fact that the individual *leges* point to a common end. He offers a threefold example particularly interesting for our study. He states that "laws are the assent (*assensu*) and the habit, or the collection of them, and their conclusions that pertain to the achievement of an entire object with the same degree of abstraction from the sensitive matter, or that they do not abstract from it." And here is where he offers the threefold example, because Molina affirms that

> as in the knowledge of moral things it can be taken the many assents and habits and conclusions that pertain to achieve moral goods, also it can be said about the economic science and about the political science, because ethics, economics and politics distinguish themselves because of the assents, habits and conclusions that pertain to achieving their goods and ends.[63]

Assensu is in philosophical Latin an "assent to the reality of sensible appearances,"[64] Molina is showing here the importance he grants to experience in the formulation of moral judgments about economics and politics.

When used collectively *lex* might refer to a collection of laws that guide us toward a good or an end, or both. Some of these laws come from our experience. The main classification of law is made according to this criterion of grouping singular *leges* according to the end they serve. The *lex naturalis* guides humans to their natural ends.[65] The Old Law guided Israel towards God before the coming of Christ. The New Law guides us to God after the coming of Christ. Human law guides the human community. These classes are not classes utterly apart. Rather many of their precepts overlap, because what makes a class is a common end,

---

[63] "Sicut scientia duobus sumitur: uno, pro assenssu et habitu cuiusque conclusionis, altero vero, pro collectione assensuum ac habituum multarum conclussionum ad unum totale obiectum attinentium, quod eundem gradum abstractionis a material sensibili habet, aut quo dab ea non abstrahit: vel in scientiis moralibus pro collectione assen suum ac habituum multarum conclusionum ad eandem finem boni moralis attinentium, puta felicitatiscuiusque moralis ac virtutum, quae ad eam spectant, boni ac finis oeconomici, auc bonis ac finis politici; quo pacto Ethica, oeconomica, et politica scientia inter se distinguuntur: sic lex duobus modis sumitur." V. 49. 23. p. 152. Molina uses the word *assensu* to mean agreement, approbation, admittance of the truth. It is based in experience and in a shared experience.

[64] Charlton T. Lewis, *A Latin Dictionary Founded on Andrew's Edition of Freund's Latin Dictionary* (Oxford: Oxford Univesity Press, 1998). 177.

[65] "lex naturalis, ad finem naturalem humanae felicitatis moralis ac speculative ordinata." V. 46. 21. p. 151.

not a similarity in the material content of the precept. Molina in passing offers another classificatory criterion that groups all types of laws: the precept of love of God and neighbor.[66] Everything depends on the end we are considering. These ends are not exclusive, but rather they tend to be inclusive.

3.2.4. Ius Naturale

Molina follows Aristotle's definition of *ius naturale*. He says that *ius naturale* is that which "has the same validity everywhere, and does not depend on our accepting it or not."[67] After employing Aristotle's definition he explains what it means. It is that whose obligation originates from the nature of the thing and not from the will of the one who orders. More than an explanation, this is an addition to what Aristotle said that gives great importance to human rationality.[68] He actually uses that criterion of dependence on the will to distinguish what pertains to *ius naturale* from what pertains to *ius positivum*. In the realm of *ius naturale* something is mandated because it is good, and something is prohibited because it is bad. That is why *ius naturale* is the same everywhere, namely because it depends on the nature of the thing and not on the will of the one who commands, it retains its binding force no matter where as long as the nature of the thing remains the same.[69]

Having said that, Molina affirms that frequently something that in the absence of other circumstances would be observed as *ius naturale*, when certain circumstances accrue, this something might no longer be considered to fall under *ius naturale*. According to Molina there are three ways by which something falls under *ius naturale*. These differences explain this mutability.[70]

---

[66] "... finem omnium praeceptorum, esse caritatem Dei, quae non est sine proximi caritate." V. 53. 8, p. 187. To back this he quotes Iª–IIae q. 99 a. 1, Rom 13, Mat 7, Mat 22 and 1 Jn 1.

[67] I take the English translation from Aristotle, *The Nichomachean Ethics*, Loeb Classical Library (Cambridge, MA: Harvard University Press, 1999). V. vii.1.

[68] "[T]his is not at all what Aristotle meant. Molina does not interpret his meaning but adds a new one: he definitely married natural law to our rational diagnosis, with reference to the Common Good, of the cases—whether individual contracts or social institutions—which we observe in research or practice." Schumpeter and Schumpeter. 109.

[69] "Hoc voluit ac docuit Aristoteles 5. Ethicorum c. 7 dum ius naturale sic definivit: Est, quod utique eandem vim habet, ut non quia videtur aut non videtur. Hoc est, cuius obligatio oritur ex natura ipsa rei, de qua est praeceptum ac lex naturalis, et non ex arbitrio voluntate praecipientis. Et quia res eandem naturam retinet se apud omnes, idcirco ius naturale idem est, eandemque vim apud omnes habet." V. 49. 1. p. 161.

[70] V. 49. 5. pp. 163–164.

There are things that *intrinsice sunt mala*, that is constitute intrinsic evils. No circumstance can excuse this category. The second way by which certain things come under *ius naturale* is if they are by a certain formal reason *intrinsice mala*. As long as that reason remains, the judgement does not change. But there can be circumstances that remove an act from the *intrinsice mala* category, making it licit. Molina gives the example of burglary. It falls under the seventh precept of the Decalogue, the prohibition of taking something against the owner's will. That can never be done. But if one receives the permission of God, the universal owner of all things, an external circumstance—God's permission—intervenes and cancels out the judgment. The act no longer falls under the prohibition of the seventh commandment. Since it does not go against the owner's will, it can be done.[71] He has a second—and more provocative—example in which God, Lord also of everyone's life, can condone the prohibition of taking another person's life. God is Lord of that life, so if he agrees on it being taken, we are no longer constrained by the fifth commandment. With these two examples Molina was addressing the problems posed by two passages of Scripture: the sacrifice of Isaac (Gen 22) and the despoiling of the Egyptians (Ex 12). The circumstances that Molina considers can affect *ius naturale* are not confined to divine interventions. When discussing slavery, he clearly states that in the beginning all people were free. But *ius gentium*—a fully human law according to Molina—agreed that the legitimate death penalty for the defeated in a just war would be commuted to the loss of freedom, therefore making slavery licit.[72] It is a case where positive law, by

---

[71] We will return to this in the next chapter. For Molina, private property has been determined by the consent of all, but in the beginning there was no private property. And although it was legitimate to change from a system of common property to a system of private property, what changes is the way the universal destination of the goods is carried out, but it remains as the goal of property, whether it is common or private. The case we have just mentioned is not a purely theoretical one, it becomes extremely important in cases where private property is contradicting its goal.

[72] In II. 32. 3. p. 86 he says: "Huius modi homines, ut *Institut. de iure personarum. sect.* servi, habetur, servi dicti sunt a servando. Quia videlicet Imperatores, quos bello capiebant, quosque fas illis erat interficere, servabant, commutata eorum morte in perpetuam servitutem." In the same disputation he justifies slavery as being just and licit: "Quod si quis nobis obiiciat l. Libertas ff. de statu hominum, est sect., servitus, Instit. De iure personarum, quibus in locis dicitur, servitutem de iure gentium, qua quis dominio alieno contra natura subiicitur: unde videtur colligi, servitutem illicitam esse, utpote contra ius naturae. Dicendum es, verbis illis solum intendi servitutem, si sola prima rerum constitutio absque circumstantiis, quibus commerita est. Licite ac iuste fuisse de

changing the circumstances, changes the applicability of *ius naturale*.[73] Circumstances greatly alter cases.

There is a third way in which something belongs to *ius naturale*. This involves things which without any special circumstance are licit, and sometimes commanded by *ius naturale*, can in some circumstances be against *ius naturale*. It is of *ius naturale* that one should give back a deposit when the one who has paid the deposit claims it. But in some cases, combining some circumstances, this might not apply. Molina is here referring to the example given by Aquinas[74] of the depositary of a sword, who claims it when we know that he is in a state of rage, and we know that he is going to use it to kill someone. It becomes a matter of *ius naturale* not to give him back the deposit.[75]

We see that different kind of circumstances change the obligations that arise from *ius naturale*. Sometimes it is God's will that changes it. At other times it is human will, as in the case of slavery, or as we shall see in the third chapter, a matter of ordering property relations. In other cases it is just a transitory state of a person. *Ius naturale* is that which has the same validity everywhere and does not depend upon our acceptance. That means that it is not subject to human whim or caprice, but that does not mean that it is eternally fixed. The nature of the thing is what determines the obligation. This nature sometimes does not change with circumstances, but in other cases it does, according to Molina.

---

iure gentium introductam, contra id quod, spectata sola prima rerum constitutione, natura rerum postulabat." II. 32. 7. p. 87.

[73] Although he considers slavery a licit institution, when he pronounces himself about the slave trade conducted by the Portuguese in Africa, he concludes with very strong language that it is most likely a mortal sin. "Sit nihilominus quarta conclusio. Mihi longe verosimilius est, negotiationem hanc emerium eiusmodi mancipia ab infidelibus illis in locis, eaque inde asportantium, inustam, iniquam esse, omnesque qui illam exercet, lethalither peccare, esseque in statu damnationis aeternae, nisi quem invincibilis ignorantia excuset, in qua neminem eorum esse affirmare auderem. Regem praeterrea, et omnes, qui regni clavum in manu tenent, nec non Episcopos promotorii viridis, et Insulae Divi Thomae, et qui horum omnium confessions audiunt, singulos in suo gradu et ordine, teneri curare, ut res haec examinetur, et statuatur, quid liceat, et quid non liceat, ut iniustitiae in posterum efficaciter refecentur: nisi eis aliquid, quod me lateat, in facto inotescat, aut principia alia eis eluceant, quae ego ignorem." II. 35. 16. p. 103.

[74] II^{a}–IIae, q. 57, a. 2. Aquinas himself is borrowing from Aristotle's *Nichomachean Ethics*, V. 7. Aristotle is taking the argument from Plato's *Republic*.

[75] "Eiusmodi est, reddere depositum domino illud petenti. Id enim de se, seclusa omni alia circumstantia, quae id impediat, aut quae limitum efficiat illud non reddere, est de iure naturali: ex circumstantiis tanem, secundum naturae cursus supervenientibus, definere potest esse de iure naturali, imo esse poterit contra ius naturali." V. 49. 5. p. 164.

A distinction made by Molina clarifies the justification for the three ways of something being a matter of *ius naturale*. In the first treatise he states that we can say that something is natural in two ways. One as when we say that fire is hot. That happens always and everywhere. But we can also say that the right hand is naturally more skillful, but if trained the left hand can also be very skillful. It works similarly in ethics. He goes on to say that in moral matters some things are naturally in a certain way and cannot change, and he gives the example of the precepts of the Decalogue, but other things can sometimes cease (*defficere*) to be of *ius naturale*.[76]

Although we will say more later about the epistemological question when we talk about the law, let us address here why, according to Molina, in so many things pertaining to *ius naturale* so many people err. Some err because of their roughness or coarseness or, because they are distracted with other things, they fail to investigate and learn about it by themselves or through others. Others err because they have many vices and are blinded by their passions. In other cases, though, ignorance and error occur because the truth is concealed (*abstruse*) and it is hard for us to penetrate it or to deduce it from its principles. This happens not only to the inexperienced, but also to the wise and the devout. This occurs particularly with matters of contracts.[77] This will be important when we discuss the matters of justice in the fourth chapter. This is so because nature does not teach us the precepts of *ius naturale* so clearly that there cannot be any error in their deduction from the first principles, especially when the conclusions are deducted in a remote way. That is why there can be many errors in talking about *ius naturale*.[78]

---

[76] "Ut enim res naturals quaedam sunt necessariae omnino, quae variationem non patitur, ut ignis ita est calidus, ut esse nequeat frigidus, et homo suapte natura ita vim habet ad intelligendum, ut nequeat ea privari; et quaedam sunt ita suapte natura tales, ut possint aliquando aliter se habere, sicut, licet dextera manus naturaliter fortior sit, quam sinistra, interdum tanem sinistra evadit fortior quam dextera: ita in rebus moralibus quaedam sunt de iure naturali eius conditionis, ut nequeant non esse, cuius modus sunt, quae in Decalogo praecipiuntur, eo modo, quo praecipiuntur, in quae, sic spectata, ne divina quidem potentia cadit dispensatio, ut Iª–IIae q. 100 art. 8 late ostendimus: alia vero ita sunt de iure naturali, ut possint aliquando deficcere, et non esse de iure naturali." I. 4. 5. p. 7.

[77] "Evenit vero multa, quae in se iuris sunt naturalis, non solum a multis ignorari, et quaedam eorum etiam a doctis et timoratis, opinative solum cognosci, quin et circa aliqua non nullos, etiam doctos et timoratos, errare, idque variis ex causis." V. 49. 2. p. 162.

[78] "Adverte tamen, naturam non ita distincte nos docere quae iuris sunt naturales, quin in deducendis aliquibus conclusionibus ex principiis facile error surrepat, praesertim quando conclusiones eiusmodi remote obscureque ex primis principiis colliguntur: quo sit, ut circa ea, quae iuris sunt naturalis, error possit aliquando evenire." V. 4. 4. pp. 6–7.

In the manuscript of his commentary on the *Prima Secundae*, when he asks if there can be an ignorance in the *ius naturale*, Molina distinguishes between the first principles that can never be ignored and the conclusions that are deduced without difficulty from the first principles. In these ones rarely can ignorance be adduced. There are then the obscure deductions in which even the wise err. There is a fourth class, the intermediate deductions, those that are neither clear deductions, nor obscure. In these there can be invincible ignorance sometimes, more so when the deduction is more remote, and vice versa.[79]

Ius naturale pertains to what is good because of the nature of the thing, although circumstances might change that nature. Not only that, we are warned that to penetrate the nature of the thing is a difficult task, more so when we move away from first principles. It will be important to recall this when we later discuss the binding force of *lex naturalis*. It is not the will of anyone—not even of God—that makes it binding, but the nature of the thing—of which God is the Creator. But to establish this, we must take up the question of *lex naturalis*.

3.2.5. Lex Naturalis

According to Molina the term *lex naturalis* can be understood in three different ways. First it can be distinguished from supernatural law, that is, the precepts that pertain to the supernatural end. The criterion by which a law is placed in the supernatural or natural class is not the legislator, but the end to which it tends. The *causa finalis* plays a determining role in this classification. A law given by the Pope and with intended effect beyond the boundaries of the Papal States is thus presumably a supernatural law, because it directs Christians to their supernatural end. The same could be said of the ceremonial precepts of the Old Law, given by God. Supernatural laws show us the way to God, *leges naturales* the way to our natural end.

A second way of understanding *lex naturalis* is to distinguish it from *lex positiva*. Here the criterion for distinction is not the *causa finalis* of the law—where does the law takes us?—but the *causa efficiens*—whence does it come? A *lex positiva* is a law that stems from the will of the legislator, whether that be God or a human authority (Pope, emperors, kings, bishops, princes). A *lex naturalis* stems from the very essence or nature of things. Actually this is the criterion that allows us to distinguish

[79] Díez-Alegría. 145–149.

a natural law from a positive law. In natural law we say that something is mandated because it is good; in positive law we say that something is good because it is mandated.

Lex naturalis can be understood in a third way. It is placed in our minds and that of the angels.[80] This affirmation is somewhat obscure, and therefore Molina hastens to explain it. Addressing the topic of the law in general, he claimed that *ius naturale* is something that pertains to creatures possessing free will, the only ones that can be self provident, the only ones that can be collaborators in God's providence. God has placed within them (*inditus*) part of the eternal law, impressing upon them part of his reason and mind because he created them in his likeness.[81] The eternal law is the law by which God provides and governs all things, the reason that directs everything to its end, and provides the means for all things to reach those ends.

Molina distinguishes two aspects of God: *ars* and *providentia*. *Ars* is the knowledge God has regarding how to make different things. It is the knowledge of the *causa formalis*—in the image of which is a thing created. *Providentia* is the knowledge of how to govern and direct things to its ends, providing the means suitable to those ends, and prescribing the laws suitable to its nature. It is the knowledge about the *causa finalis*.[82] Among the things that fall under divine providence are the things that pertain to free will. The creatures that are gifted with free will part take in God's divine providence through eternal law. *Lex naturalis* is a theological matter because it stems from our participation in eternal law. God has imprinted part of the law that from eternity he uses to provide for the world in the creatures that have free will. So *lex naturalis* in humanity is a participation in God's providence. Such a law imprinted in our minds is primarily a non-written law. This raises the important question: how is it placed in our minds?

---

80 V. 47. 2. p. 157.

81 V. 46. 18. p. 149.

82 "Ut vero haec melius intelligas observa. Hoc inter artem divinam et providentiam divinam esse discriminen. Quod ars est cognitio in Deo modi faciendi res sua omnipotentia possibiles, ac proinde est in Deo recta ratio factibilium, hoc est, modi eas condendi ac fabricandi. Providentia vero est recta ratio in Deo illas gubernandi ac dirigendi ad solos fines, providendo illis de mediis ad id accommodatis, ac necessariis, atque accommodate ad naturas diversas ipsarum leges illis praescribendo, quas servare debeant, ut universim et singulae quam accommodate se habeant in se et ad fines, ad quos eadem providentia ordinantur." V. 46. 17. p. 148.

Lex naturalis can exist within us in three different ways. First, it can be in us as the potency to make a moral judgment. Before we form any moral judgments, there are certain first principles and their necessary conclusions[83] that exist in our minds. These first principles and the necessary conclusions that we can deduce from them are innate. They are in us prior to any instruction because we are created in the image of God. These first principles correspond basically to the Thomist *bene faciendum, malum vitandum*. The necessary conclusions refer already to more precise claims: the duty to honor parents, to refrain from committing robbery or homicide or adultery. In this sense *lex naturalis* comes to be identified with conscience (both *synderesis* and *conscientia* in the way that Aquinas uses these terms). In treating the operation of *lex naturalis* within us Molina almost is equating natural law with conscience.[84]

Secondly, *lex naturalis* can also be in us as the act of the (moral) judgments we make. Moving from potency to act, the first principles and their necessary conclusions allow us to make a moral judgment. In it the *lex naturalis* that is in potency in our mind is en-acted.

Thirdly the *lex naturalis* can be in us as the habit left in us by these moral judgments. It is what is left in our memory of the commands our conscience gives us; by going back to these judgments we became more virtuous, wiser. Besides the first principles and necessary conclusions, the term *lex naturalis* is also applied to the acts of our mind in which a moral judgment is made in accordance to the first principles and their necessary conclusions. But these by definition cannot be the same in all. Each moral judgment is necessarily historically mediated and grounded. We have seen that for Molina laws are those acts of assent and habits that conduct a thing to its end, in ethics, as in economics and politics. They belong to the *lex naturalis* because they are deductions of the habit left by the deductions from the first principles. They are actualizations of what is in potency. They are *leges* because they are the rules that conduct to an end. But certainly they cannot, being operations of a mind, be as

[83] Here we have a clear example of how Molina is dependent on the Aristotelian ideal of science. There are "two essential elements in the Aristotelian ideal of science, that is, a rationally convincing body of knowledge: first it must be derived from "first principle" agreed upon as true; second, by logical argumentation the relationship of these principles with one another must be shown to result in a coherent whole." John W. O'Malley, *Four Cultures of the West* (Cambridge, Massachusetts: Harvard university Press, 2004). 82.

[84] V. 47. 3. p. 158. Vazquez will follow this opinion against Suarez. Vereecke. 581–595.

universal as the first principles and their necessary conclusions. Not only that, they cannot be the same everywhere. And as Molina would say they lead us to intermediate and semi-obscure conclusions. The acts of our mind and the habits they form within us are by themselves obscure and remote conclusions in which, according to Molina, we can easily err.[85] Even the wise and learned err in these. They are also fruit of our experience; they are sensible species, and therefore subject to error and decay.[86]

Lex naturalis is in us in three different ways: as potency, as act and as the habit left over by repeated acts. Molina is here developing what Aquinas sets in a brief treatment in the *Summa*.[87] We have to conclude that *lex naturalis* is being used in an analogical way, something very common in scholastic theology and philosophy. At the same time we have to note that Molina never elaborated on virtue in general and natural inclinations. At least in his publications these two important elements in Aquinas's moral theology seem to disappear.

I have said that one of the characteristics of *lex naturalis* is the fact that it is not written. But what is its content? We have talked about the first principles and the immediate conclusions that we can find in *ius naturalis*, something that almost anyone could know. These coincide with the Decalogue (at least the second table which treats duties to fellow humans rather than God), which works as a summary of *ius naturale*,

---

85 "Ejemplo de conclusiones oscuras "en las que aun los sabios suelen dudar", son la licitud o ilicitud de muchos contratos "y otras muchas cosas controvertidas entre los doctores". También se puede considerar como conclusión oscura, aunque tal vez en grado poco menor, el precepto natural que prohíbe la poliginia. Por último entre las conclusiones semioscuras o intermedias cuenta Molina la ilicitud de la delectación morosa y de la simple fornicación y la malicia absolutamente intrínseca del pecado solitario y de la mentira." Díez-Alegría. 149.

86 V. 47. 3–6. pp. 158–160.

87 "Respondeo dicendum quod lex naturalis potest intelligi mutari dupliciter. Uno modo, per hoc quod aliquid ei addatur. Et sic nihil prohibet legem naturalem mutari, multa enim supra legem naturalem superaddita sunt, ad humanam vitam utilia, tam per legem divinam, quam etiam per leges humanas. Alio modo intelligitur mutatio legis naturalis per modum subtractionis, ut scilicet aliquid desinat esse de lege naturali, quod prius fuit secundum legem naturalem. Et sic quantum ad prima principia legis naturae, lex naturae est omnino immutabilis. Quantum autem ad secunda praecepta, quae diximus esse quasi quasdam proprias conclusiones propinquas primis principiis, sic lex naturalis non immutatur quin ut in pluribus rectum sit semper quod lex naturalis habet. Potest tamen immutari in aliquo particulari, et in paucioribus, propter aliquas speciales causas impedientes observantiam talium praeceptorum, ut supra dictum est." Iª–IIae q. 94 a. 5 co.

and that has appropriately been revealed to ensure that it is to some extent accessible to every one. The content is not exhausted there. The content of *ius naturale* is almost infinite and difficult to understand. It is left to be investigated and taught by the wise (and virtuous) and the doctors of the Church.[88]

Lex naturalis is not binding just because of the will of God—in that case it would be a divine positive law—but because of the nature of the thing. Molina goes as far as to posit the hypothesis, one that Grotius will extend, that even if God were not our legislator and our judge, the *lex naturalis* would still exert its normative claim on us.[89] God has commanded the *lex naturalis* in the Decalogue, this brings these commands to a higher perfection, but the precept already has a claim on us before the divine command.[90]

The *lex naturalis* is for Molina an analogical concept, that pertains only to beings who have free will, and which leads them to their natural end. This makes them collaborators in God's providence.[91] It refers to first principles, but also to moral judgments, and the experience (habits) that these leave on us. This *lex* is binding because of the nature of the thing, not because of God's will, although God's command perfects and brings it to its fullness. The *lex naturalis* helps us attain our natural goal, but by doing so it drives us towards our supernatural goal.

Having seen how elaborate the concept of *lex naturalis* is, the next task is to examine how it relates to positive human law. We have already investigated how it relates to the Old and the New Law when we talk about the use of the Bible. How does it relate to other kinds of law? It

---

88 V. 56. 1. p. 195.

89 "Quare si per impossibile Deus neque legislador neque iudex noster esset ..." Further down he says again "Quare si per impossibile Deus non esset hominum dominum ..." V. 57. 5. p. 202. He is arguing the possibility of dispensation of the *lex naturalis* according to John Mair.

90 "Y a la luz de esta distinción, se ha hecho notar que la obligatoriedad de la ley natural, tomada en el primer sentido, proviene del precepto de Dios, pero que a parte esta ley natural preceptiva, hay una ley natural meramente normativa, que es plena y absolutamente obligatoria con anterioridad al precepto divino." Díez-Alegría. 193–194. It is so because of the internal order, the coherence with the nature of the thing, the normativity of its essence. That is what renders so important the knowledge of reality, because it allows us to access, somehow, the natural normativity, prior to the divine command.

91 "Por último consiguientemente, en último término podemos concluir que la ley natural, considerada en sentido propio, abarca—en la mentalidad de los maestros de Evora—la totalidad de las normas morales necesarias inteligibles como tales a la razón humana." Ibid. 146.

is intimately related to positive law, whether human or divine, because they have the power to concretize the obligations of *ius naturale* and *lex naturalis*.[92] Following tradition, Molina claims that a positive law that goes against natural law is not a law and it is not binding. There is no novelty here. Positive law is a concretization of natural law that has to be consistent (*congruentia*) with natural law.

There is nevertheless another way of relating positive and natural law. Positive law can change the applicability of natural law, by introducing a circumstance that changes not the *lex naturalis*, but the *ius naturalis* and therefore the *lex* as applied to the case. This is what brought about the introduction of so much positive law—civil and canonical—into moral theology. The knowledge of human positive law was fundamental in the task of assessing the obligations arising from *ius naturale* and the applicability of *lex naturalis*. Molina holds that *lex naturalis* is immutable, although he acknowledges that *ius naturalis* changes according to circumstances. Here we return to the beginning of our quest, which is the scholastic quest. Is *lex naturalis*, as seems to be true in some cases, dispensable?

Molina attempts a clear treatment of the issue of the dispensation of the *lex naturalis*. He starts his disputation on the topic by defining very clearly the terms of the disputation, something very typical of scholasticism. He makes a distinction between four different cases of apparently legitimate non-compliance with the law: *irritare, abrogare, dispensare* and *interpretari*. *Irritare* is to prevent the law from gaining binding power (*impedire ne vim obtineat*). *Abrogare* is to abolish a law, to put an end to the binding power of the law (*postquam lex vim obligandi obtinuit, eam tollere*). *Dispensare* is to dispense, to exempt from the obligation of the law in a particular case (*tollere a lege vim obligandi comparatione alicuius aut aliquorum*). *Interpretare* is to interpret, to explicate in which cases the law is understood not to bind (*explicare in quo eventu, aut in quibus eventibus, lex non intelligatur obligare*).[93]

We said at the beginning of the section that *lex naturalis* was a theological concept. We can see that the fact that God is Lord of all helps to explain many apparent exceptions to following the *lex naturalis*. God,

---

[92] "Unde actus illi earum virtutum non sun simpliciter de iure naturali, sed sunt de iure humano, aut divino positivo, esto ad virtutes naturales pertineat: cum hoc tamen addito diminuente, suppositis eis legibus humanis, aut divinis positivis, de iure naturali tunc est, ut fiant, si virtute illae naturales, apposita en circunstantia eorum praeceptorum positivorum, salvae debent consistere" V. 48. 3. p. 161.

[93] V. 57. 2. pp. 198–199.

being Lord, is merely making use of something that belongs properly to Him. All things are oriented towards God and this explains the apparent infractions of the law.[94] For Molina God does not dispense the law, because the *lex naturalis* has a binding force that lies not in the divine command, but in the nature of the particular realities, but cancels what is due to him as a result of that precept. Molina gives the example of Peter promising with an oath to give Paul a certain amount of money. Paul cannot dispense Peter from the oath, but he can cancel the debt Peter owes him by freeing Peter from the obligation to pay him. The oath is valid and never dispensed, but the obligation has ceased. A man-made circumstance has changed the obligations that result from the promise. This is important because here analogical language is being used for natural law. Molina uses the same type of reasoning when talking about *ius naturale*. We have also seen the example of slavery.

Part of moral wisdom is to decide whether a given case falls within the definition of a certain *lex*.[95] According to this model, to talk of a dispensation is incorrect. It is more appropriate to talk about a circumstance that takes the object affected by this circumstance out of the range of the precept.[96] With this understanding, circumstances become extremely important. In the particularities of every case, the empirical is important, because, to use Thomistic-Aristotelian language, it changes the species and is not just an accident. A critical step towards casuistry has taken place here. We shall see how casuistry plays a role in Molina's theology, but before we do that let us examine how Ignatian spirituality might influence this development.

---

[94] V. 57. 5. p. 202.

[95] "ita iudex, legum peritia instructus accedere debet ad iudicandum, caeterum utendo simul prudentia, ut pro qualitate circumstantiarum concurrentium moderamen interdum adhiebat dispositionibus universalibus legum, interdumque illa s omnino omitat, quando per epicheiam iudicaverit illas in eo eventu et cum eis circumstantiis ex mente ipsorummet legum latorum locum habere." V. 68. 2. p. 232.

[96] This is not an original idea of our author, but comes from Gaspar Gonzalvez S.J. who taught in Evora at the same time that he did "Es, por tanto mérito innegable de Gonzálvez haber señalado con claridad que es inconveniente toda aplicación del concepto de dispensa a los preceptos de la ley natural—de cualquier grado que sean—y que es preciso explicar siempre las aparentes excepciones como casos de interpretación, es decir, como situaciones en que el objeto, afectado de una circunstancia especial, escapa al verdadero ámbito del precepto, que en realidad nunca se había referido al hecho concreto aquel." Díez-Alegría. 171.

3.3. *Jesuit Spirituality*

All too often, moral theology ignores the way a person's spirituality affect his moral reasoning.[97] Sometimes the author's spirituality might be difficult, or even impossible to detect. We do not have a spiritual diary of Luis de Molina or any source of that kind, but we do have a wide variety of sources about early Jesuit spirituality. Molina's moral theology reveals to some extent some of this early Jesuit spirituality.[98] This section explores some of the traits of early Jesuit spirituality that influence Molina's moral reasoning.

3.3.1. *The Spiritual Exercises*

At the beginning of the Spiritual Exercises of Saint Ignatius Loyola we find the Principle and Foundation. The text starts by recognizing a proper end toward which every human action must be directed. This end is to "praise, reverence and serve God our Lord."[99] This end is what must determine one's relationship to any other creature. All the other creatures are oriented toward helping man reach that ultimate end. There is a degree of relativity in man's relation to other things. But this relativity is only partial. The basic rule directs us to use creatures as much as they help us to reach our end, and to rid ourselves of them as much as they hinder us as to it. This basic orientation provides a limit regarding what is allowed to the choice of our free will. Some things are completely prohibited. For the rest it is important to decide which are most likely to assist us to our ultimate end and which are more likely to hinder us from achieving it.

---

[97] The fact that Ockham was a Franciscan is identified as important to understand his moral theory in Marilyn Mc Cord Adams, "The Structure of Ockham's Moral Theory". Schumpeter also highlights the importance of the fact that most of the scholastics were vowed religious men: "Not only did the monk's sociological location—outside, as it were, of the class structure—make for an attitude of detached criticism of many things; there was also a power behind them that was in a position to protect that freedom. So far as treatment of political and economic problems is concerned, the clerical intellectual of that age was not more but less exposed to interference from political authority and from "pressure groups" than was the laical intellectual of later ages." Schumpeter and Schumpeter. 77.

[98] Molina explicitly talks about the Society of Jesus in II. 139. 1, 5, 6,7; II. 687. 3.; III. 49. 25; III. 50. 4; V. 69. 1; V. 73. 4. (I omit the page numbers for brevity sake) He also refers to Jesuits when he talks about things he has learned from missionaries, as we have already mentioned.

[99] Ignatius of Loyola, *Monumenta Ignatiana. Series secunda. Exercitia spiritualia Sancti Ignatii de Loyola et eorum directoria*, vol. II (Romae: Institutum Historicum Societatis Iesu, 1969). 165–166.

Everything that is not prohibited is not necessarily good for us in every circumstance. This forces the person who follows this spirituality to continually revise how his or her relationship to things is helping or hindering the achievement of the final end. What makes the difference in many cases are the circumstances that surround the action. This is an important working principle in Molina's fundamental moral theology. We have seen how important circumstances are for him in determining the *ius*, the right thing to do. The norms do not change, but the circumstances of particular cases do alter the way a discerning observer will apply these norms in order to determine the right thing to do—the *ius*—so as best to serve our ultimate end.

The Spiritual Exercises seek to shape the sensitivity of the person doing the exercises so that this person might be able to choose according to this relativism, a theological relativism, because everything is relative (non absolute) with regard to the God revealed to us in Jesus Christ. By the end of the exercises, the retreatant's sensitivity should have been more closely conformed to the image of Christ. The Spiritual Exercises end with the 'Contemplation to Attain Divine Love'. The purpose of this contemplation is to allow the retreatant to return to his ordinary life after a long and profound spiritual experience. In the third point of the Contemplation, the retreatant is encouraged "to consider how God works and labors for me in all things created on the face of the earth—that is, behaves like one who labors."[100] By doing so the Spiritual exercises not only fix God as the end of every human action (this is nothing new to the spirituality or the theology common at the time), but more importantly they 'picture' God at work.[101] To work in Creation is something that makes us collaborators of God in the work of redemption, and makes our work in the world a possible locus for an encounter with God. This idea is not utterly new to the Christian faith, but it is particularly emphasized in the Exercises. These were written in an era in which there was little social affirmation of the positive role of work in human life. The courtier's ideal is that of war and the gentleman of the court. The ideal model for religious life was that of the monk who flees from the world to dedicate himself to contemplation. The ideal offered in the Exercises is that of a person whose labors in the world are relevant in the economy of salvation,

---

[100] Ibid. 310.

[101] The original Spanish text turns to Latin—a sign of intentionality and of the use of a term that has a technical sense—and says that God "*habet se ad modum laborantis*." Ibid.

whose worldly actions are not merely a collaboration in the work of redemption, but in themselves an opportunity for an encounter with God.

A further locus of influence of the Spiritual Exercises in Molina's theological work concerns the eleventh of the rules for thinking with the Church.[102] Here St. Ignatius exhorts the retreatant to praise both the scholastic and the positive doctors, that is, the Church Fathers. These rules are presented against the background of the humanists' attacks on scholastic doctrine, and what Ignatius is trying to protect with this rule is the endeavor of scholastic theology. But in doing so he is also acknowledging the importance of the Fathers. In Molina's work the Fathers appear more extensively than in the early scholasticism.[103] An example of this is the discussion about when the ceremonial precepts of the Old Law lost their validity. The topic arose in the debate between Augustine and Jerome. Aquinas discusses this in Iª–IIae q. 103. Molina dedicates a very long disputation to it, giving a more extensive summary of the dispute between Augustine and Jerome, but referring also to Cyprian, Ambrose, Fulgence and Bernard of Clairvaux.[104]

3.3.2. *The Jesuit 'Way of Proceeding'*

The importance of the autonomy of earthly affairs was not just a theoretical principle for consideration at the end of the Spiritual Exercises. This principle incarnated itself in Jesuit life.[105] Jerónimo Nadal repeated over and over as he traveled throughout Europe promulgating the Constitutions of the new religious order: "We are not monks, the world is our house."[106] This affected the way theology was done, because until

[102] Ibid. 410.

[103] "En la elaboración de este pensamiento fueron herederos [los doctores de la Escuela de Salamanca] de tres corrientes de pensamiento que se remontan al mundo griego, la primera; al mundo romano, la segunda, y la tercera a los primeros padres de la iglesia." Gómez Camacho, *Economía y filosofía moral: la formación del pensamiento económico europeo en la escolástica española*. 24.

[104] "Utrum ceremonialia veteris preacepta ita cessaverint, ut absque lethali culpa servari nequeant." V. 62. pp. 212–224. Other examples of extensive use of the Fathers of the Church can be found in V. 64–65. pp. 225–228 that deal with the New Law, or V. 69. pp. 232–235 on the conditions that a human law must fulfill.

[105] It was the expression "nuestro modo de proceder". O'Malley, *The First Jesuits*. 8.

[106] "'The world is our house.' Again and again Nadal reiterated this point. Ignatius never said it so boldly. Nadal's expression caught the reality at a depth that went beyond the immediate context of his words. He referred this statement to the geographical scope of the Jesuits' ministry, but, as we shall see, it had deeper resonances—as with his

then most of theology had been written by monks and friars who lived in monasteries and convents. This type of religious life allowed for rules to determine every minute detail of everyday life. Jesuit life was different, and these novelties influenced the governance of the Society of Jesus. Saint Ignatius, a man who by character was disposed to regulate everything, was at the same time aware of the importance of experience in shaping decisions, and therefore in many of his letters to Jesuits, after a detailed account of what the person should do, he adds "unless you, who are at the work judge otherwise."[107] Experience exerted normative force, and amounted to a new set of rules that conducted the Jesuit towards the goal he pursued.[108] This principle would be extended to experience in worldly affairs.[109]

This importance accorded to experience is not just a mere fashionable empiricism of the time. It is rooted in Jesuit mysticism. We find a privileged expression of it in number 288 of the Constitutions. In it the Jesuit novice is exhorted to have an honest intention in all things, even in the most particular ones, and is encouraged to find God in all things and to love him in all of them.[110] The world is the stage for the encounter with

---

reconciliatory theology of nature and grace, the systemic relationship of the Jesuits to the *studia humanitatis* through their schools, and the "Contemplation to Obtain Divine Love" of the Exercises." Ibid. 68.

[107] "El P. Ribadeneira en su *Tratado del gobierno de nuestro bienaventurado Padre para los superiores de la Compañía de Jesús* explica la razón profunda de este "remitirse" de Ignacio a la decisión de la persona que está tocando la realidad y es que "vos, que estáis al pie de la obra, veréis mejor lo que se debe hacer". [...] Así lo expresa Ribadeneira: "Mostrava así mismo este amor ('a sus hijos') con la confianza que hacía a la persona a quien encomendaba un negocio importante, dándole las instrucciones que le parecía y firmas en blanco y crédito, y dejándole hacer según la capacidad y talento de cada uno. Y si le avisaba de algunas cosas particulares que al padre se le ofrecían, añadía: 'Vos, que estáis al pie de la obra, veréis mejor lo que hay que hacer' "." Ignasi Salvat, *Servir en misión universal*, Manresa, vol. 27 (Bilbao Santander: Mensajero-Sal Terrae, 2001). 201.

[108] A good illustration of how this worked in the early Society of Jesus with the undertaking of schools can be found in O'Malley, *The First Jesuits*. 200–208.

[109] "Molina was always willing to credit experience. Modestly deprecating his own knowledge of economic affairs, he points out that in cases where justice is not apparent and a custom or trade practice was accepted by upright men, there is probably a valid title somewhere, for "merchants understand these things better than the doctors." " Frank Bartholomew Costello, *The Political Philosophy of Luis de Molina, S.J. (1535–1600)* (Roma Spokane: Institutum Historicum S.I.; Gonzaga University Press, 1974). 21. He is quoting Bernard W. Dempsey, *Interest and Usury*. 122.

[110] Ignatius of Loyola, *Constitutiones Societatis Iesu latinae et hispanicae cum earum declarationibus* (Romae: apud Curiam Praepositi Generalis, 1937). 99–100. Pubblicazione: Romae: apud Curiam Praepositi Generalis, 1937. Const. # 288.

God. Any human activity is a possible arena for this encounter.[111] This idea, typical in Jesuit spirituality, shapes the way theological research is conducted because it gives importance to the autonomy of earthly things. It also underlines the importance of the particular. It is the place of the encounter with God. In the field of moral theology this would result in an emphasis on knowing about worldly affairs in order to be able to make sound moral judgments about them.[112]

We have seen the spiritual roots of the taste for the particular. We can now proceed to see how the conception of natural law and this 'worldly' spirituality paved the way to casuistry.

3.4. *Casuistry*

From a contemporary perspective, many observers consider that natural law and casuistry are two incompatible methods of moral reasoning. Casuistry would be accused of moral relativism, and natural law would be considered the ideal antidote for this moral relativism.[113] For some a rigid conception of natural law is the antidote for relativism, but for others it is precisely this narrow conception that drives them away from this type of moral language.[114]

De Iustitia et Iure is not a book of casuistry, strictly speaking; it is a book of speculative theology but in it cases are discussed after the more doctrinal part is set out. Albert R. Jonsen situates the maturing of

---

[111] The importance of the autonomy of earthly affairs might be an undisputed idea of Catholic theology nowadays after its recognition in *Gaudium et Spes* 36, but it was not in Molina's time. Molina himself dedicates disputation 39 of his second treatise to a discussion on whether the Pope is lord of the whole world. "Utrum summus Pontifex dominium iurisdictionis temporalis, supremamque in universum orbem habeas potestatem." II. 39. pp. 75–83.

[112] "Dazu kommt die apostolische Zentralidee des Jesuitens ordens, die nach Gustav Gundlach nichts weiter ist als die im Jesuitorden besonders ausgerägte katholische Zentralidee des "lebendigen Christus", d.h. des in und mit der Welt fotlebenden Erelösers, der hier und jetz Mitarbeiter braucht, um alles "in Christus als unter einem Haupte zu erneuen". "Diese Mitarbeiterschaft mit Christus, dieses mitleben mit ihm in und mit der Welt, enthält, wie shon gesagt wurde, neben der dynamischen Arbeitsidee ein zweites, das dem Jesuitenorden nicht ausschliesslich, aber vorzüglich eignet und ihm die harmonishce Totalität der Lebensauffassung verleiht: die positive Wertung der Welt, vor allem der in der Zeit fortschreitenden Kulturmenschheit" Weber. 13. Quotes are from Gustav Gundlach, *Zur Soziologie Der Katholischen Ideenwelt Und Des Jesuitenordens. Inaug.-Diss* (Berlin: E. Ebering, 1927). 103.

[113] Albert R. Jonsen, "Foreword," in *The Context of Casuistry*, ed. James F. Keenan and Thomas A. Shannon (Washington, D.C.: Georgetown University Press, 1995). ix.

[114] Díez-Alegría. 159.

casuistry as a discipline in the years between 1556 to 1656.[115] According to these authors conceptualization of casuistry I would not include *De Iustitia et Iure* as a book on casuistry. Keenan anticipates the beginning of high casuistry to the beginning of the sixteenth century with John Mair, and differentiates high casuistry, in which the cases were discussed at length, from the summaries of cases, which did not offer demonstrable arguments but offered already resolved cases, downplaying the theoretical discussion.[116] If we take this conception, it would be easier to include Molina in high casuistry. He is certainly not a summist. What is clear is that Molina could not have remained uninfluenced by casuistry in the years in which this way of moral reasoning was at its zenith, and his work shows this influence.

3.4.1. *Ecclesiastical Development*

Trent had repeated what the Fourth Lateran Council had ordered, that the confessor should hear the complete confession of all mortal sins of the penitent. This included the circumstances of the sin, because, as the Council declared, there are circumstances "which change the sin's nature."[117] What the Council stated dovetailed with the distinctiveness that the sacrament of confession acquired in Jesuit apostolic endeavors.[118] All this contributed to the great importance granted to cases of conscience in Jesuit formation.[119]

Shortly after Trent's decree on the sacrament of penance had been approved in 1551, in Rome, at the Collegio Romano there were daily lectures on cases of conscience for the Jesuit students. Because of broad

---

[115] Jonsen and Toulmin. 142–146.

[116] James F. Keenan, "Moral Theology," in *From Trent to Vatican II*, ed. Raymond F. Bulman and Frederick J. Parrella (Oxford: Oxford University Press, 2006). 161–168.

[117] "Colligitur praeterrea, etiam eas circumstantias in confessione explicandas esse, quae speciem peccati mutant, quod sine illis percata ipsa nec poenitentibus integre exponantur, nec iudidibus innotescant, et fieri nequeat, ut de gravitate criminum censere possint, et poenam, quam oportet pro illis poenitentibus imponere." Council of Trent, Sesion XIV, chap. 5. Trent reserves an anathema to all those deny the obligation of declaring all sins with all the circumstances, because the latter change the nature of the sin. "Si quis dixeri, in sacramento poenitentiae ad remissionem peccatorum necessarium non esse iure divino confiteri omnia et singula peccata mortalia, quorum memoria cum debita et diligenti praemeditation habeatur, etiam occulta, et quae sunt contra duo ultima decalogi praecepta, et circumstantias, quae peccati speciem mutant; [...] anathema sit." Council of Trent, Sesion XIV, canon 7.

[118] O'Malley, *The First Jesuits*. 134–145.

[119] A brief account about cases of conscience in the early Society of Jesus can be found in E. Moore E.L. Lisson, J.T. Bretske. 691–694.

interest in the subject mater and the success of the lectures, in 1563 the lectures became open to the clergy of Rome. They drew an audience of more than 800.[120]

It soon came to pass that a two-year course in Jesuit schools and universities was dedicated to the topic of cases of conscience. The *Ratio Studiorum* stated that every school should have two professors to teach cases of conscience. One had to "spend two years on the explanation of all sacraments, the censure, and the different states of lives and their duties." The other one should teach "the ten commandments, including under the seventh the subject of contracts [...] He should refrain entirely from treating of theological questions that have no essential connections with cases of conscience."[121] On Saturdays the usual lecture would be replaced by a disputation on cases of conscience. This was not taught just for men being trained for the priesthood. In 1553 the University of Evora and the school at Lisbon offered only the lower program in humane letters, but cases of conscience were also taught.[122]

3.4.2. *The Influence of Nominalism*

Besides the ecclesiastical events that encouraged the development of casuistry, there were also theological trends that contributed to its growing importance. The nominalism of Scotus, Ockham and Mair influenced theology in Spain and Portugal in the sixteenth century. Molina was not a nominalist. He is more dependent on the realism of Aquinas, but we cannot say that he was not influenced by nominalist positions. He clearly demonstrates that he had read them, and, although he positions himself with Aquinas on the possibility of dispensation from natural law, he does not remain uninfluenced by his reading of nominalism. He disagrees with Scotus, Ockham and Mair on the topic of dispensation from *lex naturalis* but Molina incorporates certain traits of nominalism that draw him close to the way of reasoning of casuistry.[123]

He clearly acknowledges that there are conclusions that are remote from the first principles of natural law and their necessary conclusions. Although he considers—contrary to Scotus, Ockham and Mair—that

[120] Vereecke. 653.
[121] *The Jesuit Ratio Studiorum of 1599*. 37–38.
[122] O'Malley, *The First Jesuits*. 218. The influence of Trent and Jesuit formation in the moral theology of the time is, also, thoroughly developed in Vereecke. 614–656.
[123] The relationship between casuistry and nominalism is treated in *The Context of Casuistry*, ed. James F. Keenan and Thomas A. Shannon (Washington, D.C.: Georgetown University Press, 1995).

all the precepts of the Decalogue are indispensable, he acknowledges that in many cases the intermediate or remote conclusions are not clear. That is why many err, even the wise and the devout. In the *Concordia* Molina moves along lines that could well be classified as Scotistic[124]—the idea that "[o]ne core element of freedom is contingency."[125] In his moral theology, though, he never uses the word contingency to refer to the uncertainty of moral judgments. He actually considers valid the binding nature of *ius naturalis* that stems from the nature of the thing, but he is actually willing to concede that this *ius naturalis* is mutable, as we have seen, and therefore—we could conclude with the Scotistic label—contingent. If it were necessary, it would have to be immutable. What is immutable is *lex naturalis*, but not the *ius*. This gives theological leeway to talk about the contingency of the situation—the mutability of *ius naturale*, without inferring from that the dispensability of *lex naturalis* and therefore its contingency. The nominalist importance of the circumstance, also stressed by Trent, is in this way incorporated in a Thomistic framework.

This claim about the mutability of *ius naturale* does not necessarily entail relativism. Besides the fact that the indispensability, and immutability, of *lex naturalis* is upheld, there are other checks upon it. An important one is the concept (one that can be traced to Scotus and that is also present in Molina's moral theology) of harmony with the first principles of natural law. For Scotus the precepts of the second table of the Decalogue are not strictly speaking dictates of natural law, but rather they are "exceedingly in harmony (*multum consona*) with that law, even though they do not follow necessarily from those practical principles known from their terms."[126] Molina, putting some distance between his position and that of Scotus, considers the entire Decalogue part of *lex naturalis*—and therefore immutable. But when talking of remote and intermediate conclusions, those in which many err, among which we find

---

[124] According to Eef Dekker, regarding middle knowledge "Molina's account bears a striking resemblance to that of Scotus, who uses, however, a completely different terminology." Eef Dekker, *Middle Knowledge* (Leuven: Peeters, 2000). 121.

[125] Shannon. 4.

[126] "Alio modo dicuntur aliqua esse de lege naturae, quia multum consona illi legi, licet non necessario consequatur ex primis principiis practicis quae nota sunt ex terminis et omni intellectu necessario nota." John Duns Scotus and Allan Bernard Wolter, *Duns Scotus on the Will and Morality* (Washington, D.C.: Catholic University of America Press, 1986). 278–279.

many contracts, he uses the same idea of harmony with the principles of natural law and their necessary conclusions.[127] Whether something is good or bad is largely based on its harmony with the first principles and their necessary conclusions.[128] In this manner circumstances become an important part of his moral reasoning. It even becomes one of the criteria that determine a sound relationship between *lex naturalis* and *lex humana*. *Lex humana* should be a harmonious concretization of *lex naturalis*.

3.4.3. *High Casuistry*

De Iustitia et Iure is not a book of casuistry. It is the development of lectures on a work of speculative theology. It was not the development of commentary in book form such as the *Summula peccatorum* of Cajetan or the *Manual de confessores et penitentes* of Martin de Azpilicueta. Molina, nevertheless, has read them and he quotes them often—especially Azpilicueta, known as *Navarrus*.

Casuistry was not theorized as a method at the time,[129] but it was widely practiced in Jesuit colleges. Molina followed the normal path of formation for a Jesuit scholastic of the time. He spent most of his academic life in Coimbra and Evora, first as a student and then as a faculty member. We have seen how important cases of conscience were in any Jesuit college. He could not have remained uninfluenced by this practice of cases of conscience. This shows up in his work, even if it is a speculative one. In the prologue he talks about how his book can help confessors.[130] The work presents in its final volume, a very good index that runs from page 269 to page 452—that is, 183 pages of index. A confessor would have found it very easy to consult this work in cases of doubt and would have found there a speculative discussion that granted a great deal of attention to circumstances.

---

[127] Where Scotus uses the term *consona* Molina uses *congruentia*.

[128] The idea of harmony in Scotus applies not just to moral theology. His proof for the Immaculate Conception of Mary runs along the same lines of rationality. In his famous "*Potuit, decuit ergo fecit*" *decuit*—it was fitting, right, proper—stands for this idea of harmony. After the Franciscans, the Immaculate Conception of Mary was strongly defended by the Jesuits.

[129] The first work of this nature is the one by Jonsen and Toulmin.

[130] "Ita enim fiet, ut Theologi in enonandis hominum conscientiis, passim non haereant, audacioresque proinde, aptioresque multo sint ad proximos suos iuvandos, et a peccatis eruendos, atque ut prelaturis, regiminisque toti Ecclesiae longe evadant utiliores." I. Prologue. p. 1.

Shannon and Keenan claim that "two major issues prompted casuistry and in both instances nominalism's claims on the particular made that turn to casuistry easier." The first of these two was "the exploration of the New World, the trade with the East, and the evangelization that accompanied both."[131] These same three issues appear in *De Iustitia et Iure*.

Molina sees the arrival of Europeans in the New World as a missiological problem,[132] and he briefly refers to this new set of challenges when talking about the New Law;[133] but living in Portugal he became especially acquainted with the problems of trade with the East. In his disputations about slavery he shows a detailed knowledge of the practices of the slave trade along the coasts of Africa and Asia.[134] When discussing this topic, Molina has always in mind the missiological problem. The possible conversion of a pagan slave owned by a Christian might constitute an argument in favor of slavery in some cases; but he insists more on his concern about the behavior of the Portuguese in Africa and Asia. It was not one that would move the indigenous to convert to the religion of the colonizers. Although he considers slavery a legitimate institution as we have noted above, he manifests himself strongly in favor of the liberation of the slaves, because of the cause of liberty itself, but also because it would be of great help for the cause of evangelization.[135] Missiological problems helped moral theology to move towards casuistry.

---

[131] James F. Keenan and Thomas A. Shannon, "Introduction," in *The Context of Casuistry*, ed. James F. Keenan and Thomas A. Shannon (Washington, D.C.: Georgetown University Press, 1995).

[132] Stegmüller. 555.

[133] V. 64. 5. 226. For the missiological ideas of Luis de Molina, especially referring to America, see Vereecke. 597–613, where he discusses Molina's missiology in the work *De bello contra insulanos* published for the first time in 1984.

[134] The entire II. 33. pp. 87–91 is a long description of slave trade of the coasts along Africa to send slaves to Portugal and Brazil. But he also discusses slave trade in India, China, Cambodia and Japan. He knows all this through the Jesuits who went to all these places as it shows in the way he concludes this disputation. "Postquam haec scipseram, ea contuli eum patre quodam ex nostra Societat, qui diu in regione Sinae commoratus fuerat, interioraque penetrarat, eaque probavit." In II. 35. 17. p. 104 he also says: "Comes patris nostri Gondisalvi a Sylveria, inter alios illorum hominum mores, quod ad nos scripsit, referebat ..."

[135] "Quod si ministry Evangelii ad nations illas barbaras idonei mitterentur, in suisque regionibus ad fidem converterentur, tunc sane omnes pii consulere potius deberent ac favere miserorum hominum libertari neque aliter servitus cuiusque illorum est permittenda, quam si luce cularius eam iustam esse constet. Tum quod libertatis causae, quippe quae piissima est, per se sit suffragandum. Tum etiam quod id magno esset adiumaneto, ut fides nostra, moresque Christiani in illis locis propagaretur." II. 35. 17. p. 105.

Jonsen and Toulmin hold that casuistry is a helpful method of moral reasoning because it is independent of rival accounts of ethics and morality.[136] But in the case of a moral theology like that of Luis de Molina, this assertion is refuted, and Molina is not vastly different from his contemporaries during whose time high casuistry flourished. A study of *De Iustitia et Iure* demonstrates that a notion of natural law based in Aquinas but also one that has taken into consideration new problems and theologians, like Scotus and Ockham, is compatible with a correct use of casuistry. We could venture as far as to say that it demands it, because it places great importance upon the particular that is incomplete if it just states the first principles and their necessary conclusions. This is why in *De Iustitia et Iure*, along with very speculative, abstract and theoretical developments, we find very detailed accounts of the life of trade, politics, economics and finances.

4. Conclusion

Natural law as potency and first principles and their necessary conclusions were in the mind of creatures that had free will; but the term could also be used to refer to the habit remaining in the creature's mind. Natural law could be the *assensu* of how to attain a certain goal. This *assensu* was based on experience and therefore contingent. To some, this meant that *assensu* based on experience was a door to moral relativism. But if this act of the creature was known and willed by the divine mind, this meaning of natural law (*ius naturalis*), without being necessary and immutable—it was actually contingent and mutable—would have divine endorsement. It was not sheer relativism.[137] It made the work of creatures God-grounded, and it accorded an intrinsic value, although imperfect. Only in God was this value perfected.[138]

---

[136] Jonsen and Toulmin, 1–20.

[137] This does not mean that this *assensu* was not subject to error. Molina himself acknowledged that the possibility of error was huge. This meant that if correct it was not just a mere human opinion.

[138] The dogma of the Immaculate Conception rested in this value of the concrete. For a strict Thomism the Immaculate Conception was an unacceptable dogma, because it was an exception to the universal essence of the human being after the Fall. "Et ideo melius videtur dicendum quod per sanctificationem in utero non fuit sublatus virgini fomes secundum essentiam, sed remansit ligatus, non quidem per actum rationis suae, sicut in viris sanctis, quia non statim habuit usum liberi arbitrii adhuc in ventre matris existens, hoc enim speciale privilegium Christi fuit; sed per gratiam abundantem quam

Molina acknowledged the possibility of error. Actually he said that it was quite common, even among the learned. This was a step towards probabilism too, because it asserted that even among the learned, there was uncertainty. His explanation of God's general concurrence and foreknowledge lent a strong theological support for probabilism. Probabilism soon became associated with the Society of Jesus; its spirituality upheld it; its pastoral practice recommended it and the common doctrine of the order on justification gave it a solid theological ground. Although vilified in the seventeenth century, it rested upon a spirituality approved by the Church, a pastoral practice that had produced immense fruits of sanctity and a doctrine of justification approved by Pope Paul V.

But probabilism was not just a moral doctrine. There is also an economic aspect to it.[139] Detailed accounts within his work prompted many theologians to study Luis de Molina's writings about property, just war, banking, just prices, usury, and political theory. We shall turn to property, usury, just price and money exchange in the following chapters and see how theology and economic doctrine interact in the work of Luis de Molina.

in sanctificatione recepit, et etiam perfectius per divinam providentiam sensualitatem eius ab omni inordinato motu prohibentem. Postmodum vero, in ipsa conceptione carnis Christi, in qua primo debuit refulgere peccati immunitas, credendum est quod ex prole redundaverit in matrem totaliter a fomite subtractio." III[a] q. 27 a. 3 co.

[139] "In most branches of academic logic, such as the theory of the syllogism or the geometry of ideal space, all the arguments aim at demonstrative certainty. They claim to be conclusive. But many other arguments are rational and claim some weight without pretending to be certain. In Metaphysics, in Science, and in Conduct, most of the arguments, upon which we habitually base our rational beliefs, are admitted to be inconclusive in a greater or less degree. Thus for a philosophical treatment of these branches of knowledge, the study of probability is required." John Maynard Keynes, *A Treatise on Probability* (London: MacMillan and Co. Ltd, 1921). 3.

CHAPTER THREE

JUSTICE AND THE ORIGINS OF PRIVATE PROPERTY

1. Grace and Property: An Often Repeated Discussion

1.1. *The Medieval Inquiry Regarding Property: Theologians, Canonists and the Spiritual Franciscans*

In the early Middle Ages the controversies regarding *dominium* were tied to the idea of original sin.[1] Society was organized around the idea of *dominium* as an act of force. The story of Cain seemed to cohere with the Stoic theory that after an initial age of equality and justice, humankind had entered into another age in which innocence had been lost.[2] Only after the Fall does private property appear in the Bible. After the Fall, freedom and the right to enjoy the goods of Creation in common had ceased. History seemed to corroborate both the theological and philosophical theories. Resulting from the exercise of military force, the Roman Empire was taken as legitimate.

The naturalistic conception of Aristotle's *Politics* offered an alternative to the idea that *dominium* existed merely as the result of sin. Aristotle's philosophy also offered reliable principles of justice. Aquinas invoked the principle that grace does not destroy nature, but rather perfects it; he used this principle to acknowledge the validity of the *dominium* of the pagan states.

Marsilio of Padua, John Wycliffe and Amarchanus had defended the theory that whoever was in mortal sin had no right to *dominium*; this included political or ecclesiastical power and property rights. According to them, real *dominium* was the result of charity, because we are all custodians of what belongs to God.[3]

---

[1] *Dominium* in the discussion of the scholastics refers both to property (*dominium proprietatis*) and political power (*dominium iurisdictionis*).

[2] Lucio Anneo Seneca, *Lettere morali a Lucilio*. Vol. 2 (Milano: Oscar Mondadori, 1995). 798.

[3] Etienne Grisel, "The Beginning of International Law and General Public Law Doctrine: Francisco De Vitoria's De Indiis Prior," in *First Images of America: The Impact*

In 1200, Pope Innocent III issued the decretal *Quod super his* on the vows of the crusaders and their dispensation. The commentators, nevertheless, appropriated the decretal into a central document regarding the legitimacy of the *dominium* of the infidels. Half a century after Innocent III, the two thirteenth-century commentators Sinibaldus of Fieschi, later pope Innocent IV, and Enrico de Segusio, known as Cardinal Ostiensis wrote a long gloss on this decretal.[4]

For Innocent IV, every rational creature could exercise *dominium*, that is, could hold property and political authority. He grounded his opinion on the principle that what concerns all must be approved by all.[5] For this reason, the Roman Pontiff could not take away infidels' property or the political authority of a non-Christian prince. The pope could only intervene if the prince placed the Christians under his rule in danger. Cardinal Ostiensis held the opposite opinion. He believed that no pagan prince had licit political authority, not even over their pagan subjects. For Cardinal Ostiensis, only if a prince submitted to the rule of the pope would he then hold legitimate political authority. The opposing views of both Innocent IV and Cardinal Ostiensis were discussed well into the sixteenth-century.[6]

At the beginning of the fifteenth century, the knights of the Teutonic Order, made use of Cardinal Ostiensis' opinion to justify their conquest of pagan land along the Polish border. The people of this land, represented by Pawel Wladüriri, rector of the University of Krakow, cited the opinion of Innocent IV as their basis for their claim to the Council of Constance against the unstoppable push of the Teutonic knights. By the end of the fifteenth century Innocent's opinion had become the common opinion.[7]

---

of the New World on the Old, ed. Fredi Chiappelli (Berkeley: University of California Press, 1976). 307.

[4] Robert L. Benson, "Medieval Canonistic Origins of the Debate on the Lawfulness of the Spanish Conquest," in *First Images of America: The Impact of the New World on the Old*, ed. Fredi Chiappelli (Berkeley: University of California Press, 1976).

[5] "Quod omnis tangit ab omnibus comprobetur." For the political and ecclesiastial use and development of the maxim during the Middle Ages see Yves M-J. Congar, "Quod omnes tangit, ab omnibus tractari et aprobari debet," *Revue de Histoire du Droit Fraçais et Etranger* (1956). 210–259.

[6] Molina quotes the opinion of Innocent IV in II. 25. pp. 68–69: "De regia potestate erga subditos, et erga regia coronae bona, et num donatio a Constantino Ecclesiae facta fuerit legitima."

[7] Hanke. 364.

The debates regarding Franciscan poverty, one of the greatest controversies at the end of the Middle Ages, called the canonical and the theological discussion together. The Spiritual Franciscans' main voice was William of Ockham. He held that Christ and the apostles had renounced any type of property or material goods. Therefore to imitate them in this was of a higher perfection. He develops this idea in the *Opus nonaginta ierum* in which he attacks the constitutions on poverty given by John XXII. This pope had suppressed the Spiritual Franciscans because of their radical views on poverty, which raised serious questions regarding any kind of ecclesiastical structure. Ockham and the Spiritual Franciscans held that property rights constituted an exclusion of the natural right that originated in God's original intention of the common use of the goods of Creation.[8]

Jurists identified private property with a right that could be claimed against anyone. The Franciscans thought that the license to use goods that they were asking for would not give them a new legal right, but instead it would restore them to the initial state of things in respect to the goods that they used. They did not claim an exclusive right of use, but a common use of goods as the one existing before the Fall.

The discussion about *dominium* was loaded with juridical, theological and political implications. The doctrine of Thomas Aquinas, which found support in Aristotle and in theological principles, did not become common doctrine until the sixteenth-century, thanks to the works of the Dominicans, such as Cajetan[9] and Francisco de Vitoria. Molina, in his *De Iustitia et Iure*, dedicated one disputation to the problem of Franciscan property: *Utrum minores frates dominium aliquod rerum habeant, an solum usum.*[10]

1.2. *Soto and the Plight of the Poor*

In sixteenth-century Spain, the problem of poverty became especially acute.[11] The socio-economic transformations discussed in the first chapter, were driving people from the countryside into the cities. Additionally,

---

[8] Josep Canning, "Introduction: politics, institutions and ideas," in *The Cambridge History of Medieval Political Thought c. 350–c. 1450*, ed. J.H. Burns (Cambridge, U.K.: Cambridge University Press, 1991). 363.

[9] Cajetan in his comments to the Summa recognizes the legitimacy of the *dominum* of the pagan princes. II^a–IIae q. 66. a. 8.

[10] II. 6. pp. 25–27.

[11] For a very detailed and interesting account of the canonist medieval discussion of the claims of the poor on private property see: Brian Tierney, *The Idea of Natural Rights:*

the wealth coming from the Americas attracted people from all over Europe, in search of what they perceived could be an easy life. Pedro Fernandez Navarrete (1564–1632) in his *Conservación de monarquías y discursos políticos* said that "all the scum of Europe has come to Spain, so that you can hardly find a deaf, a mute, a lame or a blind person from France, Germany, Italy or Flanders who has not been in Spain."[12] The first problem was to differentiate the real poor from the false ones. Once accomplished, the next step was to care for the real poor. Their lack of goods did not deprive them of the natural right to access the goods of Creation that had been granted to humanity as a whole. Two standard modes by which the poor might access the goods to which they were entitled as part of humanity were envisioned: alms and work. There was also the emergency mode which stated that, in case of emergency the exclusive right to use a thing, which private property entitled, ceased. Private property and poverty were two realities that had to be harmonized.[13]

Public authorities were worried about the plight of the poor for charitable reasons, and because this constituted a problem of public order. Bands of beggars roamed the fields and cities. Charles I promulgated laws addressing this topic in 1523, 1525 and 1540. The last of these laws found inspiration in Juan Luis Vives' groundbreaking work *De subventione pauperum.*[14] During the reign of Phillip II even more laws addressing the problems of the poor were approved. This proves that the previous ones were not very effective.[15]

Alongside the laws approved by the public authorities, doctors in the universities also began to discuss the situation. The positions of Domingo de Soto and Juan de Medina[16] on the question exemplify opposing views. At stake was not the fact that the real poor had to be helped, as this was

---

Studies on Natural Rights, Natural Law, and Church Law, 1150–1625, Emory University Studies in Law and Religion; No. 5 (Atlanta, Ga.: Scholars Press, 1997). 69–76.

[12] "... toda la escoria de Europa ha venido a España, de forma que difícilmente hay un sordo, mudo, cojo o ciego de Francia, Alemania, Italia o Flandes que no hubiera estado en España." Quoted in Francisco Gómez Camacho, *Economía y filosofía moral: La formación del pensamiento económico europeo en la escolástica española*. 111.

[13] Ibid. 109–113.

[14] Juan Luis Vives, *De Subuentione Pauperum. Siue De Humanis Necessitatib[Us] Libri.II* (Bruges: 1526).

[15] Gómez Camacho, *Economía y filosofía moral: La formación del pensamiento económico europeo en la escolástica española*. 115.

[16] Juan de Medina (1490–1547) studied at the University of Alcalá, and was professor at the Chair of Prime of the College of St. Ildefonsus of the same university from 1526 to 1546.

taken for granted. Both Soto and Medina agreed that people had the natural right to use the goods of Creation; what was at stake was how to guarantee that right.

Medina defended the measures taken by such cities as Zamora which forbade the poor to move from their places of origin. Under this doctrine the city of one's origin would be obliged to provide the needed assistance. Medina acknowledged that the poor person's liberty to move was being violated, but he argued that the common good and the interest of the poor authorized such restraint on the freedom of the poor to travel. In his view, if the public authority provided for the needy, they would not be compelled to move, therefore the evils resulting from roaming would cease.[17]

Soto took a different approach to the problem. He knew that the civil authorities' assistance to the poor was slow and not always effective. Soto, therefore, believed that it would be an injustice to limit the freedom of the needy to move. Further, such a prohibition would actually limit his right to participate in the goods of Creation through seeking alms. The particular legal measure would limit a natural right without providing a real alternative. He went so far as to argue that "those trying to do mercy could end up doing injustice."[18] For him, freedom of movement reached beyond national boundaries, which meant that the right to participate in the goods of Creation was not limited by them.[19]

Of note is that both Soto and Medina acknowledge a natural right to use the goods of creation, a right that the efforts of the Spiritual Franciscans had helped to clarify and establish. Another item to note is the conditional character of both Soto and Medina's reasoning. Both of them argue not only on the basis of issues of principle (the poor have a natural right to use the goods of Creation), but also based on the abject situation in which the poor find themselves. It is these conditions, not the principles underlying their positions, that led Soto and Medina to conflicting positions. It was the existential reality of the poor, and what each believed was a better way to defend the rights of the poor to the use of the goods of creation that led them to their different conclusions.

[17] Gómez Camacho, *Economía y filosofía moral: La formación del pensamiento económico europeo en la escolástica espanola*. 129–133.

[18] "Porque esta es la llave de la materia y podría ser que los que pretenden hacer misericordia hiciesen injusticia." Quoted in Ibid. 111.

[19] Ibid. 124–128.

The problem of poverty was the other side of the coin to the problem of private property. We have seen how the debate had been conducted so far, and how in Molina's time the circumstances were conditioning the debate. Molina's notion of private property would develop not as much as a dogmatic one, but rather as one open to the appreciation of circumstances.

2. Molina on Private Property: A Theological Problem

Molina develops the problems about *dominium* in the thirty-first disputation of the second treatise. In his time private property existed as such; however, it was believed, in line with tradition, that this was not so at the beginning of Creation. The common destination of goods is more than a principle of Catholic social ethics. According to Aquinas, and this was held as common doctrine, in the beginning everything was common.[20] What Molina sets out to do is to reconcile the fact of private property with the established theological principle of the time concerning the original common destination of the goods of Creation.

Molina's discussion demonstrates how well versed in Roman and civil law he was. The focus of our explanation, however, will be on his ideas about the foundations of private property, more than on all the different juridical nuances it can present. His wide-ranging discussion of the different kinds of *dominium*, shows that, in Molina's mind, private property is never an absolute right. There are many ways in which private property is moderated.[21] At the end of this chapter we will also refer to problems pertaining to political power—*dominium iurisdictionis*—insofar as they illuminate Molina's ideas regarding private property.[22]

[20] "*Ad secundum sic proceditur. Videtur quod non liceat alicui rem aliquam quasi propriam possidere. Omne enim quod est contra ius naturale est illicitum. Sed secundum ius naturale omnia sunt communia, cui quidem communitati contrariatur possessionum proprietas. Ergo illicitum est cuilibet homini appropriare sibi aliquam rem exteriorem.*" II^{a}–IIae q. 66 a. 2 arg. 1. He starts admitting that everything was in common in the beginning. What he refutes is the consequence that, because of this, private property is illicit.

[21] In the disputations dedicated to *dominium* he discusses *usum* and habitation, *emphyteusis*, usufruct, possession and other rights over things. He also discusses an institution very common at the time but unknown in our times, that of primogeniture that resulted in entailed estates, which as well limited property rights.

[22] Molina considers political power a right of a higher kind than private property. The explanation of political power can help understand private property. "Explicato dominio in genere, ut ad partes illi subiectas descendamus, ordiendum nobis est dominium

2.1. *Dominium: Definition and Kinds*

Molina defines *dominium* as "the right to have some material thing completely at one's disposal unless it is forbidden by law."[23] But after giving this very precise definition he widens it. He admits that *dominium* can also be applied to non-material things.

There is a first notion of *dominium* that refers to the relationship of superiority between man and all other creatures.[24] The basic division of *dominium*, though, is the one we have noted; *dominium* can be divided between *dominium iurisdictionis* and *dominium proprietatis*.[25] *Dominium iurisdictionis*, what we call today political power, can be divided between political and ecclesiastical power, however, it is more than that. It literarily means the power to declare what is right, the saying—*dictio*—of the law, the right thing, the right or the duty—*iuris*. It can be divided into *iurisdictionis temporalis*, that of the state, and *iurisdictionis spritualis*, that of the church. I will turn to this first type of *dominium* at the end of the chapter.

The *dominium proprietatis* comes from man's own nature. It is the moral faculty that allows him to use Creation for his own good.[26] It is divided into *dominium universitatis* and *dominium particulare*. *Dominium universitatis* is ownership held in common such as the common fields that belong to towns and cities whose use is reserved indiscriminately to those who dwell there.[27] This type does not include the property of public entities in which the owner is public, but the use is as if it were a

---

iurisdictionis. Tum quia nobilius est. Tum quia notitia illius conducit, ut tituli dominii proprietatis melius intelligatur." II. 21. 1. p. 58.

[23] "Est ius perfecte disponendi de re corporali, nisi lege prohibeatur." II. 3. 1. p. 19.

[24] Improperly one could also talk about a *dominium* of the beasts over the grass they eat; improperly because if animals cannot control their acts ("namque suorum actuum dominium non habent"), least could they control other things ("multo minus aliarum rerum poterunt dominium habere"). II. 3. 6. p. 21.

[25] This distinction is found in Bartolus of Sassoferrato.

[26] "Esta relación de superioridad se concreta en el hombre en la facultad moral que brota de su misma naturaleza, de utilizar los bienes creados para su propio provecho." José Caycedo, "*Ideas jurídicas de Luis de Molina sobre la propiedad privada*. Excerpta Ex Disertatione in Pontificia Universitas Gregoriana" (Pontificia Universitas Gregoriana, 1957). 8.

[27] "Dominium locorum, seu rerum pertinentium ad universitatem iure universitatis est dominium, non quidem iurisdictionis, sed proprietatis comparatione eorum locorum aut rerum quae ita sunt universitatis propriae, ut ad singolorum usum sint deputatae. Eiusmodi sunt prata oppidi aut civitatis alicuis, deputata ad pactum pecorum eorum, qui illis sunt loci. Sylvae item ad ligna scidenda similiter deputatae, et alia eiusmodi." II. 3. 11. p. 21.

single owner, for example, a fire house. It belongs to the public, but only those designated for certain duties have access to the property. The owner is a public entity, but its use is neither common nor open to everyone.

Dominium particulare, the closest to our notion of private property, is the one by which an individual owns a thing. Molina says that it is so well known that it needs no explanation.[28] He describes it, rather than define it. Defining a property right has always been difficult to pinpoint for legal experts. That may be the reason why Molina indicates that a property right is something so well known that it needs no explanation. It is certainly the reason why he resorts to his knowledge about law, in order to describe as minutely as he can the juridical traits of something difficult to define. But this is not the issue on which I will focus. My focus will be upon his ideas about original common property, the origin of private property and its justification.

Molina also distinguishes the *dominium paternum*. It was the power that a married man exercised over his wife, his children and his servants. For the scholastics, family is a natural institution and the *dominium paternum* is a power that anteceded the state and the division of property. As we shall see, this type of *dominium* is referred to in explaining the division of goods.

2.2. *The Original Common Property of Goods*

2.2.1. *The Traditional Doctrine*

In the beginning everything was in common. This assertion was accepted doctrine for scholastics. This belief was supported by philosophers of the Ancient world, by the Scriptures and the Church Fathers.[29] Molina

---

[28] "Dominium particulare, quod unusquisque in res suas habet, est similiter dominium, non iurisdictionis, sed proprietatis, et adeo notum, ut explicatione non egeat." II. 3. 18. p. 21.

[29] "Responsio ad hanc quaestionem est apud omnes unanimis: In initio mundi omnia erant communia sine ulla proprietatis distinctione. Hoc docebant philosophi antiqui (9), in hoc Patres concordabant (10), hoc commune evadit apud theologos et iurisperitos. Nec hodie quisquam invenitur, qui de hac initiali et transitoria bonorum communione dubitaret." "(9) Cfr. Cicero, De oficc., I, 7, 21, ubi resumit doctrinam Stoicorum. (10) Eorum hac de re propositiones a Gratiano saepe citantur: "Iure naturae omnia sunt communia omnibus", dictum Gratiani ad D. VIII init; cfr. c. 2, C. XII, q. 1: c. 7, d. I." Jaroslaw Skarvad, *De Iure Proprietatis Privatae Apud Ludovicum Molinam*, Dissertatio in Pontificia Universitas Lateranensi (Roma: 1950). 29.

"For Gratian and Isidor, the common possesion was of natural law." Tierney. 60. He quotes Isidor "Ius naturale est commune omnium nationum, eo quod ubique instinctu naturae, non constitutione aliqua habetur, ut uiri et feminae coniunctio, liberorum

holds this opinion in disputation 18, on the question of whether or not only those who have free will can own property or have other rights—be *domini*.[30] He is arguing against those who held that the insane and children cannot hold property or any other rights.

Molina gives philosophical and theological reasons for the assertion that everything was common in the beginning. The philosophical reason he quotes is found in Aristotle's *Politics*. According to Aristotle, nature offers indistinctly to both animals and humans what is necessary for life, in the case of human beings, even for family and political life.[31]

The theological reason for this is Creation.[32] Man is made in the image and likeness of God. God the Creator and, therefore, the Lord created humankind in his image and likeness. This is the reason why man can be *dominus* of created things, because of his likeness to the Creator and Lord.[33] For Molina justice and *dominium* are tied to free will.[34] When

successio et educatio, communis omnium possessio et omnium una libertas, acquisitio eorum, quae celo, terra marique capiuntur; item depositae rei uel commendatae pecuniae restitutio, uiolentiae per uim repulsio. Nam hoc, aut si quid huic simile est, numquam iniustum, sed naturale equumque habetur." We have already shown Aquinas' position. Scotus also taught that in the begining everything was in common and that natural law changed after the Fall making private property of natural law. *In Quartum Sententiarum*. D. 15. q. 2.

"Molina lehrt demnach im Einklang mit der patristischen und scholastischen Tradition, daß Gott ursprünglich alle materiellen Güter dem Menschengeschlecht insgesamt gewidmet hat." Weber. 71.

[30] "Utrum solae res libero arbitrio pollentes, dominii sint capaces." II. 18. pp. 50–52.

[31] II. 20. 4–5. p. 55. There seems to be some confusion in the citations when compared against the originals referring to the book numbers of Aristotle's *Politics*. In *I Politics III. 4. 1256 a*. Aristotle has an idyllic view of an original state before civic life, in which game or fishing are offered by nature without work. It is very interesting what he says about nomadic life. "The idlest men are nomads (for to procure food from domesticated animals involves no toil or industry, but as it is necessary for the herds to move from place to place because of pasture, the people themselves are forced to follow along with them, as though they were farming a live farm)." Aristotle, *Politics*, trans. H. Rackham, The Loeb Classical Library (Cambridge, MA: Harvard University Press, 1959). 35. In *II Politics* Aristotle discusses different political systems that propose common property (property understood in a large sense for they include commonality of women and children) as Plato's *The Republic* and *The Laws*. He dismisses them as impracticable.

[32] Molina quotes Gen 1, Salm 8 and 113 and Deut 4. He also refers to IIª–IIae q. 66, a. 1 and Soto's *De Iustitia et Iure* I. 4. 1.

[33] "Confirmatur ex illo Gen 1. Faciamus hominem ad imaginem et similitudo nostram, et praesit piscibus maris, volatilibus coeli, et bestiis universae terrae, quasi dicat, et eo ipso, quod ad imaginem et similitudinem nostram sit, praesit, et dominus fit, sicut nos domini sumus." II. 18. 2. p. 51.

[34] "Quae namque arbitrio praedita non sunt, ut iniuriae non sunt capacia, ita neque iutis, atque adeo nec dominii." II. 18. 1. p. 51.

saying this, he is pointing to the fact that animals cannot have *dominium* or suffer injustice. He is aware that he could be asked whether children or insane people can suffer injustice and be *domini*. He thinks that children and insane people are in potency created in the image and likeness of God, therefore they are capable of *dominium* but that given their situation their right should be protected by legal guardians.

Human *dominium* is a result of creation, not of a particular divine gift. It affects all humankind. Because this likeness is common, this *dominium* is also common. Property over goods is common, as was, in the beginning, political authority. It is the fact that God, the Lord, has created the universe and has created humankind in his likeness which made all humankind common owners of all created things.[35] Through this ownership, all humankind participates in God's Lordship over the world.[36]

Property is tied to creation and free will, and not to redemption and grace. This fact might seem of little importance, but it guarantees that all have access to the goods of Creation,[37] because every person is a creature, but not every person is necessarily in a state of grace. As we have shown, Wycliffe and others had claimed that only those in a state of grace could hold *dominium* of any kind. According to Molina, God's original intention is the common ownership of created things. After the Fall, the system of division of goods became more in harmony with this original intention and state of things. If the original situation and intention is common property, what has to be justified—judged just—is not the access of all to the goods of Creation, but the accumulation of goods and the exclusion of many from this original and divinely intended common destination of goods.[38]

---

[35] "Quod cum naturae author ita res omnes alias corporeas condiderit propter genus humanum, ut nihil, constitutione ipsa rerum, ciuquam hominum proprium effecerit, sed omnes indistincte in hominum commodum et utilitatem condiderit; efficitur, ut, si solum ius naturale, primamque rerum constitutionem spectemus, dominium aliarum omnium rerum corporearum omnibus hominibus sit commune, nullaque rerum dominia sint inter hominess divisa." II. 18. 17. p. 52.

[36] Weber. 70.

[37] It is also a theological caveat against any doctrine that tends to identify possession of material goods with God's blessing.

[38] Molina acknowledged that certain things in the beginning were not in common. He refers to qualities of persons such as beauty, intelligence or strength. "Dona tanem sive corporea, sive incorporeal, sive indita a natura, sive propria industria comparata, quae cuique hominum inessent, illius essent propria quad dominium, ut pulchritudo, artes, scientia, et id genus alia, imo et honor, fama propriis meritis comparata, quamvis ab alienis suppositis, quoad opinionem vel honorem externum, penderent." II. 18. 17. p. 52.

Molina ties the problem of property to the problems of rationality. Nevertheless, the human being in God's image, that is a rational and free creature, is what makes him capable of ownership. This is in accord with the tradition, and this notion will continue to inform the subsequent discussion. However, briefly after Molina, the original intention of God in Creation will be lost in the discussion, and property, as many other rights will be given merely to rationality. By dissolving the theological link that keeps creation and property together there will be an inversion of the original idea of the tradition.

2.2.2. *Molina's View of the Original Community*

If original common property of goods is the traditional and inherited doctrine, what is specifically original to Molina is how he conceives this original community.[39] Out of the nature of things, that is, out of *ius naturale*, man has *dominium* over creatures. It was in common that God gave man the goods of the earth. This original community was not a 'negative community'.[40] A negative community is one in which we can talk about a common destination for all goods; however, that destination is a potential one. That destination is possible but not yet realized. In actuality no one owns anything, and things await someone to take possession of them. Molina's original community is also not a 'positive community' in which all men collectively own all goods of creation, the same way a corporation owns property. Therefore, the idea of the initial community for Molina is a middle one, set between a negative and a positive community.[41]

What Molina says about the original common property is that all was once owned by all,[42] because God created and gave this to all of humanity

---

[39] Molina has no comprehensive doctrine about private property. He answers the questions about it that arise from the problems of the time. For the systematization of this doctrine, other that in the texts of DII, I rely on Caycedo and Johann Kleinhappl, "Die Eignentumslehre Ludwig Molinas," *Zeitschrift für katholische Theologie* 56 (1932).

[40] I take the terminology negative community and positive community used to refer to the original community of goods from Kleinhappl, Weber and Skarvad.

[41] "Betrachtet man diese Sätze unbefangen, so wird man sagen mussen: bei Molina ist von einer negativen Gütergemeinschaft nicht die Rede. Fast mit einem gewissen Nachdruck finden wir immer wieder in verschiedenen Wendungen betont: omnibus omnia sunt communia. Es ist eine wirkliche Gütergemeinschaft, nicht bloss das Fehlen von Sondereingentum, denn sie wird für den Zustand der urspünglichen Gerechtigkeit als das Entsprechende und Geziemende hingestellt." Kleinhappl 51.

[42] "Stando a solo iure et constitutionem rerum, omnibus omnia sunt communia" II. 20. 6. p. 55.

as a community, and not individually or separately.[43] There is a right to all things by each and every member of the community. It is not a case in which a member of the community has some right over a part of what the community owns in common, but rather each member has a full right over all the things in creation, because of the very nature of those things.[44] This means that it is a natural right over all things.[45] This peculiar way of conceiving the original community, along with his notion of *ius naturale*, allows him to explain the movement towards the division of goods,[46] because what *ius naturale* demands is not a particular type of juridical arrangement, but the defense of the natural rights of the community members.[47]

2.3. *The Origin and Justification of Private Property*

The original common property of things is for Molina, as for all the scholastics, a given. They differ on how to conceive the original community and how to explain the lawfulness of the transition towards the system of division of goods. The question requiring an answer is how the division of goods, the situation in which we live, came about and

---

[43] "Cum enim res a Deo conditae et donatae fuerint toti generis humani congregationis indistincte." II. 20 7. p. 56.

[44] "Hoc commune dominium competit omnibus et singulis hominibus non in quantum sunt membra cuiusdam societatis, quae ipsa esset subiectum dominii, quod illis ex parte communicaret, sed competit unicuique eorum directe ab ipsa natura." Skarvad. 33–34.

[45] We have seen how for Domingo de Soto the poor had a right over all goods that transcended national borders, because it affected all goods of creation.

[46] Caycedo insists in talking about division of goods rather than private property. The term certainly helps to convey the idea of a common destination of goods better than the expression private property. "Cuando decimos en el enunciado de la Proposición: "regimen de División de Bienes", entendemos lo que ordinariamente se llama "propiedad privada", o sea, el Derecho-facultad de apropiarse una parte de los bienes de la tierra para ejercer sobre ellos un dominio exclusivo y duradero, y usarlos en conformidad a este derecho." Caycedo. 22.

[47] "Molina no quiere probarnos que el Derecho Natural exija que la propiedad de los bienes deba ser común; el se coloca en un plano más elevado y nos dice que si consideramos las cosas en su estado primitivo antes que la voluntad de los hombres hubiera introducido cualquier cambio; como según su manera de pensar los bienes de la tierra habían sido dados por Dios en propiedad común a todos los hombres, el Derecho Natural exigía que se respetara ese derecho de cada uno; y que a ninguno se le prohibiera el uso de bienes cuyo dominio, por ser común, también a él le pertenecía. El Derecho Natural, pues, no exigía que la propiedad fuera común y mucho menos que así permaneciera; únicamente exigía que en ese estado de cosas no se violasen los derechos de los miembros de la comunidad." Ibid. 20.

whether or not this is valid.[48] The title of the disputation, where Molina discusses this question is precisely that of the Summa: Was the *dominium* over things lawfully divided and if so, in accordance with what law?[49]

Private property, as political power or slavery, was for the scholastics a postlapsarian institution. It appeared in history after the Fall of Adam and Eve. For Molina it was necessary to institute political power after the Fall in order to preserve peace and tranquility.[50] The division of goods works in a similar way. Before the Fall, in an age of innocence, common property was more appropriate. After the Fall, though, the division of goods was both expedient and necessary. This need, however, is not a logical necessity, but a historical and existential one. Three considerations led Molina to conclude that it was more expedient and necessary to have a system of division of goods. First, nature was not as generous as it was before the Fall. Secondly, the conviction that if things were kept in common, no one would want to work; and lastly, the concern that if no one worked, there would be an absolute scarcity of things, which would lead to a struggle over existing things. In such a situation the strongest would oppress the weakest.[51] The division of goods thus appears as a means to an end. The end is the enjoyment of the goods of Creation by all men. In the circumstances after the Fall, the means, the division of goods,[52] seems more appropriate than common

[48] "Es erhebt sich danach notwendigerweise die Frage, wie es dann zu einer Verteilung der Erdengüter unter die einzelnen Menschen kommen konnte." Kleinhappl. 71.

[49] The title of the disputation is "*An licite et quo iure, rerum dominia fuerint divisa. D. Thomas. Q. 66. art. 2.*" II. 20. p. 54.

[50] "Etenim statim ac genus humanum ab innocentiae statu per peccatum corruit, necessarium fuit iurisdictionis dominium cum vi quadam coercente introduci, quo homines in officio continerentur, propulsarentur et pinirentur iniuriae, paxque et tranquillitas inter eos servaretur." II. 120. 1. p. 54.

[51] "Posterior vero pars probatur. Quoniam cum ex una parte post peccatum terra, ut hominibus necessaria suppeditet, nimio eorum labore et sudore indigeat, ut experientia testatur, spinasque et tribulos, etiam culta, germinet, ut Genesis 3 habetur: ex alia vero parte homines post peccatum segnes ac debiliores ad laborandum effecti sint, abundentque pravis affectibus et cupiditatibus, sane si toti hominum communitati essent omnia communia, nullus culturam et administrationem temporalium rerum propter laborem et molestiam, quam adiunctam habet, curaret: cum tamen singuli optimis quibusque rebus potiri vellent. Unde necessario sequeretur penuria et rerum egestas, orietuntur rixae et seditiones inter homines circa rerum temporalium usum, ac consumptionem, robustiores opprimerent debiliores." II. 20. 5. p. 55.

[52] We shall use with preference the term division of goods over private property because it conveys better the idea that there is a right to commonly enjoy the goods of creation, and that this right is enforced through the division of goods. The term private property tends to evoke absolute rights to sole enjoyment of the goods of creation.

property. It is a prudential necessity, not a strictly logical one because the division of goods does not solve all problems.[53]

To explain the logic of the transition from one system to another, Gómez Camacho talks of two models.[54] Model A denotes a state of innocence, where the earth furnished everything that was necessary in abundance and with little effort. Beyond that, man had no disorderly affection for things, and therefore had no desire to take things to the disadvantage of others. It was more suitable to have everything in common. Model B addresses the changed circumstances after the Fall. After the Fall earth is not so generous, and it takes great effort to make it produce what is needed for man's sustenance. The earth itself was not solely affected by the Fall, human nature was also affected adversely, becoming weaker and more lazy. Man exhibits disordered affections. If things were in common, no one would work. The result would be poverty and need. In this case the system of division of goods was more suitable. The logic of the decision is not the logic of a syllogism, it is more like the prudent judgment in which human freedom and responsibility are called to decide according to the end established by *ius naturale*—the access of all to the goods of Creation—and the social circumstances in which the person deciding lives.[55]

This division could have happened for Molina in three moments.[56] The first possibility is that it originated from paternal authority. Adam or Noah, because they enjoyed the *dominium paternum* over the people of their time, had the authority to divide the goods of creation among their descendants. They held a natural authority over all, thus instituting the system of division of goods. The second possibility is that as men multiplied, they elected a leader, under whose authority proceeded a

[53] "Observant Conradus et Sotus locis citatis, quamvis rerum divisio non tollat, omnino absurda omnia et mala, quae sequerentur, si rerum dominia non essent divisa, ut tanem expediens et necessarium omnino sit ea dividendi, satis esse si magna parte tollantur." II. 20. 5. p. 55.

[54] Francisco Gómez Camacho, "En torno a unos textos de Luis de Molina sobre la propiedad privada," 163–166.

[55] "Naturalmente que esta es una conclusión a la que se llegue mediante una cadena de razonamientos lógico formales, como si nos halláramos ante la conclusión de un silogismo. Se trata más bien de una conclusión de tipo existencial, coherente con los supuestos existenciales que especifican el modelo. La misma expresión que utiliza Molina para estableces el nexo entre los supuestos y la conclusión deja a las claras que no nos hallamos ante un raciocinio formal, sino ante un razonamiento existencial: 'era muy conveniente esa posesión en común, lo que no significa que fuera lógica y estrictamente necesaria'." Ibid. 163.

[56] II. 20. 9. p. 57.

division of what was once common. The third possibility was a general agreement of men, whether implicit or explicit, to divide the goods of creation. Molina gives as an example the case of Abraham and Lot. When it became impossible for both to herd their livestock by using the same pastures, Abraham said to Lot: "Let there be no strife between you and me ... Is not the whole land at your disposal? ... If you prefer the left, I will go to the right; if you prefer the right, I will go to the left ... Thus they separated from each other."[57]

Although he discusses three possible scenarios, there are only two possible sources of lawfulness for the transition from common property to division of goods. Molina here is following Aristotelian sources of authority, quoted shortly before giving this triple scenario.[58] For Aristotle there are two sources of authority. The first source comes from *ius naturale*, such as paternal authority—this authority would legitimize the case of Adam or Noah. The second source is civic authority that comes from the general consent of men. Such a source of authority would legitimize the two later cases. But let this be clear, *ius naturale* does not validate the division of goods. It only validates the authority that decreed the division. *Ius naturale* will never be used by Molina to validate the division of property. What is important for Molina, when he discusses the different possible scenarios for the transition from common property to division of goods, is not the question of which one of these possibilities was the actual and historical one. Rather, his point is to emphasize that the system of division of goods was legitimate and the result of a human law. It was the result of *ius gentium*, which for Molina is without nuance a human law.

To prove the division licit, Molina sets forth two sets of reasons. The first is that this division through human law was licit because it was not against *ius naturale*. *Ius naturale* prescribes that all of humankind should have access both to use[59] and enjoy the goods of creation, but it does not prescribe a certain system of property. Before the Fall the system of common property was better suited, but it was not prescribed.[60] After

[57] Gen 13: 8–11.

[58] II. 20. 8. p. 57. He quotes Aristotle's *I Politics*.

[59] Remember the discusion of the Spiritual Franciscans.

[60] Molina concedes that it would have been licit to divide the goods of Creation before the Fall, there was no prohibition against it, although it would have made no sense because the historical circumstances common property suited better God's original intention. "Potuissent namque homines in illo statu de communi consensus dividere inter se et appropiare absque cuiusquam iniuria res omnibus a Deo concessas non secus ac

the Fall, the division of goods seems to guarantee to all greater access to the goods of Creation than the original prelapsarian system.

For Molina, following Aquinas, a principle of the natural law cannot change, but our circumstances can. Something as significant as the Fall is for him circumstantial, but circumstantial means for him important. Thus in light of the Fall circumstance changes, therefore the obligations arising of *ius naturale*—of the very nature of the thing—also change. The division of goods not only is it not against *ius naturale*, but it is also in accordance with the *recta ratio*, and therefore should be followed. I shall show in the next chapters how circumstances affect what is in accordance with *ratio*, something that links any moral reasoning to prudence.

A second class of reasons, less important than the previous one, takes into consideration scriptural passages, where Molina finds divine commands. These passages do not have for Molina great normative significance. God gave[61] the Promised Land to the people of Israel, in the same way he gave the kingdom of Israel to David. Therefore, there can rightfully be private property. Another scriptural argument for Molina is the existence of a commandment forbidding theft, and this must mean a licit right to private property.[62] If everything were in common, theft would be impossible. Additionally, he quotes the Council of Constance in condemnation of Wycliffe's proposition that it was illicit for the clergy to own property.[63] For Molina, nevertheless, the division of goods is set by the first argument.

The reasons recommending the division of goods are weighty according to Molina. The division of goods, however, was not of *ius naturale*.[64] The importance of these circumstances, though, is so great that Molina considers the possibility that the obligation to divide things is a matter of *ius naturale*. The division of goods was licitly done by human law out of an obligation that arose from *ius naturale*. If the nature of a social situation whereby not dividing the goods would lead to serious evils, then

in statu naturae lapsae iustissimis de causis effectum est. Quia tanem id tunc non erat necessarium, contrariumque erat decens" II. 20 6. p. 56.

[61] Molina uses the term "tradidit" which is a technical term to express the transfer of ownership. He has to talk about it in II. 2. pp. 17–19 and II. 13. pp. 42–45.

[62] For Proudhon private property was theft. For Molina the existence of theft actually proves that private property is legitimate.

[63] II. 20. 6. p. 56.

[64] Like any scholastic Scotus acknowledges the original community of goods, but for him this changed in such a way that, after the Fall, private property became a matter of natural law. We have seen in the last chapter that, for Scotus, except the commandments of the first table, all the other laws of the natural law could change.

there exists an obligation arising from *ius naturale* to undertake such a division, but we cannot say that the division itself pertains to *ius naturale*.[65]

2.4. Ius Naturale *and* Ius Gentium: *Virtue and Human Law*

In the previous chapter, we set out Molina's conceptualization of natural law—the nature of the thing—as well as the importance of circumstance and the significant distinction between *ius naturale* and *lex naturalis*. In this section we will explore how this plays out in his doctrine regarding private property. We will also examine the different scenarios he contemplates concerning private property.

The division of goods was neither of divine nor of natural law. It was a human decision because, for Molina, *ius gentium* is a purely human law. This decision was adopted taking into consideration both the demands of *ius naturale* and of specific circumstances. The decision sought to harmonize *ius naturale* and circumstances. But this does not end the moral problem. Molina knows that he has solved the problem of the nature and lawfulness of the division of goods, but he also knows that this institution will always pose problems, many of them problems of justice. This is why he takes the discussion further.

The way in which private property has been justified in *De Iustitia et Iure*, renders clear that the division of goods is a means to an end. Being neither a matter of divine nor natural law, it involves the prudent decision of men. As such it is not something absolute. Therefore, the only absolute we could consider is set as an end, and not as a rule, that would be the common use and enjoyment of the goods of Creation. Ends in scholastic philosophy create rules,[66] and affect them. We noted, in discussing natural law, that an important criterion for grouping laws was their common end. And one of the ends that justifies the division of goods

---

[65] "Quare non fuit de iure naturali, sed humano: obligatio tamen, ut fieret, esse potuit de iure naturali, non semper, sed quando ex eo quod non fieret, imminenter gravia mala. Neque inter omnes, sed inter eos tantum, inter quos ea mala imminetrent. Atque hoc tantum est, quod Joannes Medina voluit." II. 20. 7. p. 56. He says this at the end of a long excursus in which he discusses the opinion of Juan de Medina who held that the division of things was of *ius naturale*. He discusses Medina's opinions and concludes with the quote we have just copied as a way to reconcile his doctrine with that of Medina.

[66] "Regula autem et mensura humanorum actuum est ratio, quae est primum principium actuum humanorum, ut ex praedictis patet, rationis enim est ordinare ad finem, qui est primum principium in agendis, secundum philosophum." Iª–IIae q. 90 a. 1 co.

is the protection of the weakest.[67] This purpose should always inform the system of division of goods, because we are in the presence of a system that takes different shapes in different times and places.

Molina also notices that in his time there were still places in which goods have not been divided. He then deals with this fact, mentioning religious life and the original community of Jerusalem.[68] He compares community of property to the practice of celibacy, inasmuch as it is not for all: because it would lead to the annihilation of humanity, it remains a counsel that pertains to individuals.[69] He also knew because it had been reported by the Conquistadors, the missionaries and the Spanish and Portuguese settlers, that the colonial powers were arriving in lands where there were systems of common property.[70] All these cases posed an intellectual challenge. Although the division of goods had taken place, systems of common property had persisted in some corners of the world, and so were still possible. In fact they happened, and in good scholastic logic against facts you cannot claim reasons.

Molina even contemplates the possibility of a reversal of the system; in his first treatise where he discusses the nature of *ius gentium* and whether it can be repealed, he argues precisely the case for the division of things. For him it could lawfully be repealed because it was instituted through human consent. He considers, however, that it would most likely be a mortal sin, because it went against an obligation that arose from *ius naturale*. It is in one of those cases, where we see how there is an

---

[67] II. 20. 5. p. 55.

[68] Acts 2: 44 and 4: 32.

[69] "Observa quod quemadmodum coelibatus consilim est singulis, non vero toti hominum collectioni: alioquin periretgenus humanum, ad cuius conservationem quilibet in aliorum defectum, sub reatu lethalis culpae teneretur ducere uxorem, et vacare generationi: sic quoque paupertatem, abdicationemque rerum temporalim in particulari, consilium est singulis, non vero in hominum collectioni: eo qui nec expediens orbi statum conservari posset, si multiplicatis hominibus omnes universim res possiderent." II. 20. 13. p. 57.

[70] "El descubrimiento de América ejerció decisiva influencia en el desarrollo de las doctrinas sociales y replanteó con caracteres nuevos el problema doctrinal del comunismo. Los mitos de la edad de oro, estado de naturaleza, retorno al principio, que venían gravitando un poco estelarmente sobre el espíritu de aquella sociedad, reciben un nuevo impulso, y se concretan y cualifican en la corriente de las utopías al encontrar en América una presunta realidad. Allí había, en efecto, una sociedad en estado de naturaleza, y la visión idealizada de ella, en contraste con la europea, hizo creer existente en América el primitivo modelo feliz de vida en la aurora del hombre y la historia" quote from Carmelo Viñas, *Doctrinas de los tratadistas españoles de los siglos XVI–XVII sobre el comunismo*, ed. Biblioteca de Clásicos Sociales Españoles (Madrid: 1945). in Gómez Camacho, "En torno a unos textos de Luis de Molina sobre la propiedad privada." 166.

obligation that arises from both end and circumstances, but it is not of *ius naturale*, because otherwise not only would it be a mortal sin but also unlawful.[71]

Molina develops in Vitoria's wake the interplay of *ius naturale* and *ius gentium*. *Ius gentium* in Molina has, in Wilhelm Weber's words, great elasticity.[72] It shapes private property. An example of this is the institution of prescription.[73] Prescription is the acquisition of property by possessing the thing under those circumstances determined by law.[74] Through prescription, what legally belongs to one person is passed on to another. Political authority has the power to declare that for some reason, usually legal security, the property rights of a person have prescribed and now belong to another person. This power, according to Molina, is related to the common good.[75] If property were a natural right this could have not happened, but being of *ius gentium* it can be done. This is because it does not go against what is right in itself (and therefore can never be contradicted) but against what is right according to human regulation and will. What results from human will can be overridden by human will, if it is according to *recta ratio* and executed by the legitimate authority.[76]

[71] "In totum autem vix abrogari posset quod ad ius gentium pertineret. Ratio est, quoniam ad id necessarius esset communis consensus omnium, aut fere omnium nationum, qui difficili haberi potest. Atque, quod ad rerum divisionem attinet, si prorsus tolleretur, tot inde orirentur mala, ut proculdubio culpa esset lethalis eam omnino tollere. Si tamen tolleretur, non dubito, quin factum teneret. Ratio est, quoniam quemadmodum humana voluntas sufficiens causa fuita ad rerum divisionem inducendam, sic quoque sufficiens videtur ad illam tollendam." I. 5. 5. p. 8.

[72] "eine große Elastizität, wodurch verschiedene Einrichtungen des Jus gentium" Weber. 85.

[73] Molina dedicates to the topic of prescriptio II. 60 to II. 80. pp. 143–178.

[74] "Esse acquisitionem dominii per continuationem temporis lege definiti. [...] Cum enim, quod unus ea via et ratione dominium amittat, et alter illud acquirat, humano iure in commune bonum, ne videlicet rerum dominia sint incerta, et ut litibus obvietur, sancitum sit." II. 60. 7. p. 143.

[75] Juridical prescription appears as an institution oriented towards the common good. "Poterit tamen quatenus administrator Reipublicaest, et quatenus ad commune bonum omnes illi subiiciuntur, condere leges, quas ad idem bonum commune viderit expedire, quibus dominia amittatur, et transferatur ad alios, ut legem praescriptionis, et alias similes: idque non solum in poenam culpae, sed etiam in solum commune bonum, nulla interveniente culpa." II. 25. 1. p. 68. Note also the explanation of prescription that Molina gives in the previous footnote.

[76] "La prescrizione d'altra parte "prova solo, che le leggi civili possono per giusti motivi cambiare o rasferire iura dominandi, e fatto questo, si può dire che per un motivo estrinseco è cambiato il diritto naturale, perché cambiata la materia, cessa il

Legal security is not the only reason to override property rights. The case of necessity is also one in which property rights, based on a human law, yield to the access of all men to the use of the goods of creation, based in *ius naturale*. At the end of his disputation on the division of goods, Molina discusses the issue of extreme need. Under cases of extreme need, the use of goods becomes common, under the penalty of mortal sin.[77] This is in complete agreement with the deepest theological foundation Molina cites regarding property, his notion of participation.

As we noted in the beginning, human beings are capable of owning property because they participate in God's image. It is because of the human faculties and human free will—a way of participation in God's intelligence and will—that we are able also to participate in his Lordship over things. In Molina there is a theological link between being human and being *dominus*.[78] This is stronger than any human regulation and, therefore, in cases of necessity—in cases of conflict between the human law on division of things and the nature of humanity—the basic requirement of human nature prevails.

2.5. *Conclusions on Private Property*

The papal social encyclicals *Rerum Novarum* (1891) and *Quadragesimo Anno* (1931) affirm that private property is a matter of *ius naturale*.[79] It is worthwhile to conduct a brief review of the evolution of the doctrine in the Catholic Church in order to understand what was being said at different times.

We have seen that the common destination of goods before the Fall was the common assumption of the Church Fathers and the scholastics. This was commonly stated with the phrase that common property existed according to *ius naturale*. The problem for scholastic theology was not to justify that the poor had a right to the goods of Creation. Rather, it was that for scholastic theology we now seemed to live in a world with

primo diritto, ed obbliga un altro (diritto)." Gianpiero Mancioni, "Il "Dominium Altum" nella dottrina di Soto, Molina, Suarez: studio per un ridimensionamento della dottrina scolastica sulla proprietà privata." (Pontificia Università Gregoriana, 1966). 51.

[77] "Bona nihilominus temporalia comuna esse debent omnibus quopad usum, tempore quidem extremae aut paene extremae necessitatis, sub reatu lethalis culpae." II. 20. 14. p. 158. In other cases the failure to share the goods of creation is a venial sin: "Aliis vero temporibus, quando id prudentia ac recta ratio postulat de consilio, aut sub reatu venialis, iuxta ea, quae dum de eleemosina esset sermo dicta sunt." Ibid.

[78] II. 18. 4. 51.

[79] RN 11and 22, and QA 49.

institutions that were contrary the original will of God. The way the question was framed was different from today, and therefore the solutions were different. In the contemporary discussion, we might discover that the very frame of the discussion begs the question.

For Aquinas the division of goods is a matter of human agreement because *de iure naturale* property is common. This division is an addition devised by human reason. The reasons supporting this device are very similar to, but shorter, than those set out by Molina. For the Angelical Doctor "man ought to possess external things, not as his own, but as common, so that, to wit, he is ready to communicate them to others in their need."[80]

Scotus solved the problem by saying that natural law had changed after the Fall, and therefore what was not originally of natural law became of natural law. Molina, who held that natural law was immutable, solved the problem through his original treatment of *ius naturale*, *lex naturalis*, and the circumstances and the obligations arising from them.

It was Lugo who contributed to the success of the idea that private property was of natural law. He held that position, because he did not understand the complexity of Molina's natural law theory. While praising Molina, who clearly said that private property was not of natural law, Lugo concluded that private property was of natural law, because, according to Kleinhappl, Lugo thought that if an obligation to do something arose out of natural law that institution must also be from natural law.[81] Lugo's development was passed on to Alphonsus Liguori who collapsed the difference between *ius naturale* and *ius gentium*. Weber traces the evolution of the doctrine from Lugo to Liguori, then to Luigi Tapparelli d'Azeglio S.J. (1793–1862), and then to the Magisterium. Ironically Tapparelli, a polemicist against liberalism, made room for the Lockean concept of private property in Catholic doctrine.[82] Sometimes in intellectual controversies one assumes and then retains some of his opponent's fundamental ideas.

Molina's notion of private property is very different from that of Locke, whose view is now the prevailing perspective on property. For Locke, property is a natural right and is based on a primeval state, where none

---

[80] II^{a}—II ae q. 66, a. 2.

[81] It is interesting to see that for Kleinhappl, writing in a capitalistic society, Lugo's development is a misconception of Molina's doctrine. For Skarvad, a Pole in the time of communism, Lugo's development is the culmination of a long development.

[82] RN 5 follows the Lockean idea that labor is the justification of property.

had the right to anything and moreover people could simply use whatever things were found in nature. In this negative community, this right to take possession of whatever was available, caused many evils, leading to the institution of private property, whose basis, for Locke, is labor.[83] That was neither the conception found in Molina nor the traditional scholastic view. For Molina the goods were communally owned, and although the *diviso rerum* was in harmony with the situation after the Fall and desirable within Molina's perspective, this original destination and the defense of the weakest still obliged private property.

Some Catholic theologians seem to forget the integrity of the natural law tradition; while they claim that property rights are a matter of natural law, they forget all the limitations, that even those in the tradition who express this view place on private property.

Michael Novak in his book *The Catholic Ethic and the Spirit of Capitalism* affirms that "since ancient times—in Aristotle, in Cicero, in St. Augustine, and consistently in the Catholic tradition—this universal destination as a final end has led to the selection of private property as its necessary means."[84] That private property has been defended in the Catholic tradition is undeniable, but Novak commits a pivotal mistake: in the Catholic tradition private property was never thought of as a necessary means. It was a means that was relative to its end. It is hard to find Catholic writers who advocate for the suppression of private property, but most theologians believed that in the beginning everything was in common and defended the notion that there were cases in which it should still be so.

In modern thought it is the future that acts as a model to follow or pursue. Utopias serve as horizons towards which we move. Such horizons are never reached, merely approached asymptotically. This Enlightenment model of progress was preceded by a model which saw the past as the normative paradigm. Before the eighteenth century the model lay in the past. For the problem of property, it was clear to the entire tradition of the Church that the desirable model was that of common property and that this might not be possible after the Fall. The primeval situation nevertheless still exerted a moral claim over the present. It reflected God's will and the inherent nature of things. Theologians subordinated the division of

---

[83] Frederick Copleston S.J., *A History of Philosophy*, vol. V. Modern Philosophy: The British Philosophers (Garden City, NY: Image Books, 1964). 139.

[84] Michael Novak, *The Catholic Ethic and the Spirit of Capitalism* (Toronto: Free Press, 1993). 149.

goods to the common destination of those goods. Novak fails to see this because he has a positivistic view of natural law. He also overlooks the fact that private property throughout history has taken different shapes. He might want to defend the modern American idea of property, however it is hard to reconcile it with the ideal example of the Catholic idea of private property.[85]

To some extent there has been a reversal in the line of thought. Today we take for granted that there is private property justified by labor. Then we ask ourselves whether or not distribution of goods should be affected by the plight of those in need. But in scholastic thought, and in the Fathers of the Church, an inverse question was posed. For them, it was clear that in the beginning everything was in common. The question then was, is private property lawful? If so, under what circumstances? There has been a narrowing in the tradition, one that is not especially attributable to the Magisterium, but rather to the entire theological quest and its desire to conform to normal science. The normal scientific standards of our time demand a one-to-one correspondence of concepts, but this one-to-one correspondence does not exist in scholastic science where ideas can have analogous meanings, and be used in a metaphorical sense.

Being a matter of *ius gentium* and the result of the consent of all people, the way in which private property is regulated does not depend on natural law, but on human law. The main influence of natural law on it would be the safeguard of the original common destination of the goods. Molina's stance, reflecting scholasticism, is much less rigid than others. Those following the Lockean tradition (which is supposedly anti-metaphysical), defend private property as a natural right, although even in this Locke was moderate and nuanced.[86] Those in the communist tradition (whether

[85] Even Chafuen, whose book seems more a defense of classical liberal economics that an enquiry in the way of thinking of the Scholastic Doctors, is forced to concede that according to the scholastics "God created visible goods so that humans can live by their use; the division of goods can never abolish this first destiny of material goods. Rights to life and liberty are, in a sense, superior to property rights. These rights evolved to preserve life and liberty. In extreme cases when these rights seem to be in contradiction, life and liberty should prevail." It is striking though how an economist and a historian can fail to see the importance of the particular circumstances and the real situation of the poor in the Scholastic analysis. Chafuen seems only preocupied with matters of principle and misses the importance of the particular in the theologians of the sixteenth-century. Alejandro Antonio Chafuen, *Faith and Liberty: The Economic Thought of the Late*. 45.

[86] Locke "raises the objection that if gathering the fruits of the earth confers a right to them, anyone may amass as much as he likes", and he answers, "Not so. The same law of nature that doth by this mean give us property does also bound that property too." The

Marxist or not) deny any rightful type of private property.[87] For Molina the question is not whether private property should exist, but what type of private property.

It is important to note that *dominium*, whether it is property or political jurisdiction, is a postlapsarian phenomenon. We cannot have extreme confidence and optimism about either one. Strangely, the liberal creed has inherited this suspicion regarding political power, but has not done so with the suspicion of private property.

In the beginning there was no private property, for all things belonged to all. The idea of Molina is that after the Fall humankind negotiated the institution of private property in order to preserve this common destination of goods, because community of property in a world of sin would frustrate the common destination. Human will can create this second nature, but it does so in order to preserve the intentionality of the first. The object of property, people's use, has not changed; rather circumstances have, so as to recommend a change in the law. Justice is being worked out here as a second nature, according to the Thomistic view, as a virtue.

There is no possible discussion about justice if there is not a previous discussion about how we conceive property. Where does the right to property arise from, what are the consequences of how property rights and the way of dealing with them are conceived?[88] The problem of

---

fruits of the earth are given for use and enjoyment; and "as much as anyone can make use of to any advantage for life before it spoils, so much he may by his labour fix a property in: whatever is beyond this is more than his share and belongs to others." Copleston S.J. 140.

[87] The Spanish scholastics were also very reluctant to embrace communism. We have seen Molina's opinion about a return to a system of common property. See also the opinion of Vitoria, for whom "communism requires many things which society [after the Fall of man] does not have; (it) requires modesty in life, union of heart, obedience of will and just distribution. Society is in lack of all these things, and communism can not subsist without all these. How shall it be possible in the world when it is so troublesome in the convents?" From his commentary In II^{a}–IIae q. 62, a. 2, n. 3. Quoted in Gómez Camacho, "Later Scholastic: Spanish Economic Thought,". 519.

[88] Think of a case: A mining company operates a mine in one country. The company operates the mine because it has obtained mining right from the government. The mining company pays the government, but the money benefits just a small ruling oligarchy. The mining rights belong to the people of that country, but these people are not receiving the benefits of letting the company enjoy those rights. Can the mining company be held responsible for not paying the legitimate owner of the mine? Or is the fact that the mining contract was done according to some formal legality enough to exonerate the company from further responsibility?

property goes hand in hand with the problem of justice.[89] For Molina only those capable of *dominium* are capable of *iniuria*.[90] From Molina's theory on private property we learn not only a way of thinking about that property that does not consecrate private property, but also much about the relationship between private property and justice. We cannot speak about justice if we do not analyze the origin and justification of property.

For Molina it is clear that any type of *dominium* exists under a constant mortgage owed to morality. If only rational beings are capable of *dominium*, only rational beings are capable of morality. They are not two phenomena that randomly coincide, they are actually, related and stand on the same basis. Private property finds its ground in the postlapsarian world, precisely because of it; private property is subject to the changes of the postlapsarian world. It can never be presented as an absolute right, but as a harmonious realization with circumstances of the original common destination of goods which would be the absolute right. This has not been damaged by sin; what was damaged by sin is the particular realization of this end. As Gómez Camacho has put it: private property is for man and not man for private property.[91]

3. The Common Good of the *Respublica*: Politics and Economics

According to Harro Höpfl "it was beyond contention for Jesuits that the end and justification of government, law and policy was the common good (or the common *felicitas*, *beatitudo*, *utilitas*, all impeccably

[89] "Explicatio integre dominio in genere, de illius, et de iuris subjecto est dicendum. Pars, quae affirmat, ex iis quae disp. I dicta sunt, satis perspicua est. Quae namque arbitrio praedita non sunt, ut iniuriae non sunt capacia, ita neque jutis, atque adeo nec dominii." II. 18. 1. p. 51.

[90] According to Tierney a similar connection had initially been established by Jean Gerson in the works he wrote for the reform of the Church. "In pursuing the aims of a whole generation of church reformers, he formulated a theory of individual subjective rights that included a natural right of each person to fulfil God's law, a natural right to liberty, a natural right to self defense, a natural right to the necessities of life. Moreover these doctrines were not forgotten. Transmitted by writers like Almain and de Soto and Vitoria and Suarez they entered the mainstream of early modern thought on natural rights and so influenced the whole subsequent development of Western political theory." Tierney. 233. Although not mentioned Molina is also a link in this chain.

[91] "Es el hombre quien decide, pues, diciéndolo en una frase clara y concisa, no es el hombre para la división de los bienes, sino la división de los bienes para el servicio del hombre." Gómez Camacho, "En torno a unos textos de Luis de Molina sobre la propiedad privada." 167.

Aristotelian and Thomist synonyms)."[92] Private property and political authority are topics with which Molina deals in parallel, because political power and private property are two related topics for the scholastics.[93] He acknowledges that political authority is of a greater rank than property, therefore the explanation of it can help us better understand the idea of property.[94]

For Molina, in line with the Thomistic tradition, man is a social animal. Because man has more needs that he himself cannot meet, man is more inclined by nature to live in a society than other animals.[95] This does not mean, however, that society as an institution belongs to natural law. Political bodies are not of *ius naturale*, even if man is inclined by nature to live with other men. While setting out how this social inclination takes place, Molina affirms that the *respublica* is ordained to preserve peace, security and justice among men.[96] This is the best definition of how he conceives the common good that we might find, given that he does not discuss the topic in any disputation.

The *respublica* has its end and justification in the common good, to the point that the common good becomes the measure against which to decide whether a law that assigns a burden to some part of the polity should be accepted or not. Only if this burdensome law is strictly necessary for the common good should it be accepted; otherwise the

---

[92] Harro Höpfl, *Jesuit Political Thought. The Society of Jesus and the State, C. 1540–1630* (Cambridge, UK: Cambridge University Press, 2004). 283. He also says that this concept was never clarified, because it "was not a standard question of the Thomist corpus."

[93] "Molina setzt die Frage nach der Entstehung des Privateigentums in Parallelitatjzu der Frage nach der Einrichtung der politischen Gewalt. Er hat dieses Parallelverhältnis sehr scharf erfaßt. Sobald das Menschengeschlecht durch die Sünde den Stand der Unschuld verloren hatte, ergab sich die Notwendigkeit einer politischen Gewalt, die Frieden und Ruhe unter den Menschen wahren sollte. Die Ausbreitung der Menschen über die ganze Welt brachte es mit sich, daß diese Gewalt geteilt und daß für die einzelnen Städte, Provinzen und Völker jeweils ein besonderer Gewaltträger bestimmt wurde. Ähnlich verhält es sich mit der Entstehung des Privateigentums." Weber. 72.

[94] "Explicato dominio in genere, ut ad partes illi subiectas descendamus, ordiendum nobis est dominium iurisdictionis. Tum quia nobilius est. Tum quia notitia illius conducit, ut tituli dominii proprietatis melius intelligatur." II. 21. 1. p. 58.

[95] "Ut homo, propter rationes, quas subiiciemus, societate plus indiget cum aliis hominibus, quam reliqua animantia cum animalibus suae speciei: sic etiam natura, quae in necessaries non deest maiorem, tum aptitudinem, tum propensionem ad societatem illi, quam caeteris animantibus, contulit." II. 23.23.p. 61. Locke's stance about society is strikingly similar. To see the scholastic influence on Locke through Grotius, see Tierney. 317–342.

[96] "Indiget homo vita non solum in communitate plurium familiarum, sed etiam integrae perfectaeque Reipublicae ut pax, securitas et iustitia inter homines conservetur." II. 22. 9. p. 63.

ruler commits an injustice if he forces a subject to obey that law. The power of the ruler cannot be greater that the commonwealth that created the ruler. Although for Molina, once a king is created the commonwealth looses its power in favor of the king and cannot withdraw the power it has given. By the same token, the king cannot increase the powers that the commonwealth granted him. His power cannot contravene the terms of under which he received power.[97] The *respublica* is for the common good, and this, in Molina's thought, is a not a source of absolutist rule, but rather a limit to the power of the ruler.[98]

A similar argument could be made for private property, although Molina did not undertake this project.[99] In Molina, political power has an origin that resembles private property. If for him private property is the result of human consent, so is political power. It comes from God, but not directly, rather through the commonwealth that elects and consents to have a ruler with certain powers. Talking about political power, which is for Molina more important and advances our understanding of private property,[100] he avers that political power is of natural law, but not in an immediate way but through human society. The power of a ruler is of natural law, but not coming immediately from God, but from the men that gather and confer it to him. And he has no more power than that which has been given to him by them. According to Molina this

[97] "Et quemadmodum Respublica variare non potest, auferendo aut minuendo potestatem, quam in principio concessit, tametsi possit illam ampliare, et concedere maiorem: ita princeps, renuente Republica, ampliare sibi non potest potestatem, neque quicquam forum transgredi, qua a principio fuerint constituta." II. 23. p. 65.

[98] "By this Molina means that the power conferred upon rulers by the commonwealth is in nature of a *communicatio* or a *concessio*. The commonwealth does not thereby divest itself of all authority. Of course, the power once granted cannot be withdrawn without weighty reasons. What the commonwealth grants is the immediate use of power; the natural power of the commonwealth is inactive while governmental power lasts. When governmental power is abolished, the commonwealth recovers the use of its natural power. But this natural power must be institutionalized anew since it cannot be exercised in the natural state. The power of the commonwealth remains inalienable; the people cannot surrender or abdicate this power because it is natural. In establishing a government the people merely relinquish the use of their natural power. Should the government be abolished, the power returns to the commonwealth—the people as a whole." Costello. 57.

[99] "che per lo stesso motivo per cui venne fatta la divisione delle cose, e cioè per diminuire i mali e salvaguardare la pace del popolo, è necessario che esista una concretizzazione del potere per regolare le cose fra i cittadini e ordinare tutto al bene comune." Manccioni 27. Manccioni does it in the reverse way.

[100] "ordiendum nobis est a dominio iurisdictionis. Tum quia nobilius est. Tum quia notitia illius conducit, ut tituli dominii proprietatis melius intelligatur." II. 21. 1. 58.

illuminates the way we conceive private property.[101] Private property is the result of a human law, the result of the consent of all or almost all men. Any particular and historical realization of private property cannot contravene the original consent which was given to preserve peace and guarantee the access of all to the goods of creation, and the protection of the weakest. If this does not happen there might be a cause for disobedience because there is an injustice being committed. According to Manccioni private property has a '*quasi servitutem*' towards the common good.[102] The scholastics, as Tierney points out, "emphasized both individual rights and the common good as complementary rather than conflicting aspects of the human condition."[103]

Property created by human law is also subject to the common good. There are different examples of this. One is the plight of the poor. In the case of extreme necessity, all becomes common. This case has already been discussed. There are other cases in which the commonwealth could and should regulate the exchange, the use of property on behalf of justice and the common good. This leads us to our fourth chapter in which we will see three instances regarding how justice works according to Molina in an economic context.

---

[101] "potestatem hanc non oriri ex eo, quod homines se illi volunt subicere, eamque pro suo arbitratu in seipsos ad commune ipsorum bonum eligunt, quasi perinde oriatur, ac si congregati aliqui ad quodvis aliuud, eligeret sibi communem aliquam otestatem, haec namque posterior potestas ortum non haberet a Deo immediate per ius naturale, sed a hominibus ipsis libere se illi subicientibus neque esset potestat maior, quam homines pro suo arbitrio illi tribuisset." II. 22. 9. p. 63.

[102] "giacché i beni privati hanno nei riguardi del bene comune una "quasi servitutem" " Maccioni 54.

[103] Tierney. 334.

CHAPTER FOUR

THREE SPECIFIC TOPICS: USURY, PRICES AND MONEY EXCHANGE

1. Introduction

Both historians of economic thought and moral theology display a predilection for focusing on the problem of usury when they study the economics of the Middle Ages and early Modern Age;[1] bibliographical research reveals what is nearly a fixation on this topic. One might erroneously be led to believe that the return of a sum above the principal of a loan—for this is what most historians take as the scholastic definition of usury—was the major problem in the business and economic practices of the time. The scholastics, nevertheless, dealt with many other economic topics. The table of contents of Molina's *De Iustitia et Iure* reveals that he also dealt with such matters as types of companies, leasing, renting, insurance, mortgage and just wage. In this he was not different from other scholastic theologians.

Usury was a much debated topic of scholastic theology, because it was a point of friction between moral theology and approved business practices. For many centuries the teaching office of the Church was emphatic in condemning usury. Theologians had to deal with this fact, but they also needed to offer practical advice to those merchants who wanted to be good Christians. In other topics addressed in the scholastics' treatises there was less divergence between the opinions of the scholastic doctors and the opinions of the honest businessmen. The divergence is what makes the study of usury interesting because it shows how moral theology and economic doctrine developed. The same can be said about two other topics that have received less attention, although they were also much-debated issues: prices and money exchange. Economics was

[1] See: John Thomas Noonan, *The Scholastic Analysis of Usury* (Cambridge: Harvard University Press, 1957). Pribram. 17–20. Jonsen and Toulmin. 181 and ff. Schumpeter and Schumpeter 74–115. An exception seems to be Vereecke. In his book the Belgian historian of moral theology deals with economic problems other than the ones the scholastic theologians approached.

in the sixteenth century part of moral theology: it did not exist as an independent discipline. In this unity we can find patterns in the relationship between moral theology and economics that can be illuminating.

This chapter will deal with three specific topics addressed by Luis de Molina in *De Iustita et Iure*: usury, just price and money exchange. I have chosen these three topics partly because, as stated above, usury, just price and money exchange illustrate the development of moral and economic doctrine. In this development Molina's contribution was important. A second reason for choosing these three topics is that they involve both the individual conduct of merchants and certain structural elements of the economic system. My goal is to make my research a fruitful historical investigation that will shed light on the sometimes contentious contemporary dialogue between economics and ethics.

2. Usury

Molina dealt with usury in disputations 303 to 335 of the second treatise, the one dedicated to commutative justice, of *De Iustitia et Iure*. Strikingly, he managed to uphold the traditional prohibition of usury while allowing for different ways of money lending, in which the return exceeded the principal. Molina was the first theologian to acknowledge an honest livelihood based on lending.[2] Molina knew the tradition well. He was aware that the Church had been condemning lending for profit for over seven hundred years. I will demostrate Molina's command of the tradition in the course of presenting his discussion on usury. John T. Noonan's book *The Scholastic Analysis of Usury* provides us with a detailed account of how the discussion on usury appeared and evolved. The book allows us to trace how Molina used the sources and how he read the tradition. One easy interpretation of what he did would claim that he merely accommodated to the practices of the time. Molina's work, however, was not mere accommodation; it was a sincere effort to find the right thing to do in light of the nature of the case that he was addressing. I will draw on the teaching on natural law that I set out in the second chapter to illuminate Molina's position and his contribution to the development of the tradition.

[2] Noonan. 309.

2.1. *The Classical Definition and its Unlawfulness*

Disputation 303 defined usury; it was profit from a loan, an intended or accepted return above the principal, motivated by the loan itself. This was the object of usury. The word, however, also referred to the act and the habit that the repetition of an act created; therefore, usury also referred to a sin and a vice.[3] In giving this definition, Molina was not going beyond the first definition of usury that we find in the Nynweger capitulary of 806, according to which usury occurs in a loan "where more is asked than given."[4] Molina's definition only added intention, though that was not his creation but part of the evolution of the doctrine in those seven hundred years. For scholastic theology, the mere intention of a sinful act was itself a sin. The early canonical treatment of usury had added the criterion of intention, and this element had become part of the standard definition of usury from the early canonical discussions.

Having defined usury, Molina proceeded to discuss its unlawfulness. The case against usury had been slowly built up since the early Middle Ages. John Noonan found the origin of the scholastic doctrine of usury in the economic conditions of ninth-century Europe, which were similar to the ones that prompted the Mosaic Law's prohibition of usury. According to Noonan, "the facts that the economy was almost completely agrarian and that borrowing was nearly always for consumption" can help to explain the zeal with which usury legislation appeared "as a last effort to save small free farmers from absorption by the landholders who were the usual lenders."[5]

The prohibition of usury had been first developed in canonical texts. In 1006 Anselm of Lucca treated usury as a sin against the seventh commandment. This classification is important because it called for restitution as it did with stolen goods. In Gratian's *Concordia discordantium canonum* (1159) usury was treated as a special topic, evidence suggestive of the growing importance of commerce. In this important collection of canons, usury was condemned and restitution demanded.[6] The warp of Molina's discussion of usury was shaped by this early canonical

---

[3] "lucrum ex mutuo, hoc est, incrementum, quod vi mutui intenditur, aut accipitur, supra id, quod mutuo est datum ... Quia vero nomen objecti interdum trahitur, et extenditur, ad significandum actum habitu ... ut nomen, usura, sumptum etiam sit ad significandum actum et peccatum." II. 303. 2. p. 134.

[4] Noonan, 15.

[5] Ibid. 13.

[6] Ibid. 17–18.

discussion. Usury appeared as a separate and relevant sin, calling in all cases for restitution. As he discussed various cases, Molina always ended up each case in which he found usury with the concluding tag line "and it is bound to restitution."

Usury was, in fact, a special kind of sin. St. Antoninus of Florence had pointed out that, unlike other sins, where the sinner did not linger in them—the adulterer was not always in the act of adultery or the murderer always in the act of murdering—the usurer lingered in the act of usury as long as he did not restore his illicit gain.[7] The canonical treatment of usury, however, was not what caught Molina's attention, because it was a positivistic argument, not solid moral reasoning.

Usury had become an important topic because the magisterial teaching of the Church had declared it a sin; but as long as the discussion about usury had remained primarily in the canonist's purview, the theological reasons against usury remained feeble. Innocent IV, Pope and renowned canonist, writing just a generation before Aquinas, thought usury bad not in itself but because of the evil consequences derived from it.[8] This had prompted theologians to enter the discussion and stimulated the development of biblical and natural law arguments against usury. Molina began disputation 304 addressing the natural law arguments against usury. He then turned to the other types of law. For the sake of the exposition and to match the historical development, I shall follow the inverse order. I will first set out the canonical, biblical and civil law arguments against usury that Molina offered; the natural law argumentation will follow.

2.1.1. *Divine and Human Law*

The Third Council of the Lateran (1179), presided over by Pope Alexander III, had declared usury condemned by both Testaments, excommunicated usurers and denied them Christian burial.[9] Molina cited this piece of legislation and offered four quotations from the Old Testament endorsing the prohibition of usury.[10] The quotes he gave were standard ones,

---

[7] Ibid. 78.

[8] Ibid. 49.

[9] Ibid. 19.

[10] Ezekiel 18: 8. Psalm 14: 5. Psalm 54, 12. Here there is actually a misprint because it says Psalm 45, but the quote is from Psalm 54. Psalm 71, 14. Here there is also a misprint because the text says Psalm 7, but the quote is from Psalm 71. These were standard quotations. Besides Jesus' words in the New Testament they found biblical prohibitions

and he did not grant them much importance; in fact at the beginning of the disputation, he had actually offered two Old Testament quotations that could be used to approve usury.[11] He even offered the parable of the talents as a New Testament quotation in favor of usury.[12]

The only biblical passage that Molina discussed at length was Lk. 6: 35. In 1187 Urban III, in an effort to support and confirm the measures of the Third Council of the Lateran, issued the decretal *Consuluit*, where the pope quoted the words of Christ "Lend freely, hoping nothing thereby." In these words, the pope saw an authoritative command of the Lord. Until Domingo de Soto, that is, for almost four hundred years, this interpretation was not challenged. But then Soto held that Christ's words were not a command, but a counsel.[13] Adhering to Soto's opinion, Molina argued that the pope did not intend to mandate that the literal interpretation of the New Testament passage was the only possible one. Molina offered a second reason to support the view that Christ's words were not a command but a counsel; the words do not appear in any other place in the New Testament. The passage had no parallel. We can see that for Molina the biblical argument against usury carried little weight. He certainly thought that it was more pleasing to God to lend without hope of repayment, but Molina did not see in Christ's words a divine command, but a piece of advice to achieve a greater level of perfection.[14]

Having dealt with divine law, Molina turned to human law. He knew that "according to the sacred canons, usury was illicit, and forbidden under grave penalties."[15] He offered as a proof of this the prohibitions of the Council of Nicea and the Council of Lyons. The most up-to-date piece of legislation he furnished was in *Clementina unica de usura*, from which he offered a long quotation. Molina was citing a piece of canonical legislation found in the *Constitutiones Clementinae*, a collection of

---

of usury in Psalm 14:5; Exodus 22: 25; Leviticus 25: 35–37; Deuteronomy 15: 7–10; Amos 8: 4–6; Ezekiel 18:8. The biblical commands, however, were not conclusive.

[11] Deuteronomy 23: 20–21. Deuteronomy 28: 12.

[12] Luke 19: 11–27.

[13] Noonan. 19–20. In chapter II, we saw the importance of evangelical counsels in moral reasoning.

[14] "Cum tamen non appareat locus alius novi testamenti, in quo ita aperte usura damnetur. In contrarium vero obiicitur, quod eo in loco Christus tradere videatur consilium ut mutuum fiat absque intuitu similis retributionis, ut ea rationis magis sit gratum, et meritorium, apud Deum, ut ex ipsamet serie contextus videtur manifestum." II. 304. 14. p. 139.

[15] "Iam vero usuram iure humano, id est, sacris canonibus, esse illicitam, atque sub gravibus poenis prohibitam." II. 304. 15. p. 139.

decretals promulgated by John XXII in 1317. Most of the decretals were drawn from the Constitutions of Clement V at the Council of Vienne (1314). The decretal in question resolved that whoever denied that usury was a sin should be punished as a heretic. Instructions were given to the ordinaries of the place, as well as to the Inquisition, to act accordingly in proceeding against such people.[16] Molina resolved the canonical aspect of usury in a succinct way, but he did it with forceful arguments against it.

The canonical injunctions against usury had certainly not eradicated the problem. The regularity of magisterial declarations against usury is a sign of how widespread the practice was. People needed to borrow money, and those willing to lend it wanted to get a return on it. Throughout the Middle Ages public money lenders charged a rate that was never lower than 35 % per year.[17] Civil authorities had to deal with the problem. Roman law allowed a return above the principal in loans with rates that varied from 6 % to 12 % per year. The laws of Castile and Portugal also permitted some practices that were considered usurious, something that for dialectical purposes Molina acknowledged at the beginning of the disputation as a reason in favor of the rightness of usury. Molina knew that one was not obliged to follow unjust laws. He also considered that canon law was above civil law in those matters that pertained to the spiritual well-being of Christian people. He nevertheless conceded that, as happened with prostitution or the toleration of heretics, public authorities could tolerate usury to avoid greater evils.[18]

Molina furnished all these reasons against usury after he had discussed the natural law case against it. As I have shown, he did not find them conclusive. They were actually proofs supplied after the case had been decided. Now I shall turn to Molina's natural law argumentation against usury, because the way he set the case was what allowed him to later admit payments above the principal without breaking from the tradition.

---

[16] "Novissime autem in Clementina unica de usura sic definitum est: Si quis in illum inciderit, ut pertinaciter affirmare praesumat, excercere usuras non esse peccatum, decernimus eum veluti haereticum puniendum. Locorum nihilominus ordinariis, et haereticae parvitatis inquisitoribus, districtius iniugentes, ut contra eos, quos de errore hiuius modi diffamatos invenerint, aut suspectos, tamquam contra diffamatos, vel suspectos, de haeresi, procedere non omitant." II. 304. 15. p. 139.

[17] Noonan. 294.

[18] "Et sicut inter nos permittitur meretricium, quod cum iure naturae pugnat, ad maiora mala vitanda." II. 304. 18. p. 140.

2.1.2. *Natural Law Case against Usury*

What really encouraged theologians to argue against usury was the teaching of the Church authorities against it, and the resulting canons prohibiting it.[19] Because the biblical injunctions were not conclusive, and the canonical prohibitions were not a reason in themselves for the moral wrongness of usury, a convincing argument had to be grounded on natural law.

Molina accepted that usury was wrong according to natural law, but he was not satisfied with some of the arguments given for the prohibition. He set out the reasons why usury was wrong, and then proceeded to refute some of the traditional arguments against usury. In fact he refuted all the major medieval arguments against usury.

In the introduction I pointed out that Joseph A. Schumpeter had distinguished in the natural law ideas of the scholastics, and particularly in those of Molina, an analytical natural law that referred to the investigation of the nature of things, from a normative natural law, dependent on the analytical, that offered normative guidance based on the nature of things. I shall show that Molina was being faithful to the received tradition, but that, while remaining faithful to the normative natural law, his solutions changed by virtue of his explanatory natural law.

Molina presented his argumentation against usury in the form of a syllogism: It was illicit by reason of the nature of the case and against commutative justice to demand or to accept in an exchange more than the value of the good that was given, unless there was some reason that justified receiving more than what was given. To receive something above the capital on behalf of the exchange that occurred in a loan was to receive more than the value of the thing, unless there was another reason to justly receiving more. Therefore by virtue only of the loan, it was wrong, because of the nature of the contract, to receive anything above the capital, and against commutative justice. Hence usury was illicit, against commutative justice and liable to restitution.[20]

---

[19] Noonan, 14.

[20] "Ex natura rei est illicitum, et contra iustitiam commutativam, in rei unius commutatione pro alia plus exigere, aut accipere, quam valeat res quae datur, nisi aliquid aliud interveniat, ratione cuius illud amplius juste accipiatur: sed accipere aliquid ultra sortem pro mutuo, est pro commutationte rei mutuo datae, accipere plus quam valeat, nisi interveniat aliud ratione cuius illud iuste accipiatur: ergo, vi solius mutui, nefas ex natura rei, et contra iustitiam commutativam est, aliquild ultra sortem accipere, ac proinde usura illicita est contra commutativam iustitiam, restitutione obnoxia." II, 304, 4, p. 136.

In this syllogism, a matter of principle and a matter of fact made usury wrong. The matter of principle was the failure to respect the equality of exchange. But to judge when this had happened, one had to turn to a matter of fact, the value of the exchanged goods. It was by working in value theory that Molina managed to adapt the received theory to the new circumstances. He respected the received notion of normative natural law—there should be equality in an exchange—but was able to rework the analytical natural law. What had to be compared was the economic value of the goods exchanged, not their quantity or their fixed legal value as had been done previously.

Molina gave an example of what he was saying. To receive repayment beyond the capital was nothing other than receiving above the value of the goods lent; therefore it would be always licit to receive the entire value of the good lent, even if that would mean to receive a larger quantity of the good lent, and this would not be usury. The key to the argument is the recognition that values attributed to goods may change over time. It was not usury if one lent a number of measures of wheat when the price of wheat was high, and asked the borrower to return a higher number of measures of wheat when prices were low. Although the lender was receiving a greater quantity of the goods than he had lent, there was no usury in the contract, because the change in the price of wheat kept the equality of the value of the exchange.[21] The example given was in direct opposition to Aquinas's doctrine on usury, with the very example given in the *Summa*.[22] Molina must have been familiar with it, and therefore he immediately proceeded to refute some objections against his explanation of usury.

Saint Antoninus of Florence presented in his works, at the end of the Middle Ages, the three standard medieval arguments against usury: 1) consumption and use were one in consumable goods—and money is a consumable, 2) money had a fixed legal value and 3) money bore no

---

[21] "Accipere namque ultra sortem, non est aliud, quam accipere ultra valorem rei mutuo datae. Semper enim licitum est accipere integrum rei valorem quae mutuo datur, esto plus in quantitate sit accipiendum, neque in eo ulla intervenit usura. Ut, si tempore, quo triticum plus valet, mutuo des mensuras aliquot restituendas tempore mensis, quando vilius speratur valiturus, fas tibi est pacisci, ut tot plures mutuatarius tunc restituat, quod sufficiant, ut pretia tritici temporis utriusque aedequatur; eo quon nihil tunc accipere ultra sortem." II, 304, 4, p. 136.

[22] "Et simili ratione, iniustitiam committit qui mutuat vinum aut triticum petens sibi duas recompensationes, unam quidem restitutionem aequalis rei, aliam vero pretium usus, quod usura dicitur." IIª–IIae q. 78 a. 1 co.

fruits.[23] The first two arguments came from Aquinas, and the last had been passed on by Scotus, although it was prior to him. These three arguments were discussed by Molina at length, though without explicit mention of their authors, probably because of their great authority. The arguments were heavily dependent on a particular notion of the nature of money. I shall now present each of the arguments and explain how Molina refuted each of them.

As in many other theological topics, Thomas Aquinas held a preeminent position in the discussion of usury, because of the weight of his arguments. His main arguments against usury can be found in his later works such as the *Summa*, *De Malo*, in *III Quodlibetales* and *In Psalmos Davidis*.[24] In the *Summa* he stated that making a charge for the use of money amounted to selling something non-existent.

Aquinas distinguished two types of goods: consumable and non-consumable. Aquinas took the distinction between the consumable and non-consumable good from Roman law, but made an original interpretation of his sources.[25] Consumable goods were those goods that were consumed, that is, destroyed, in their use, like wheat or wine. Non-consumable goods were those in which use and consumption could be differentiated. A house or a horse were not destroyed by using them. It was just to charge separately for the use of a house and for the destruction of a house, because in a house—or any other non consumable good—use and destruction were two different things. It was not the same thing to use a house as to destroy it. According to Aquinas it was unjust to charge for the use and the consumption of a consumable good, because it meant charging twice for the same thing or selling something non-existent. Using grain and consuming grain were, according to this way of reasoning, the same thing. Money was, according to Aquinas, a consumable good, therefore charging for a loan was unjust in itself, for one party sold the other something non-existent, namely the use of money that could not be separated from its consumption; this obviously set up an inequality contrary to justice.[26]

Aquinas' case rested in a merely formal consideration of money. Money's value was derived from the legal value given by the legislator. Aquinas did not take into consideration the variable purchasing power of money

[23] Noonan. 81.
[24] *De Malo* q. 13, a. 4; *III Quodlibetales* q. 3. a. 19; *In Psalmos Davidis* 14; 5.
[25] Noonan. 54.
[26] Ia–IIae q. 78 a. 1 co.

nor the consideration of money as capital, as a productive good. He knew that the same amount of money could buy different quantities of goods according to variation in the prices, but these changes were, in his view, accidental and therefore not relevant for his moral analysis. Additionally, because Aquinas took into consideration only the fixed legal value of money, and not money as capital, any intentional act by a person holding money to produce an alteration in the value of the money would make him guilty of seeking to alter a legal measure. Alterations in the value of money could and would happen, as Aquinas well knew; but if such alterations happened through the intention of the holder of money, it was a case of usury. Although he used Aristotle, Aquinas departed from Aristotle's arguments on the nature of money and gave more importance to its legal aspect.[27] Aquinas had relied upon Aristotle selectively. Molina would do the same thing with Thomas' reasoning.

Aquinas' main objection against usury involved the impossibility to separate use and consumption in money. Molina denied that impossibility; for him it was clear that in lending something, the goods could be received in two different ways. The goods could be used for trade and profit, by selling, exchanging, transforming or taking them to another place. A second type of use of the goods would be to merely consume the goods. Among the different ways of consuming the goods he included the purchase of necessary things, but also spending on superfluous things, or with prostitutes or making donations.[28] Molina denied Aquinas' assertion that it was impossible to separate use and consumption in a consumable good. Money, at least, was not similar to wheat or wine, as Aquinas affirmed. Molina knew that money from a loan could be used for consumption, but he also knew that money was a productive good whose value varied, and this meant that money's value was not necessarily its fixed legal value. I will develop his ideas on this when I explain the titles of interest.

---

[27] Noonan. 52–53.

[28] "observandum est: Duplicem usum rei, quae mutuo datur, posse distingui. Unus est ad negotiationem et lucrum, illam lucri causa vendendo, permutando, vel transferencdo in alium locum, vel reservando in tempus, in quo plus valeat, aut, si sit pecunia, illa eodem fine emendo, transferendo in alium locum, aut in cambium dando. Alter usus est, qui non est negotiatio, sed consumptio nuda rei mutuo acceptae. Ut, si sit pecunia, ea emendo necessaria, aut etiam curiosa, et superflua, vendo debitum, donando illam, aut vane cum meretricibus, et in aliis similibus rebus eam insumendo. Si vero sit triticum, vinum aut oleum, ea in quotidiano usu insumendo, aut quovis alio modo." II, 304, 6, p. 137.

The Thomistic arguments had been attacked by Scotus, as the Franciscan had done in other matters. Scotus attacked the Thomistic argument against usury by saying that use and ownership, and therefore use and consumption, could be separated in consumables. He did so referring to the bull *Exiit, qui seminat* that Nicholas II had issued to try to mediate the quarrel between Spiritual and Conventual Franciscans on issues regarding Franciscan poverty. Scotus still marshalled natural law arguments against usury. For Scotus the main argument against usury, borrowed from previous theologians, was that money did not fructify.[29] The argument went back to Aristotle and had been introduced into theological discourse by Albert the Great.

Aristotle's argument against usury was also based on his notion of money. Money, according to Aristotle, had been created through a law on behalf of the community as a measure to value things, as a means of payment and as a guarantor of future necessities.[30] If money were only these three things, it would be consistent to hold that usury was the unnatural breeding of money by money, as Aristotle had argued. Usury was a distortion of the natural purpose of money, and therefore morally wrong.[31]

Molina shared the Aristotelian claims about the origin of money. Money had been invented in view of a social need, a need which originated from the deficiency of barter. When coming to barter something, people would not always find another person who would have what they lacked, and who would be willing to exchange it for what they had. To overcome this difficulty money was invented, because no one was self-sufficient. According to Molina, "money was created by public authority, with certain value to be price and measure of all other things."[32] However,

[29] Noonan. 60–61.

[30] Aristotle's writings about money can be found in *I Politics III*, 1257a and *Nichomachean Ethics* V, 1133a and b.

[31] Noonan. 45–47.

[32] "a principius solum inter homines fuisse usum permutationis, qua vinum pro tritico, oleum pro melle, bovem pro equo, calceum pro domo, et ita de caeteris rebus, commutabant, unoquoque rem, qua non ita indigebat, pro alia, qua egebat, permutante. In ea autem permutatione res una non magis habebat rationem pretii, aut mercis, quam alia, eaque de causa contractus eiudem rationis erat ex utraque parte, neque contrahentes diverse sortiebantur nomina. Postea, vero, propter rerum iaequalitatem, ut calceorum ad domum, bovis ad equum, etc., et quia saepe multi non indigebat rebus, quibus alii abundabant, quo facilius commutationes, ad vitae sustentationem, atque ad societatem humanam, necessaria, eo quod nemo sibi sit sufficiens, sed rebus, operaque alirum indigeat, adinventa, introductaque fuit moneta, quae publica autoritate certum valorem haberet, essetque pretium ac veluti mensura caeterarum rerum." II, 336, 1, 202.

Molina's distinction regarding the use of a loaned good shows him aware that money was more than that. Money could be used to trade; this made money more than a sterile measure of value, a means of payment and a guarantee for future necessities. In the hands of a merchant, money was an instrument to create wealth. Molina realized that money could be also considered as capital; for merchants money was a tool. If it was legitimate to ask for a return when a craftsman lent his tools, because he would be unable to perform his trade during that time, it must also be legitimate to charge money for the work and the trade that a merchant was not able to undertake with the money he had lent.[33]

With this reasoning Molina dispelled the three main traditional arguments against usury, leaving the door open for what we understand today as business money-lending. Still, Molina considered that usury was a sin and a vice to be condemned, and he discussed different cases in which usury occurred and where restitution was necessary.

In disputations 305 to 313 Molina discussed various cases of usury. I will present three to show where the idea of usury stood once commercial money-lending was considered to be legitimate.

In disputations 309 to 310 Molina discussed the broad case of a loan granted, in which, beside the obligation to return the capital, the borrower was burdened with some obligation. He considered many obligations: an obligation to buy something, or to sell or to rent. He also considered the obligation of granting a public office, or an ecclesiastical benefice or a tax exemption. These examples present a case of borrowing on the part of a public power. He also referred to the obligation to till someone's fields or to mill in a particular mill. The most unusual obligation mentioned here is that of fulfilling a service through speech (*praestare munus a lingua*). Nonetheless, Joseph Höffner presents a case that might illustrate what Molina had in mind. In sixteenth-century Germany some merchants held royal monopolies. The Fugger, Höchstetters and the Welsers monopolized the use of mines. In 1523 the Imperial Attorney in Augsburg opened a lawsuit against them on account of that. They were saved, however, by Charles V, who from Burgos in Spain wrote a letter declar-

[33] "si quis item mutuo petat ab opifice instrumenta artis, idque in causa sit, u tille laborare omittat, et ut lucrum illi ex suo labore et industria cesset, sane licite poterit exigere non solum quantum valet usus instrumentorum, sed etiam insuper quantum suo labore et industria erat lucraturus: ergo pari ratione mercator qui destinatam habebat pecuniam ad negotiandum, ex eaque, tamquam ex instrumento suae industriae subjecto, sperabat certum lucrum, poterit licite exigere aestimationem lucri sibi ex eo cessantis, quod mutuo illam det petenti." II, 315, 11, p. 162.

ing that what these merchants did was not to be considered a monopoly. Those bankers not only held those monopolies, they were also the ones who had lent Charles V the money that had allowed him to be elected Holy Roman Emperor five years earlier.[34]

What becomes clear after reading these lengthy disputations is that Molina thought that certain common practices of the time that linked loans to other contracts that were not essentially related to lending were usurious. In those cases the borrower was being burdened with an obligation not naturally related to the loan, even if some of the services demanded were in themselves legitimate. It was an abuse of a dominant position in lending.

Molina discussed a second group of cases, in which the currency had been devalued between the beginning and the end of the loan. Should the loan be paid in the old currency or in the new one? Was there usury if the value of the good was repaid, even if that meant a higher amount of money? Molina would hold that the borrower should repay the equivalent of the old value, not just the face value of the loan.[35]

A third group of cases referred to civil servants. It was a common practice for civil servants to receive something for the payment of a debt of the Crown, always short of funds and late in returning loans. The titles of debt were traded as government bonds are today, but they were traded at a discount because of the delay in the payment. There were two moral issues at stake. The first issue was the priority of the payment of the debt. Civil servants could decide to pay one person before another. This would make the loan usurious because the lender was obtaining a profit, that of the priority in the repayment of the loan, without a just cause.[36] The second issue at stake was that sometimes the civil servant would receive a reward for the priority given. This amounted to bribery.

Usury was not only money paid in return for a loan; usury—for Molina and for the tradition he had received—could be any burden imposed on the borrower because of the loan, even a burden not related to the loan

---

[34] Joseph Höffner, *Wirtschaftsethik und Monopole im fünfzehnten und sechzehnten Jahrhundert*, Freiburger Staatswissenschaftliche Schriften, Heft 2 (Jena: G. Fischer, 1941). 24.

[35] "Priorem vero partem ex eo mihi persuadeo, quod in mutuis, et in aliis contractibus, ac dispositionibus, potissimum habetur ratio quantitatis valoris: appositio autem illa, ut pecuniam talis qualitatis solvatur, fieri solet, ne in villori moneta solvatur debitum, et quae multum onerat." II. 312. 10. p. 156.

[36] "ergo sicut imponere mutuatario illa lata onera, est usura, ut disputationibus citatis ostensum est, ita etiam illicitum, usuraque erit, imponere illi hoc alliud gravamen." Ibid.

itself. Usury was wrong by its very nature, but there were accidents that allowed a return above the capital in a loan. These accidents had received the name of *titulus extrinsecus*. I will consider them in the next section.

2.2. *Titles of Interest*

I explained in the first chapter how theologians sympathetic to the cause of merchants tried to find a legitimate rationale for the charging of interest. The *titulus extrinsecus* was an extrinsic reason to charge interest—a reason external to the act of lending—that justified a return beyond the principal.

2.2.1. *Forced Lending and* Mons Pietatis: *The Development of the Titles of Interest*

The late Middle Ages saw the emergence of forced borrowing on the part of the state. The first to resort to it were the Italian city states; when short of cash, the cities would forcefully borrow money from rich citizens, who belonged to the same social class as the magistrates who decreed the forced borrowing. Sometimes they not only came from the same social class, but were the same people. The usury theory had always allowed a return above the capital in certain exceptional cases.[37] These cases included the case in which the higher return was not a payment for the use of money or the selling of time, but the just compensation for some loss that the lender had incurred because of the loan. In the case of forced lending, merchants—for the forced lending was usually imposed on them—lost opportunities to trade and to obtain some profit. The forced lending called for some type of compensation; otherwise sure injustice would be committed against those affected by it. And so the practice of forced lending led to the development of titles of interest.[38] As we shall see from accepting forced lending theologians moved slowly to accept commercial lending.

Interest, in our times, refers to the amount of money paid on a loan above the principal; however, in Roman law *interest* was the compensation a delinquent party had to pay to an injured party to compensate for the damage caused. In Roman law the money paid for a loan—*mutuum* or *foenus*—was called *usura*. The word interest comes from the expression *quod interest*, "that which is the difference" between the position of an

[37] Noonan. 100–132.
[38] Ibid. 121.

injured party before and after the injury. *Quod interest* was the amount of money the delinquent would have to pay the damaged party. The Roman formula was taken up by the Bolognese school in the 12th century. Laurentius Hispanus was the first canonist to use the word *interesse* to refer to the payment for the damage in failing to execute one's obligations in a loan. If a debtor failed to return the loaned good on time, the lender had a right to compensation for the damage he had endured. Initially, a title of interest was something that originated at the end of the contract. A title of interest came up when some irregularity occurred in the fulfillment of the contract.[39]

Forced lending, however, consecrated the legitimacy of interest from the beginning of the loan. When cities such as Florence, Venice or Genoa forced people to lend them money, the loan was organized in the form of a fund called *mons*. Every lender received a share in the *mons* according to the amount of money the person had been forced to lend. The city guaranteed some return on the loan as compensation for the damage endured by the forced levy of money. The practice met with opposition from moral theologians because they regarded it as usury. It lacked, however, one of the essential characteristics of usury mentioned above. The loan was certainly not voluntary, so there was no doubt that it was something being imposed on the lender. Thus he could hardly be conceived as entering the loan with the intention of usury, and this was part of the standard definition of usury. There was a second reason not to consider the loan usurious. It was clear that the merchants who were forced to lend money to the city—and this was the majority if not the entirety of the lenders—could not use that money for their trade. They were losing the possibility of a profit and experienced what economists would later label an opportunity cost. St. Bernardine of Siena—who wrote extensively on usury, and was by the end of the Middle Ages one of the major authorities on the topic along with Saint Antoninus—accepted as a title of interest the damage that came from the idleness which a merchant incurred when he lent his money. The merchant had to be compensated, that is, paid an interest, due to the labor he was not able to perform because of the temporary loss of that money.[40] For Molina too in these cases it was clear that it was legitimate to charge interest.[41]

---

[39] Ibid. 105–106.

[40] Ibid. 127.

[41] "si Rex, insurgente bello, postulanteque id bono publico, licite accipiat mutuum a mercatoribus invitis, mercatores licite posse tunc pacisci de lucro cesante accuperenque

In parallel to the *mons*, through which the Italian city-states organized their forced lending, the Church developed another type of *mons*. The institution of the *mons pietatis* was born out of Christian charity and is an example of how the Church did not just condemn a social practice but offered an alternative to the condemned practice. In doing so, the praxis of the Church caused both the financial system and moral theology to evolve.

The *montes pietatis* took their name from the *montes* that cities such as Florence, Venice or Genoa used to supplement their exhausted finances. The *montes pietatis* were not intended, however, to help the public funds. The goal of the *montes pietatis* was to help the poor. The persistent condemnation of usury during the Middle Ages is a sign that it was a widespread practice. Some theologians reasoned that, although a sin, usury should be tolerated by the state as a lesser evil—a similar reasoning was applied to prostitution. We have seen Molina employ this argument. There were occasions when people of a fragile economic condition would have to resort to a loan when some type of emergency arose. The *montes pietatis* were developed in Italy to meet this need, and charged a moderate 5 % annual rate on the money lent, an advantageous one for people of meager economic resources. The rate was supposed to help preserve the fund and pay the people who worked in its administration. The title of interest of labor was invoked to justify charging interest. The *montes* promoted by the Franciscans were soon attacked by the Dominicans. Cajetan held them to be usurious. Nevertheless, the Fifth Lateran Council (1512–1517) approved them. Still, Domingo de Soto attacked them in his *De Iustitia et Iure*. Molina demonstrated his surprise at Soto's argumentation against the decrees of an ecumenical council.[42]

Navarrus was the first leading scholastic to defend the *montes*, and the first one to extend the argumentation in favor of them to other lending institutions.[43] The acceptance of the *mons pietatis*, in fact, led to

competentem aestimationem ultra sortem, etenim tunc nulla in eo fit illis iniuria." II. 315. 11. p. 161. In the text we see how Molina considers this a case of *lucrum cessans*. As I shall soon set out Molina equated *damnum emergens* and *lucrum cessans*.

[42] "Ac sane Cajetanus et Sotus (quod pace doctissimorum virorum, ac de Theologia, christianaque religione bene dixerim) parum reverenter nimisque audacter, circa summi Pontificis, ac generalis Concilii definitionem, ad mores pertinentem, loquuntur, et plus iusto potestatem, quae in Ecclesia est ad definiendum et declarandum quod ad fides et mores spectant, coarctant, neque est tuta eorum opinio. Ita praeterea frivolum est, quod Sotus ait, multa videlicet ilius Concilii recepta non esse." II. 325. 5. p. 177.

[43] Noonan. 301.

the acceptance of lending as a livelihood.[44] Molina supported Navarrus's defense of the *mons* claiming that commutative justice imposed the obligation to compensate for what another did on one's behalf. The borrowers must compensate the lenders for the expense undergone in order to have the money ready for a loan.[45]

By the middle of sixteenth century, some type of commercial lending had become theologically acceptable. The critical point had been reached when interest had been accepted from the start of the loan, which certainly represented a departure from the case in Roman law; and this change in accepted practice was what began to change the theory. The causes were labor, loss on the part of the lender, the forfeiture of profit, and risk. The situation was ripe for someone to dare to express acceptance of titles of interest not only in forced loans or charitable ones, but also in voluntary commercial loans. It was Luis de Molina who took that step when he suggested that it would also be legitimate for a *mons* to be established not by the city or a pious association, but by a private citizen.[46]

2.2.2. *The Acceptance of Lending:* Labor, Damnum Emergens, Lucrum Cessans *and* Periculum Sortis

By Molina's time, titles of interest had been admitted into the theological discussion as legitimate causes for the lender to receive a sum above the principal. In the beginning the titles had been minor exceptions to the prohibition of usury. The canonists and the theologians of the Middle Ages and early modern times knew that there were exceptions to every rule.[47] What Molina did was to fully accept four titles that had been tentatively introduced in the theological discussion: labor, *damnum emergens*, *lucrum cessans* and *periculum sortis*. Accepting these titles and giving them a strong theoretical foundation is what leads Noonan

[44] Ibid. 294.

[45] "Etenim quamvis ad pecuniae dominum spectet facere sumptus ad sua conservationem necessaries, neque posit deducere illos inpactum, ut mutuarios solvatur, quando ad mutuum, commodumque mutuatariorum eos non ordinavit: quando tanem praecise sunt facti, ut ea pecunia ad mutuun in aliorum commodum deserviret, ad mutuatariorum maius damnum vitandum, licitum est deducere mutuatariis in pactum, ut ad illos contribuant, si mutuum accipere velint, non minus, quam sit licitus deducere eisdem in pactum lucrum cessans, aut damnum mutuanti ex mutuo emergens." II. 325. 6. p. 177.

[46] "Ex dictum patet, limitum esse communitatibus, aut etiam privates hominibus, eiusmodi montes pietatis erigere, retinendo dominium pecuniae ad mutuum eo modo deputatae, et cum potestate revocandi eiusmodi montes, et convertendi pecuniam illam ad alios usos, quando fine mutuatatiorum detrimento voluerint." II. 325. 6. p. 177.

[47] Noonan. 101–132.

to consider Molina the first to legitimate a livelihood of lending.[48] His pioneering work was based on his analysis of reality (*natura rei*), in this case money theory, to the development of which he contributed greatly.[49]

In the previous section, I have shown the reasoning behind recognizing the title of labor, and how it justified the moderate interest rate of the *montes pietatis*. I will discuss below the other three titles. For Molina *damnum emergens*, *lucrum cessans* and *periculum sortis* were three legitimate titles of interest, that is, accidental circumstances that allowed a return above the principal. He discussed thoroughly the first two; the last he dealt with more briefly.[50] The return above capital in a loan was not because of the loan itself, but on account of some circumstance not essentially connected with the loan.

Molina defined *damnum emergens* as the loss in the lender's own goods—whether it be in present goods or in possible future goods—, the expenses which he incurred, the inferior return on his capital or the destruction of his goods as a result of the loan.[51] We can see that Molina gave a very wide definition of *damnus emergens*. It did not need to be an actual loss, it could be a possible future one[52] that legitimized the payment of interest.[53] Molina gave two examples of *damnum emergens*. One example was that of a man who, having some money ready to repair a house, offered the money as a loan, as a result of which the house collapsed. The second example was the case of a man who gave out in a loan the money he had ready to buy wheat for his family's consumption, subsequently having to buy the wheat at a higher price.[54] In both cases

[48] Ibid. 309.

[49] Marjorie Grice-Hutchinson, *The School of Salamanca; Readings in Spanish Monetary Theory, 1544–1605*. 46.

[50] "Interesse licitu, cuius qui iacturam patitur, ut alteri mutuum, vela liquid aliud concedit, aut ut aliquid faciat, vel omittat, damnum emergens, aut lucrum cessans, dicitur." II. 314. 0. p. 158.

[51] "Si enim factura interesse sit in bonis acquisitis, saltem quia in futurum de bonis, quae tunc habuerit, cogetur ea de causa aliquid plus insumere, quam alioquin insumpsisset, aut aliquid suorum bonorum deterius redit: aut destrui omnino, apellatur damnus emergens." II. 314. 1 p. 158.

[52] Francisco Belda, "Ética de la creación de créditos según la doctrina de Molina, Lesio y Lugo," *Pensamiento* I (1963). 58.

[53] It is interesting to note the parallel between possible grace and possible title for interest.

[54] "Si quis pecunias habeas ad reficiendas domos et quo mutuo illas det, passurus est ruinam, aut detrimentum aliud domorum, factura haec domorum emergens damnus in bonis ipsius nuncupatur. Si item pecunias habeat ad triticum messis tempore in familia

Molina considered it just to ask for some compensation, namely interest, for the loan.

Molina defined *lucrum cessans* as the cost due to the omission of an acquisition. If a person desisted from an acquisition in order to grant a loan, he incurred a *lucrum cessans*. The example was more generic that that of *damnum emergens*. A person who had money ready for trade was prevented from profiting with the money he had lent. The merchant did not incur a direct loss, but there was a profit he never obtained because of the loan.

Damnun emergens had been accepted earlier by the tradition because of the forced loans. Molina found in the authorities of Aquinas and Soto some support for *damnun emergens*.[55] He considered that it could be estimated and agreed upon before the loan. Molina's bold move was to equate *lucrum cessans* with *damnum emergens*.[56] In doing so he extended the reasoning for one to the other, but, significantly, he extended the acceptance by important authorities from one to the other, although Aquinas rejected *lucrum cessans* as a title of interest. Noonan states that "in Molina's hands, the title *lucrum cessans* is not completely unrestrained, but is securely entrenched and firmly believed in."[57]

Molina's disputations on *damnum emergens* and *lucrum cessans* show that he had a concept of money more refined, at least from an economic point of view, than previous theologians. Karl Pribam points out that

> the Jesuit interpreters of the canonist doctrines [Pribram is referring to Molina and Lugo] practically ignored the Aristotelian reference to the 'sterility' of money. They distinguished between 'money per se', or money considered by and in itself, on the one hand, and money that is fruitful 'per accidens', in certain special situations. They permitted taking interest as the common price for the 'privation of money,' otherwise lenders would generally experience a loss resulting from forfeited benefits or opportunities.[58]

---

sustentationem emendum, et, quod illas mutuo det, empturus est illud postea longe maiori pretio incrementum illud, quod postea de bonis suis insumet, damnum ex mutuo emergens appellatur." II. 314. 3. p. 158. This reasoning is very close to the modern economic idea of opportunity cost, as mentioned above.

55 IIª–IIae q. 78 a. 2 ad 1. de Soto. q. 1. a. 3.

56 "Quo loco observa, lucrum cessans posse etiam dici damnum emergens, late sumpto vocabulo damni, prout, non comparare lucrum, quod quis licite poterat, et a quo desistit, damnum in bonis, quae alioquin habiturus erat, iure optimo dici potest." II, 314, 5, p. 158.

57 Noonan. 262.

58 Pribram. 30.

It was this more refined concept of money that prompted Molina to extend the reasoning for *damnum emergens* to *lucrum cessans*. Money was able to create wealth in the way other assets did. This was shown in the discussion of *lucrum cessans* as a legitimate title for interest. Unlike the case with the title of *damnum emergens*, with which he had dealt concisely, Molina knew that he had the authorities of Innocent IV, Aquinas and Soto against the legitimacy of *lucrum cessans*; he therefore felt compelled to provide a rather long explanation regarding why the title was legitimate.

Molina offered five arguments in favor of *lucrum cessans* as a legitimate title of interest. The first reason was that profit ceasing could be estimated, as could the occurrence of a loss. Soto said against *lucrum cessans* that it could not be estimated because it depended on the diligence of the owner of the money. Molina said that a prudent merchant could always estimate the *lucrum cessans* of a certain amount of money.[59]

The second reason was the argument of the forced loan. If it was fitting that when the king went to war and seized some merchant's money, the former should pay the latter compensation for the loss, a loan that occurred willingly but with a pact of compensation for the trade the merchant forfeited because of the loan ought also to be licit.[60] The reasoning of Molina shows how the acceptance of *damnum emergens* led to the acceptance of *lucrum cessans*. We see here an expansion of a case and the moral reasoning involved in it.[61]

The third argument in favor of *lucrum cessans* was taken from Aquinas, although Aquinas did not favor *lucrum cessans* as a legitimate title of interest. In IIª–IIae question 62, art. 4 Aquinas affirmed that when a thief robs a merchant not only does he take something away from him, causing him damage, but by taking away goods from the merchant, the thief deprives him of the possibility of exercising his purposeful activity and therefore from obtaining a profit.[62] Restitution in this case

[59] "Primo quoniam lucrum ratione mutui cessans, non minus est pecunia aestimabile, quam damnum ex mutuo emergens: neque enim prudens mercator, qui ad negotiandum paratam habet aliquam pecuniam, ex qua sperat lucrari centum, minus aestimabit lucrum illud ita in spe, quam pati iacturam viginti cum aequali probabilitate, imo longe plus: ergo sicut fas est pacisci de damno illo emergente, rationeque illius accipere aliquid ultra sortem, ita erit licitum eidem pacisci simili modo de lucro cessante." II. 315. 11. p. 161.

[60] II. 315. 11. p. 161.

[61] Jonsen and Toulmin. 191–194.

[62] IIª–IIae q. 62 a. 4 co.

means more than just returning the stolen good; it means some kind of extra compensation. Molina applied this type of reasoning to a loan. A merchant might licitly make a profit out of lending money because of the profit he had ceased to obtain with the money he lent.

I have already referred to the fourth reason Molina advanced. He argued that if a worker rented his tools, he could charge justly, not only for the use of the tools, but also for the gain he was failing to obtain because of his idleness. The same applied to money in the case of a merchant. Money was the merchant's 'tools.' In a loan a merchant was not only 'renting his tools' but also ceasing to do his trade. According to Molina he should be compensated for both.

The fifth and final reason went against the objection that admitting *lucrum cessans* amounted to selling something unpredictable that would occur in the future. Molina stated that, according to the Digest, a fisherman could sell the catch of a day before going out to sea.[63] For the same reason a merchant could sell the use of his money for what he expected to get as a return from it.[64]

From an economic point of view that affects the moral judgment, it should be noted that Molina fully understood the notion of money as capital, that money was a productive good. In this he was influenced by previous theologians, mostly the nominalists. John Eck had defended the triple contract at the beginning of the sixteenth century. In doing so he had declared that industry associated with money was productive. Discussing a contract that was supposed to be a company contract, Eck said that a capitalist giving the commodity of his capital was entitled to his share of profit. Eck's career as a theologian did not follow the path of moral theology because of Martin Luther, but Eck's teachings about capital were passed on by Mair, and Mair agreed with Eck.[65] Molina had read Mair for he referred to him, along with other authors, before giving the five reasons in favor of *lucrum cessans*. One of the other authors whose authority Molina referred to in favor of *lucrum cessans* was Conrad Summenhart, who had earlier said that "money was the merchant's tools",

[63] Molina is refering to Digest 19.1.12.

[64] II. 315. 11. p. 162.

[65] "Sed omnino sic est in proposito, quia pecunia est instrumentus negociatoris et industria ejus artificium, ergo si mutuaris debitor venit at mutuantem creditorem petendo instrumenta artis, scilicet pecunia; poteset cum eo pacisce, ut aliquid habcat ratione lucri cessantis, sicut de fabro diximus." Major, J., *In Quartum Sententiarum*, dist XV, q. 30, fol. 101 r. Quoted in Vereecke. 354.

although he had not accepted *lucrum cessans* as a legitimate title of interest.[66] Eck had been Summenhart's pupil in Tübingen.[67]

Molina was also influential in sanctioning another title of interest. He readily accepted the title of risk. In the Middle Ages the decretal *Naviganti* outlawed the risk of *periculum sortis* as a legitimate title for interest. This became the common opinion.[68] During the Middle Ages profit out of other's risk became synonymous with usury. One could expose his own goods at his own peril and profit from it. One could not, however, make a profit out of someone else's peril. Risk could not be passed from one person to another unless there had also been a transmission of ownership. In a loan it was understood that the money lent changed owners. The Latin name of a loan *mutuum* helped the acceptance of this idea. The word *mutuum* was held to come from *meum tuum*. A *mutuum* was the contract in which what was mine became yours. Because ownership had been transmitted in a loan, risk was not a licit title. Aquinas considered that a merchant could not charge for bearing the risk of another merchant's money.[69] Saint Bernardin also used risk and ownership as the litmus test for usury.[70] There was another reason for the rejection of risk as a title of payment. The insurance contract, the basic commercial tool for charging for a risk, was assimilated to gambling by some moralists, although some other theologians as Mair rejected this assimilation.[71] Nevertheless, profit for a risk was often frowned upon by moralists.

Molina fully admitted the paying of a price for a risk, so fully that he did not consider himself obliged to cite authorities in favor of his opinion. According to Molina risk diminished money's value, and therefore a return above the principal was not usury, but a legitimate return for the lender's preoccupation and trouble.[72] Still he admitted some kinds

[66] Noonan. 251.

[67] Ibid. 208.

[68] Ibid. 281.

[69] "Ad quintum dicendum quod ille qui mutuat pecuniam transfert dominium pecuniae in eum cui mutuat. Unde ille cui pecunia mutuatur sub suo periculo tenet eam, et tenetur integre restituere. Unde non debet amplius exigere ille qui mutuavit." II^{a}–IIae q. 78 a. 2 ad 5.

[70] Noonan. 150.

[71] Vereecke. 462–470. James F. Keenan, "The Casuistry of John Mair, Nominalist Professor of Paris". 88–93.

[72] "Nemo item negat, si, quod datur periculo exponatur, vel quod non solvetur, vel non sine labore et molestiis mutuantis, fas esse pretium accipere pro periculo illo et molestiis, quibus mutuis se exponit. Res enim mutuo data, cum morali, aut verisimili, eiusmodi

of usury in cases of risk. An unequal sharing of risk meant usury. Risk justified some interest, and depending on the risk more or less interest could be charged, but an excessive interest or an unequal sharing of risk would descend into usury.[73]

In Molina's treatment of these topics we readily observe the interplay of three key factors: the Thomistic tradition, nominalism, and the new understanding of economic reality. Molina never contradicted the teaching that usury was illicit. He even left many cases of usury standing, those in which according to him, commutative justice was broken.[74] These were cases where in a loan, something not essential to the loan was asked as a return. He found cases, nevertheless, in which 'accidental' components begged for a return above the principal in strict commutative justice. His notion of money as capital made him realize that in certain cases the right thing to do was to make a return above the principal of the loan. The *ius* of the case was to pay more. Because the *lex naturalis* prohibition against usury could not mutate according to his conception of natural law, Molina had to work out why it was *ius* or *fas* to pay more, why the law was not applicable to this case, and why it did not apply to the nature of the reality he was analyzing.

He had learned the nature of the case by talking to merchants. We can see in this development how nominalism affected Molina. We can also see how the theoretical development of analytical natural law resulted in a modification of moral judgment through normative natural law. Molina was being faithful to his own fundamental moral theology that considered it was the nature of the case that determined its justice or injustice.

---

periculo subest, tanto minus valet, quantus maius aut verisimilius, est tale periculum. Neque ea de causa acciperer pretium, est lucrum ex mutuo, sed alio licito capite, cum tali coniuncto." II. 304. 8. p. 137.

[73] "Illud vero observandum est, quando periculum incrementi et decrementi pretii non est aequale sed longe minus est, ne decrescat, quam ne accrescat: tunc mutuantem, esto ad restitutionem teneatur, si res quae ei est reddita tempore solutionis accreverat in valore, non tanem restituere teneri totum incrementum valoris, sed partis. Etenim partem incrementi potest licite retinere ratione periculi decrementi." II, 311, 5, 153. The first ecclesiastical approval of charging interest for risk came from a request from Jesuits in China who demanded that the practice of Chinese Christians of charging 30% interest under the title of risk be approved. In 1645 *Propaganda Fidei*, approving, Innocent X, answered that nothing could be charged by reason of the loan, but it could by the danger of non-repayment. Noonan. 289.

[74] II. 312. pp. 154 and ff.

3. The Just Price

Along with usury, prices were also a controversial topic for scholastic doctors. The problem of the just price arose prior to scholastic theology. Discourse regarding the just price began with Roman law, and it was presented as a legal, not an economic problem. The Code declared that a seller could recover the *iustum pretium* from a buyer who had taken advantage of him, if he had received less than half of the just price. The problem was to arrive at a satisfactory determination of the just price. There was, additionally, the problem of pricing goods in order to repay debts. The goods of the debtor were worth what one could obtain in selling them,[75] yet Roman law acknowledged that different circumstances caused the price of a good to change.[76] Roman jurists knew also that affection could influence prices, but this was disregarded for purposes of damage compensation.[77] The price of a good was ultimately determined by the common price in the market place.

The idea of a just price was passed on to scholastic theology. As in many other issues, all the scholastic doctors agreed that there was such a thing as a just price, but they disagreed on how to determine it. Historians of economics have been interested in the various rationales that the scholastic doctors proposed for the fixation of prices. Adrien de Roover found the heart of the disagreement in different economic theories of value. The canonists and the Thomists considered the just price to be the common estimation; the Scotists would favor a theory in which value was the result of work; the nominalists would favor a price determined by authorities;[78] however, most scholastics agreed that the just price varied according to time, place and circumstances.[79]

In the sixteenth century, a period of heavy inflation, fixing a just price became an even more difficult problem. Labor and other expenses were especially inadequate criteria when prices had lost their stability, leading to the advancement of the criterion of the *communis aestimatio*. Molina's was among them. Nevertheless, the formula *communis aestimatio* had many and varied interpretations.[80] Many historians of economics, and some historians of moral theology, have found in the *communis aesti-*

[75] Digest 35.2.63.1.
[76] Digest 35.2.63.2.
[77] Digest 35.2.63.pr.
[78] de Roover, *La pensè èconomique des scolastiques: doctrines et mèthodes*. 52.
[79] Noonan. 85.
[80] Pribram. 28.

matio the idea of market price.[81] I shall show below that for Molina, the market was to be taken into account in arriving at a just price, but his idea of the just price was richer than the idea of the market price of classic economics.

3.1. *Molina and His Predecessors*

Molina dedicated disputations 336 to 366 to the private sale contract. He began by discussing the juridical aspects of it, dedicating to these the three first disputations. In these disputations he dealt with the notion of contract, and the conditions under which it was considered fully binding. Apart from the legal interest of what made a contract take effect, the moment a contract was considered fully binding was important for fiscal matters, a contract becoming taxable when it took effect. Nonetheless, the legal aspects of Molina's disputation do not directly relate to our quest as much as the economic aspects of these disputations. From disputation 339 on, Molina dealt with the economic aspects of buying and selling, addressing the problem of the just price.

In the above section on usury, I presented how Molina, following the Aristotelian-Thomistic tradition, thought of the introduction of money as a result of the shortcomings of barter. In attempting to trade different goods, people had realized how hard it was to find someone who both had precisely what one needed and was interested in the goods one could offer; the result was the introduction of money. Money was a measure by which to value things, a means of payment and a guarantor for future necessities, making trade easier, but generating new problems.

The introduction of money created inequality in the exchange.[82] Where once each person held an equal position in the exchange, now

---

[81] Noonan. 85–86. Höffner. 161. Schumpeter and Schumpeter. 98–99.

[82] Locke would hold the same view: "But since gold and silver, being little useful to the life of man in proportion to food, raiment, and carriage, has its *value* only from the consent of men, whereof *labour yet makes*, in great part, *the measure*, it is plain, that men have agreed to a disproportionate and unequal *possession of the earth*, they having, by a tacit and voluntary consent, found out, a way how a man may fairly possess more land than he himself can use the product of, by receiving in exchange for the overplus gold and silver, which may be hoarded up without injury to any one; these metals not spoiling or decaying in the hands of the possessor. This partage of things in an inequality of private possessions, men have made practicable out of the bounds of society, and without compact, only by putting a value on gold and silver, and tacitly agreeing in the use of money: for in governments, the laws regulate the right of property, and the possession of land is determined by positive constitutions." John Locke, *Two Treatises of Government*, Everyman's Library (London: Dent, 1975). 141.

the introduction of money differentiated buyer and seller, the former paying money for a good and the later offering a good in exchange for money. In barter the equivalence of the goods exchanged was left to the mutual agreement of the two people bartering; the use of money, however, introduced the element of the legal value of money in the transaction. The equality of the exchange ceased to be a matter between the two people bartering, but now involved the community, which had created money and guaranteed its value. A wider circle suddenly became part of the transaction. Money had thoroughly transformed the question about justice in trade, now giving a new role to the community.

The scholastic idea of commutative justice—the section under which Molina dealt with the problem of the private sale contract—meant that in any exchange the equivalence of the exchanged goods, that is, the equality of their value, had to be maintained. There had to be parity in the exchange, lest commutative justice be violated. How to achieve that equivalence was the difficult and controversial question.

For Scotus the price should be tied to the cost of production.[83] Labor was for him the main criterion for the determination of a just price, one that assured that what was exchanged was equal. In this, again, he contradicted Aquinas, for whom the value of goods, and therefore their price, depended on their usefulness to man.[84] Thomistic scholastics viewed the Scotist position with suspicion because they thought that it would allow merchants to overcharge for their goods simply by claiming a high production cost. It was rather utility that determined the price. Molina followed Aquinas's theory; he rejected Scotus's theory[85] and declared that the value of a good and, therefore, its price depended on the preference of the buyers. He gave two examples of how price depended on the preference of the buyers, saying that the Japanese were willing to pay high prices for rusted things precisely because of their age; he also

---

[83] de Roover. *La pensè èconomique des scolastiques: doctrines et mèthodes.* 61.

[84] Noonan. 83.

[85] "Ex dictis hactenus liquido constat, falsam esse illam Scoti regulam in 4 dist. 15 q. 2 ad finem a. 2, quam sequitur Maior eadem distintione q. 41. Aiunt enim non iustum rerum pretio in manu mercatorum esse hoc. Computare debent expensas omne, quas emendo, asportando, aut conservando, tales res fecerunt, et insuper iustam mercedem quam pro industria, laboribus appositis, et periculis, quibus se exposueriunt, non secus as si mercede conducti ea in re servissent Reipublicae, et quidem, si res vendant pretio correspondenti, plus minus, his omnibus erit pretium iustum, si vero notabiliter excedat, erit iniustum, quoad excessum." II. 348. 7–8. p. 230.

mentioned that the Ethiopians liked cheap jewelry and were ready to pay a higher price for it than that of gold.[86]

Utility, however, was at once one of the elements of the problem and its solution. The problem had its economic dimension, but also a moral one. The moral relevance of the discussion resided in the fact that the price of goods actually determined the access of everyone to the goods of Creation. An unjust price would deprive some people of access to the goods of Creation, an access to which they were entitled.

3.2. Communis Aestimatio: *A Decision within the Community*

In pricing goods Molina distinguished three types of prices: legally fixed, natural and just prices. When goods had a legally fixed price, the just price would be the one determined by law. Most goods, however, did not have a legally fixed price; when this was the case, the just price would be the natural price. This distinction between legally fixed and natural prices shows that the notion of just price, even in authors such as Molina, who favored the utility theory of value, did not coincide with the market price. I shall first discuss Molina's idea of the natural price and then cases in which the just price was not the natural price.

3.2.1. *Natural Prices*

The natural price, for Molina, was the price of a good determined by the nature of the good itself, without the intervention of a human law or decree. The consideration of the nature of a good, however, did not exclude the consideration of the circumstances in which that good was priced.

The first example of the importance of circumstances, and not just of the nature of the thing, was the distinction made between two kinds of natural prices. One natural price was that of goods that were new and unknown in one place. Molina gave the example of some of the new goods that were arriving in Europe from both the West and East Indies; for these goods, Molina acknowledged the difficulty of determining a just price and gave a list of the many variables to be taken into account in fixing the price: expenses and risk run in procuring them, quantity, usefulness, scarcity and unusualness of the good. The government or the

[86] II. 348. 3. p. 229.

buyers and sellers could determine the price in this case.[87] Yet this clearly indicates that, for Molina, the just price of commonly traded goods was more than the result of the game of buyers and sellers. I shall demonstrate this by turning to Molina's explanation of the just price of commonly traded goods.

According to Molina there was a natural price for goods that were commonly traded in a region. This natural price was the price at which these goods were usually sold. The natural price of these goods varied according to different circumstances. Scarcity increased the price of a good, abundance acting conversely. The number of buyers, as well as their eagerness for the good, also affected the price. The needs of a particular time increased the price of certain goods, as happened with horses and weapons at the approach of war. These factors account for the demand side of pricing. The money supply was also a variable of the just price. Molina was well aware that lack of money decreased prices, as abundance pushed them up.[88] The ways in which a good was sold also affected its pricing, retail trade being a cause for a higher price for a good.[89] The multiplicity of diverse circumstances accounted for a range in the just price; the just price was not to be found in a specific figure, but within a range, as there was a maximum and a minimum just price. A sale would be just if the price was within the range of the just price.[90]

---

[87] "Quando de novo aliquid in provinciam aliquam asportatur, pretium iustum prudentium arbitrio est constitutendum ac iudicandum, atenta qualitate, utilitate, multitudine, aut paucitate rei, quae asportatur, attentisque expensis, et periculis, ac difficultatibus in ea afferenda, rei etiam novitas pretiosiorem illam efficit. His itaque, et aliis circumstantiis expensis, pretium iustum eius rei est constituendum, vel per Reipublicae moderatores, vel per ipsos emptores ac venditores. Neque idcirco pretium tamquam iniustum est damnandum, quod lucrum multum sit, si res suis raritate ac novitate pretiosa habeatur plurimosque emptores, habeat: neque certa alia regula hac re potest statui." II. 348. 9. p. 230.

[88] "... plurimas circunstantias esse, quae pretia rerum augent aut minuunt. Ut rerum penuria, propter sterilitatem aut aliud simile, accrescere facit pretium iustum. Multitudo emptiorum concurrentium plus uno tempore, quam alio, et maiori aviditate, facit illud decrescere. Item indigentia maior apud multos rerum aliquarum ad aliquem usum plus uno tempore, quam alio, posita eadem reum quantitate, facit pretium accreccere: ut equi plus valet bello imminente, quam tempore pacis. Defectus item pecuniae in aliquot loco, facit pretium aliarum rerum, et abundantia accrescere. Quo enim minor est pecuniae copia aliquot in loco, eo valor illius plus accrecit aequalique proinde copia pecuniae multo plura, caeteris paribus, emuntur." II. 348. 4. p. 229.

[89] "Item vendere res minutim ac per partes, eo modo, quo ii, quos regatones vocamus, vendere consueverunt, efficit acrecere pretium earum: vilius quippe regulariter venduntur res, quando eadem res ventuntur per partes." II. 348. 7. p. p. 230.

[90] "Atque hoc ab Aristotele loco citato et ab aliis Premium naturales nuncupatur ... sed naturale dicitur, quoniam ex ipsismet rebus, seclusa quacumque humana lege ac

3.2.2. Communis Aestimatio

The idea of a natural price, as well as the tendency to identify the just price with the natural price if there is not a legally fixed price, leads many historians of economics to attribute in Molina, and in other scholastic doctors, an identification of just price with market price. This leads these historians to present Molina as a forerunner of economic liberalism. Admitting the importance of the variables to pricing mentioned above, Molina still connected the just price to the *communis aestimatio*, *fori aestimatio*; there was no direct transition from natural price to just price. I have already said that when the price of a good had been legally fixed, it was the just price. Even when there was no legally set price, a just price was not just the result of the nature of the case and its circumstances. The just price was also the result of the *communis aestimatio* or the *fori aestimatio*. Molina used these two terms interchangeably, although he favored *communis aestimatio*. The English translation for these terms would be common valuation and market valuation. Still we cannot precipitously say that Molina referred with these terms to what we understand today by the term market price. When saying *communis* or *fori*, Molina was referring to the people who come together in the market, to buy and to sell. This community, decisive in establishing the just price, was not an abstract reality in which blind forces fixed the price, but rather a concrete group of people. The *communis aestimatio* referred to a specific group of merchants, buyers or sellers who came together in Seville, Lisbon, Cuenca or Medina. *Communis aestimatio* was the valuation by a particular group of people, so concrete that Molina called on prudent men to judge difficult matters and factor in the different variables of the market. This kind of pondering was more than just a mathematical calculation; it was a moral act that took into account the communal dimension of the market, and the social nature of trade.

---

decreto consurgit, dependenter tanem a multis circumstantiis, quibus variatur, atque ab hominum affectu, hac acstimatione, comparatione diversorum usuum, interdum pro solo hominum beneplacito et arbitrio. Quia ergo eius modi pretium non mere ex naturis rerum consurgit, sed a circumstantiis, quibus variatur, pendet, et quod plus est, ad hominus affectu, et aestimatione rerum pro suo beneplacito, inde proficiscur, ut non consistat in indivisibili, sed habeat certam latitudinem iusti ac commensurari merci, etiam spectantis circumstantiis omnibus, quae re ipsa hic et nunc in comercio humano concurrunt. Hoc autem non intelligas ex eo solum provenire, quod humanum iudicium incertum sit in se, ac virium in diversis hominibus, quasi ex ipsa quiddem rei natura retium re vera in indivisibili consistat, humanum tamen iudicium nesciat illud attingere, sed etiam quod rerum aestimationes, atque affectus ad res, unde pretii variatio pendet, variae sunt." II. 347. 3. p. 228.

I shall discuss other cases that Molina took into account when discussing the just price to show that, although he took into consideration market circumstances when discussing the just price, his notion of market and of the private sale contract was richer in ideas and nuances than the market pricing procedures of classical economics.

3.3. *Economics and Chrematistics*[91]

According to Molina there were three types of buying and selling,[92] the first being exchange broadly understood, in which a person bought what was necessary for his family's sustenance or sold what was superfluous from what he had. This kind of exchange—not directed at obtaining any profit—was licit because it was in harmony with the need to support one's family.[93]

The second type of buying and selling was directed toward the transformation of goods before reselling them, turning the good into a more useful one thanks to the diligence of the buyer-reseller. A person might buy wool to sell the cloth produced from that wool or perform any other kind of transformation of the good. In modern economic terms this would be to add value to the good before reselling it, resulting in a transformation of the good that accounts for the price increase.[94] The value added to the good justified this type of trade.

In *negotiatio*, however, the third type of buying and selling, the good was sold again and remained unchanged. The first two types of buying and selling did not present any moral problem; the third was discussed because it had been condemned by John Chrysostom.[95] Molina explained

---

[91] Chrematistics is defined as "of money making." *The Concise Oxford Dictionary of Current English*, (Oxford: Claredon Press, 1979). 176. As I shall explain it had in Aristotle a more precise meaning.

[92] "Triplex emptionis et venditionis genus distingui consuevit." II. 339. 2. p. 210.

[93] "Idem intellige de commutatione late sumpta. Quadam enim emptio atque venditio est, qua ab unoquoque ea emuntur, quae ad suam falmiliaeque sustentationem necessaria sunt, superflua vero venduntur. Atque haec quasi naturalis est, de se bona ac licita, ut Divus Thomae IIª–IIae q. 77 art. 4. et doctores communiter, cum Aristotele I Politicorum, affirmant. Ordinatur quippe non ad lucrum, sed ad congruam sustentationem, atque ad economos et politiocs, non vero ad negotiatores presse sumptos spectat." II. 339. 2. p. 210.

[94] "Alia est, qua emitir aliquid, ut, per industriam, commutatum, venditur ... Ad hoc emptionis et venditionis genus pertinet, non solus siquis lanam emat, ut inde pannum, quem vendat, conficiat, vel ferrum ut gladios, quos ex illo efficiat, vendat, sed etiam si aves, aut equos emat, ut postquam eos educaverit, et ad aliquid assuefecerit, illos vendat." II. 339. 2. p. 210.

[95] *Eiiciens* was erroneously attributed to John Chrysostome, and as such was incorporated into Gratian's Decretum. The *Eiicciens* was one of the earliest injunctions

why this *negotiatio* could be licit through successive arguments and conclusions. First he stated that this type of negotiation was neither good nor bad, but indifferent in itself, as the intention of the seller that determined its morality. Molina was following Augustine, who said that, unlike fornication, business might be sometimes licit and sometimes illicit.[96]

The second argument in favor of *negotiatio* was that, if it was responsibly entered into and ordained to a good end, such as the sustenance of one's family, or to direct the profit to works of charity, it could be considered licit.[97] In these cases the increase in price could justly be attributed to the toil, diligence and risk of the merchant. It could also be attributed to the different just prices that goods could have with the passing of time. The reason for the price increase could also be found in the range of the just price. Within the range of the just price, a merchant could sell at a higher price than that at which he had bought the goods.[98]

There was a third argument in favor of *negotiatio*, namely that it was necessary and useful for the commonwealth. Molina knew that there was no region capable of producing everything needed for life, and that this made it useful and necessary that some people take from what was abundant in one place to some other place where those goods were scarce

against usury that offered any explanation of why usury was wrong. Gratian's *Decretum* d. 88. c. 11.

[96] "Negotiatio hac presse et propissime sumpta, de se, neque virtutis, neque vitii est opus, sed indifferens ad utrumque. Quod si debite fiat, ad bonumque finem ordinetur, licita est ac moraliter bona, estque Republicis utilis ac necessaria. Prima pars, quod scilite indiferens sit, ut virtutis, aut vitii sit opus, est Aug. c. fornicari, et c. quoniam 88. dist. In quorum priori ait. Fornicari hominibus semper non licet: negotiari vero aliquando licet, aliquando non licet. In posteriori vero docet: vitiaquae negotiando interveniunt, negotiantium esse, non vero artis atque negotii, quasi sive vitioexercri non posit." II. 339. 3.p. 210. He is quoting from *Quaestionis Veteris et Novi Testamenti*. PL vol. 35. 2378.

[97] "... si debite fiat, ad bonumque finem ordinetur, licitam esse ac bonam moraliter, satis perspicuaest, si in sensu conditionali, in quo est prolata accipiatur. Caeterum conditionem posse ad actum redigi, probatur. Primo ex parte finis: quoniam lucrum intendi ex negotiatione potest ad sustentandam propriam familliamque vitam, hic autem finis bonus est moraliter caritatis propriae, ac surum. Item intendi potest ad divitias excerdum opera misericordia, liberalitate, aliarumque virtutum, tam in statu, in quo quis est, quam in altiori, si multiplicatis divitiis, conscedere ad illum contingat: ergo negotiati, ac lucrum ex illa referri ad finem bonum moraliter possunt." II. 339. 4. p. 210.

[98] "... quoniam pretium iustum non consistit in indivisibili, quare licite ac iuste poterit quis intra latitudinem iusti pretii vendere carius, quam emerit, nihil impediente, quod nec loca, nec tempora, nec aliae rerum ciccumstantiae varietatem susceperint, ob quam pretium iustum accreverit." II. 339. 4. p. 211.

and vice versa. This service justified the possible profit of the operation. The other way in which *negotiatio* was necessary for the commonwealth was that in times of abundance the merchants would buy those goods that abounded, and in times of scarcity they would sell the goods that were scarce. As long as they did not use fraud or tricks to increase or decrease prices the merchant would not be wronging the community.[99]

Despite his openness regarding the three different kinds of trade, Molina nevertheless provided at the end a caveat against *negotiatio*, pointing to the fact that greed was always possible and should be avoided. To stress this point, he cited Chrysostom's *Commentary on Mathew* and some other Biblical texts to stress that in every person there could be disorderly desire for profit.[100]

Molina's threefold distinction shows that he had adopted the Aristotelian distinction between economics and chrematistics. Economics was for Aristotle the natural acquisition of wealth, which belonged to household management. Chrematistics was unlimited wealth getting.[101] The point of departure for judging the morality of buying and selling was this very distinction. The constant element in the three types of buying and selling analyzed was that the three of them met a social need.[102] What made sense of business was the goal of meeting some social need, not that of merely making money. Money for the sake of money was for Aristotle sheer madness, and from a Christian mindset constituted the capital sin of greed. Ultimately the two elements that justified trade were intention and the common good.

3.4. *Monopolies and the Genovese Wool Trade*

Molina's caveats against seeking immoderate profits were not mere theoretical caveats. He must have had in mind business practices that occurred at the time. I have already alluded to monopoly problems when discussing usury. The discussion about monopolies was common in scholastic theology when dealing with the problem of just price. In this section I shall present Molina's theoretical discussion of monopolies and the specific case he dealt with, the Genovese-controlled wool trade in

---

[99] II. 339. 5. p. 211.

[100] Psalm 70: 15; Sirach 26: 28; 1 Timothy 6: 6.

[101] Aristotle elaborates this difference in *I Politics III*, 17. 1257b. Aristotle, *Politics*, trans. H. Rackham, The Loeb Classical Library (Cambridge, MA: Harvard University Press, 1959). 45.

[102] Molina. 40–41.

Cuenca. Cuenca was Molina's hometown and also the city where he lived the last years of his life, while preparing *De Iustitia et Iure* for publication.

Disputation 345 was titled: "About monopolies; to what extent do they render the sale unjust; and about hiding and holding back goods in time of scarcity."[103] The title itself tells us that the term monopoly, for Molina, included all commercial practices intending price-fixing.

In the strict sense, Molina defined a monopoly as the situation in which a person or a group of persons was able to impose and force an unjust price in the sale of a certain kind of goods, thereby doing wrong to the commonwealth.[104] This practice included the pact among merchants not to sell under a certain price or not to buy over a certain price.[105] A monopoly wronged the commonwealth in the first place, not the individuals. But because a monopoly was a wrong against the commonwealth, there could be cases in which the public authorities of the commonwealth could permit monopolies for the common good. The case put forward in disputation 345 was that in which a good was needed in a certain place; and for that sake the commonwealth could decide to set up a monopoly to provide for it. The opposite case could also occur, when the commonwealth wanted to favor the export of a good produced in the country. Portugal had opened up navigation to India at the king's own expense, in itself a justification for the transportation monopoly that existed between Lisbon and India, but the danger and difficulty of the navigation were also important reasons in favor of the monopoly.[106]

Following Juan de Medina, Molina considered monopolies as an indirect way of taxation, a common practice at the time for a prince to engage in. When in financial difficulty the sovereign would sell some monopoly

---

[103] "Monopoliis quousque emptio et venditio illicita, aut iniusta, reddatur: et de recondentibus ac asservantibus merces in tempus caritatis." II. 345. p. 224.

[104] "Est autem monopolium proprie, quando aliquis, aut aliqui, obtinet, ipsos tantum merces aliquas vendere, quod regulariter est iniquum, Respublicae iniuriosum: eo quod cives emere cogatur carius merces de eorum manu: caeteri vero de Reipublica impediatur iuste et commode negotiari, benignosque esse in pretio aliis civibus: quod in detrimentum cedit civium, esto monopole iusto pretio vendatur." II. 345. 1. p. 225. Price fixing is defined as the "agreement between two or more firms about the prices they will charge. This is considered to be anti-competitive, and is forbidden by monopoly legislation in many countries." *A Dictionary of Economics*, (Oxford University Press, 2002, accessed January 24 2007); available from ⟨http://www.oxfordreference.com/views/ENTRY.html?subview=Main&entry=t19.e2421⟩.

[105] "Eadem lege prohibetur, ne mercatores inter se conveninant de non vendenda merce aliqua infra certum Premium; aut non emendo ultra certum pretium." II. 345. 2. p. 225.

[106] II. 345. 3. p. 225.

to a merchant, who would advance the sum of money the prince needed, or guarantee some regular payment. I have mentioned the case of the monopolies over mines in some parts of Germany that Charles V had granted to the Weslers and the Fuggers. Another contemporary example was that of the salt monopoly that brought Phillip II a significant revenue. Hanseatic merchants bought salt in Spain and Antwerp, filling their ships with it when they returned home.[107] Molina saw in this practice an alternative to taxation that could be justified. Just as the prince had the right to tax his subjects, he could impose a higher price as another way of contributing to the common good.[108] The rule for just monopolies was that in establishing one, the burden of the monopoly should be shared according to one's obligation to contribute to the common good.[109]

For Molina, to buy under the minimum just price or to sell above the maximum just price was unjust and liable to restitution. But not every action on the part of the merchants directed at price fixing was liable to restitution. As long as the price stayed within the range of the just price, no harm was done, what we nowadays call collusion—an action that fell under the broad definition of monopoly for Molina—was a sin, but one against charity, not a sin against justice. Any practice seeking price-fixing in times of scarcity, although it harmed the commonwealth, would be a sin against charity and not against justice if the price charged stayed within the range of the just price.[110] Molina knew some first hand examples of these practices.

---

[107] Höffner. 27–28.

[108] "Sicut enim Rex exigere a sudditis poterat, ut contribuerent a publicae illi necessitate subveniendum: ita subiicere illos potest a gravamini; modo tamen moderatum sit, et cum minori ipsorum ac detrimento." II. 345. 3. p. 225.

[109] "Quo loco observa, hac de re commodiore aliam tradi non posse regulam, quam nunc licere eius modi privilegia concedere, quando id postulat recta ratio ac commune bonum, attentis atque expensas circumstantiis omnibus, tam ex parte Regis, atque illorum quipus conceduntur simulque attento, ut subviniendo comun bono, quoad fieri possit, non magis graventur, quaedam Reipublicae partes, quam aliae, quando ad omnes aequaliter subvenire spectat." II. 345. 3. p. 225. It is interesting that there is a sense of concern for proportionality. There are people who should contribute more than others.

[110] "Quando mercatores convenient inter se de pretio, quod ea conventioine seclusa esset iustum, sed rigurosum, peccarent contra proximorum charitatem, dignique essent, qui a potestatibus publicis gravissima poena mulctarentur, tamquam hominess Reipublicae praeiudicales, non tamen video peccare illos contra iustitiam ac proinde ad restitutionem teneri: modo nullus eorum fraudibus vi, aut metu, prohiberet alius mitius vendere." II. 345. 6. p. 226.

In disputation 359 Molina gave a detailed account of the practice of anticipated sale of wool that took place in many places in Castille, and particularly in Cuenca. This disputation, along with the following one, actually constituted a case study for which Molina did field research in order to be able to pass a well informed moral judgment on the matter.[111]

Wool was a major raw material in sixteenth-century trade, Castille being the largest wool exporter in Europe.[112] According to Molina, wool could be numbered among the natural resources of Castille.[113] The importance of the wool trade had led to the creation of the Burgos Consulate to which Isabella and Ferdinand granted the monopoly of wool trade in the ports of the Cantabric Sea—those trading with Flanders. The wool trade had also led to the creation of the *Honrado Concejo de la Mesta*, the powerful sheep-owners association that regulated the seasonal migration of livestock from winter pastures to summer pastures and back. The *Mesta* paid the Crown large amounts of money in exchange for many privileges.[114]

---

[111] "Dicemus vero quo pacto in hac civitate Conchensi, et in finitimis oppidis fiat: ubi id, diligenti inquisitione facta, indagare potuimus: si quae autem circumstantiae alibi fuerint, ut fortasse in Segoviensi civitate, quo audio Genuenses, et alios exteros, ad emendas lanas non accedere, sed inibi lanis civitatis illius, ac finitimorum oppidorum, confici ingentem pannorum multi valoris copiam, qui ad Hispanos omnes, variaque alia loca, deferuntur: si quae, inquam, aliae cicumstantia in ea civitate, aut alibi fuerint, eorum erit, iuxta illas: nostrum vero iuxta notitiam nobis traditam, de hac loci." II. 359. 1. p. 258.

[112] A list of wool purchases from 1531 to 1534 from a Florentine firm of cloth manufacturers belonging to some members of the Medici family shows how most of the wool bought came from Spain. Only small quantities came from Provence and Italy itself. de Roover, "The Scholastic Attitude toward Trade and Entrepeneurship." 113.

[113] "Inter praecipuas Castellae naturales divitias, non immerito lanae computatntur, pecoraque quorum illae sunt fructus." II. 359. 2. p. 258.

[114] For the importance of wool production to the Spanish economy see Ramón Carande, *Carlos V y sus banqueros. Edición Abreviada* (Barcelona: Crítica, 2000). 20–43. There he quotes Byron on the importante of wool production for Spain:

> More bleak to view the hills at length recede,
> And, less luxuriant, smoother vales extend;
> Immense horizon-bounded plains succeed!
> Far as the eye discerns, withouten end,
> Spain's realms appear whereon her shepherds tend
> Flocks, whose rich fleece right well the trader knows—
> Now must the pastor's arm his lambs defend:
> For Spain is compass'd by unyielding foes,
> And all must shield their all, or share Subjection's woes.
>
> Lord Byron, *Childe Harold's Pilgrimage*, Canto the First, 31.

Towards the end of the sixteenth century, the Genovese had achieved in Cuenca a de facto monopoly on the wool trade. Important Genovese merchants had in the city representatives who bought wool; because of their small number and their great purchasing power, these commodity brokers controlled the demand side of the market. A reduced number of brokers easily agreed on a maximum price over which they would not buy wool, forcing the producers to sell at the set price.[115] The control of the Genovese over the market led Molina to say that in the city of Cuenca the wool price depended on the will of the Genovese.[116]

The weak bargaining power of the producers forced them not only to sell at the price fixed by the brokers, but also to sell at a discount. Wanting to ensure that they met the orders received from Genoa, the brokers dealt with wool futures, forcing the producers to sell in advance the wool not yet shorn. In doing this, the brokers also took advantage of the cash shortage of the flocks' owners.[117] Futures in wool usually began to be exchanged on Saint Michael's day, just before flocks would go to their winter pastures, a move that meant expenditure for the flock owners. The wool would not be delivered until July, when the shearing of the sheep took place.[118] The problem of monopoly converged with the problems of usury. The credit sale being operated could be considered disguised usury. For Molina, if the difference in prices could be explained because of the just price range or the risk run, there was no usury, but if the difference in price was due to the advance of money, it was a case of disguised usury.[119]

---

[115] "Quia item illi, ad quos comisiones mittuntur, pauci sunt, facilius inter se conveniunt, ut nullus emendo certum pretio excedat, quam venditores, qui multi sunt, et qurum multi egestate premuntur, ut nullus infra certum pretium vendat: tametsi quidam interdum ad id alios suadeant." II. 359. 9. p. 259.

[116] "Ex eodem capite proficiscitur, ut lanarum pretium multum in hac civitate pendeat a Genuensium voluntate." II. 359 9. p. 259.

[117] "Accedunt variae aliae multorum necessitates, quae, una cum praecedentibus eos cogunt, vel partem, vel totam suma lanam vendere pecunia anticipata, si non totum pretium anticipare solvatur, certe ut pars aliqua, aut partes variis temporibus, quipus pecunia magis indigent, vel ad mittenda pecora ad loca distantia, vel ad illa reducenda, vel ad alios sumptus in rebus aliis faciendis persolvatur, quod in causa esse solet, ut frumentum servet, et multa alia, neque anticipate vendant." II. 359. 10. p. 259.

[118] "Anticipatae hae venditiones toto tempore anni fiunt, a tonsione anni unius usque ad tonsionem sequentis, regulariterque mense Iulio incipient. Fiunt vero frequentiores propre festum sancti Micaelis, quo tempore domini gregum se preaparantad mittendum illos ad hyemandum." II. 359 14. p. 240.

[119] II. 360. 2. p. 262.

Molina criticized these monopolistic practices that arose from an unregulated market and that allowed a few economic agents to fix the prices. In today's terminology we could say that he opposed practices by which big business controlled the market. Nonetheless, Molina was not in favor of an excess of public intervention. This becomes clear in his discussion about the fixed price of wheat.

3.5. *Fixed Legal Prices*

Ferdinand Braudel pointed out that the scarcity of wheat was a constant feature in the countries around the Mediterranean. In years of bad crops the wheat prices became exorbitant. Of course the ones to suffer the most were the poor.[120] Even in good years the adjustment between two harvests could drive the prices to levels that endangered the livelihoods of the poor.[121] The scholastic doctors were well aware of that fact. In 1540 Domingo de Soto had been dispatched by the University of Salamanca to Toledo to buy wheat and bring it to Salamanca to provide for the poor.[122]

Molina dedicated disputation 365 to the task of discussing the advisability of setting the price of wheat as was done in Portugal.[123] He was well informed, not only from the long years he had lived in Portugal, but also because, as he tells us, while teaching in Evora he received by chance a copy of the document in which Cardinal-Infante Henry of Portugal disputed the advisability of a fixed legal price for wheat.[124]

In times of scarcity the price of wheat went up. Some wanted to help the poor by setting a maximum price for what was then the basic staple. They thought that in doing so the poor would be helped. Those who held this position argued that the common good of the commonwealth was preferable to the particular good of those individuals who owned the grain.[125] The second argument in favor of a set price was that in

[120] Fernand Braudel, *The Mediterranean and the Mediterranean World in the Time of Phillipp II*, vol. II (New York: Harper and Row, 1976). 575–584.

[121] Pierre Vilar. 55.

[122] Francisco Gómez Camacho, *Economía y filosofía moral: La formación del pensamiento económico europeo en la escolástica espanola*. 37.

[123] The title of the disputation is "Utrum expediat, in Lusitano praesertim Regno, taxari frumentum eo de consuevi modo." II. 365. p. 274.

[124] "Dum haec Evorae exponerem, casu evenit, ut me inscio, nescio, quis rationes Cardinali Henrico nondum Regi offerret, ob quas contendebat taxas frumenti in eo regno non expedire, quin potius ex illis multa oriri mala." II. 365. 1. p. 275.

[125] "Etenim commune Reipublicae bonum praeferendum est particulari sigulorum: quare, cum bonum commune Reipublicae id efflagiter, licite statui potest, nihil impediente quod in aliquorum detrimentum cedat." II. 365. 8. 8. p. 277.

time of extreme need everything became common. I elaborated on these theological principles in the last chapter when discussing the idea of *dominium*.

Molina accepted both principles, that the poor should be helped and that in case of extreme need everything became common.[126] Yet Molina opposed a legally fixed price for wheat. I have described the organic conception of society in Molina's time, a view reflected in his thought. Molina's organic conception of society led him to oppose the legally fixed price of wheat, considering that a legally fixed price imposed the burden of helping the poor on the owners of wheat, a burden that should be organically shared in the commonwealth and not arbitrarily imposed upon the owners of wheat.[127] A second argument he advanced against legally fixed prices for wheat was that the well-intended measure usually backfired, benefiting those commissioned to seize wheat and sell it at the legally fixed price. Such officials would become richer at the expense of the poor and of the owners of grain. Magnates and powerful people would use their commission to create companies that benefited themselves, their relatives and their friends.[128]

---

126 "Ut vero summatim dicam, solum in eo evento potest Respublica cogere divites, ut pauperibus vendant frumentum minori pretio, quam ex rei natura valeat, in quo posseut illos cogere, ut facerent illis eleemosynam in illam eadem quantitate: quod, ut cum Soto, et Covarrubias In Materia de elemosyna, q. 32, art. 5. diximus, solum est quando illi essent in extrema necessitate eius subventionis, aut iuste extrema necessitate timeretur, nisi illi subvenitur." II. 365. 9. p. 277.

127 "Neque tunc soli domini tritici essent cogendi subvenire pauperibus, sed cogendi simul essent alii divites contribuere eleemosynam, ut Respublicam tota aeque proportiione quadam gravaretur. In aliis autem eventibus, ut divites cogi non possum facere eleemosynam, sic ne cogi possunt vendere illis res suas minori pretio quam valeat: si autem divites minore pretio illas emant, etiam principis autoritate interviniente, tenetur illis restituere pretii decrementum." II. 365. 9. p. 277.

128 "In pragmatica autem, qua frumentum tempore sterilitatis taxaretur minori pretio quam valeat, non solum divites cogerentur de suo gratis dare pauperibus, sed etiam multi pauperis; et quin magnis laboribus et sumptibus triticum collectum cogerentur gratis dare divitibus. Praesertim cum Rex in hoc Lusitaniae Regno usurpare sibi illa pretio solebat triticum ad classes praeparandas, et ad pleraque alia, et concedere soleat magnatus et potentibus facultates, ut dominis triticum etiam invitis, magantibus pretio taxato vendatur. Et praesertim, cum iudex ceterique ministri publici, qui non solum sibi, sed consanguineis, atque amicis, quin aliis, qui illud lucrum alio transportent, inita cum illis societat, accipere soleant pretio taxato, invitis illius dominis, ut interim abusus alios, ac vexationes, quae tritici dominis fiunt, omittanm. ... Pauperes autem, ut nunquam tenetur facere divitibus eleemosynam; ita nunquam cogi possunt vendere illis res minori pretio, quam valeat: si autem divites minori pretio illas emat, etiam principis auctoritate interviniente, tenetur illis restituere pretii decrementum." II. 365. 9. p. 277.

Wheat trade at the time was a complicated business. The law that fixed the price of wheat did not apply to everyone. Foreign merchants bringing wheat from abroad were exempt from the legally fixed price. It was a sensible measure. No merchant would have imported wheat into Portugal if he could not make a profit from it. In order to ensure that wheat would be imported, the state had to exempt foreign merchants bringing grain into the realm from a law that would have certainly deterred them from their trade and hampered the good of the commonwealth.[129] Molina knew this. He had lived in Lisbon for seven years, where he would often converse with the merchants to learn about their trade.[130]

Molina offered a final argument against a legally fixed price for wheat, one that refers to man's ultimate end, salvation. Molina was aware that the law prescribing a legally fixed price for wheat was a law that many people transgressed. According to Molina's legal theory, civil positive laws were binding in conscience, and therefore the people who were breaking the law were committing sin. Molina argued that this law was actually hampering the salvation of many, because it led them to commit sin. The purpose of the law was not to condemn, but to instruct. If the result of a positive law was that it endangered people's eternal salvation, instead of helping them to lead a better life, the law should be revoked, because it was certainly not fulfilling its end.[131]

Molina nevertheless did not think that the only thing to do was to repeal the law that fixed the price of wheat in Portugal. Means to help the poor had to be arbitrated. 90% of the wheat sold in Portugal belonged to the nobility and to the clergy, who, if left unchecked, would sell wheat at an unjust price, thus driving out the poor and their families. Molina

[129] II. 365. 15. p. 279.

[130] When talking about the slave trade, he acknowledges that he would talk to the merchants to learn about their trade. "Denique quantum intelligere potui ex mercatoribus, qui eiusmodi mancipia in Aethiopia emunt, eaque inde huc asportat (cum quipus locutus sum, quique nihil eorum, quae retuli, diffitentur) illi nihil aliud currant in negotiatione, quan suun lucrum et commodum." II. 34. 6. p. 92.

[131] "Secundum est ad legislatorem (praesetim christianum) spectare, attendere, non solum ad commoda aut incommoda temporalis, quae ex lege suae sequuntur, sed etiam ad spiritualia subditorum. Cum enim finis ipsius politicus ordinetur ulterius ad supernaturalem finem vitae aeternae, sane attendere debet ad sirituaem bonum, slutemque animarum suorum subditorum in legibus condendis, neque sistere debet solo temporali commodo Reipublicae. Atque ea de causa, si ex aliqua sua lege videat grave detrimentum spirituale multorum oriri, vel fragilitate, vewl etiam malitiae subditorum, tenetur charitatis praecepto ab ea lege ferenda abstinere; preasertim si lia via aeque ben consequi possit intentum, ac finem eius legis." II. 365. 13. p. 178.

proposed public regulation of the market. Public authorities would have to take wheat from places where it abounded to places where it was scarce. To do so, they could force the selling of wheat. Forced selling meant that those who had it were compelled to sell it, eliminating by this measure any type of possible accumulation and future speculation regarding the price of grain. But forced selling did not mean selling at a legally fixed price. Seized wheat would be purchased at a moderate price sensitive to the case and its circumstances, as well as the price at which wheat was commonly sold at that place.[132]

We can see that Molina's argument against fixed legal prices is not a position in favor of deregulated markets or pure free markets; Molina favored regulation or deregulation depending upon the cases. What moved him to favor one or the other according to the cases he discussed was his concern with the communal nature of the market and the social needs trade was meant to meet. On this I shall elaborate further in the concluding part of this section about the just price.

3.6. *Information, Economic Expectations and Justice*

In *De Officiis* Cicero presented the case of an honest businessman who imported a large cargo of wheat from Alexandria into Rhodes at a time of dearth and famine. The businessman knew that other imports were arriving shortly after his. Cicero asked whether the importer should disclose the fact of the near future arrival of wheat to the Rhodians or not.

---

[132] "Dices. Quid ergo? Permittendine sunt omnes vendere quo pretio voluerint? Inde sane reipublicae sequeretur pernicies. Cum enim decem partibus frumenti, quod in Lusitania venditur, novem ad conductores redituum Ecclesiaticorum, ac nobilium, pertineat: hi autem quantum possunt, conentur ascendere in pretioquibus vii possunt; sane, si vendere permittantur, quo velint pretio, ultra iustum vendent, sanguinemque pauperum fugent, ut fiet, ut brevi omnia bona ac praedia filiorum comparent. Hace video esse ration potissiman, qua senatores affirmant, necessiam omnino esse in Lusitania Regno taxam frumenti. Ad quam dicendum est, malum hoc (si er hyperbolem no sit dictum) nullo modo esse ferendum. Facile tamen posse illi occurri sine taxationis lege, quae tot pariat mala, quot supra commemoravimus. Cum enin eius modi homines, si id efficiunt, iniusti sint, Reipublicaeque perniciosi, compelli utique possunt, rationem reddere frumenti, quod in unoquoque oppido ex commendis, reditibusque aliis ecclesiasticis, ac nobilius habent: quo sciri non est difficie in unoquoque oppido. At tunc cogi possunt illud vendere, moderato pretio, ut natura rei, spectatis circumstantiis concurrentibus, postulat, atque ut communiter ab aliis in eodem loco venditur. Imo autoritate publica vendi posset ac distribui, ut commune bonum eius populi efflagitaret, redditio illis pretio iusto, relcitoque eisdem frumento toto, quod communi bono, ac necessitatibus populi, in quo illud habent, necessarium non esset." II. 365. 15. p. 279.

Cicero's solution was affirmative. The merchant ought to disclose the fact. Cicero's argumentation rested on the assessment that withholding from others something that one knew and that would be for their advantage to know amounted to concealment, and thus the importer would commit an injustice and would be liable to restitution.[133] Molina reported the case to Summenhart and Juan de Medina with whose solution they agreed. Aquinas, Cajetan, Soto, Biel, and Molina himself, however, held the opposite opinion, stating that the importer did not sin against justice by not revealing what was his private knowledge. The importer, therefore, was not liable to restitution. Nevertheless, that was not the end of the discussion. Although, along with Aquinas, Molina considered that it would be more virtuous for the man to reveal what he knew; he still gave four reasons why the merchant would not sin against justice in not revealing his private knowledge. First, if one accepted that the merchant was liable to restitution, one would also have to accept, for the sake of consistency, that those selling wheat at a high price without knowing of the coming vessels would not commit sin, but would also be liable to restitution once the new arrivals reached Rhodes.[134] No author would hold that absurdity, and Molina knew this. The second argument was that the price of goods was tied to common knowledge, not to private knowledge; therefore *communis aestimatio* prevailed over private knowledge. Thirdly, if Cicero's solution was followed, when drought had increased the price of wheat and someone had sold at a high price, this person would be liable to restitution in case of rain. This again was absurd. The last argument was a Biblical one. If this was a case of injustice, then in Genesis 41, Joseph would have acted unjustly, whereas the Bible actually praised Joseph for his wisdom.[135]

Having determined that it was not a sin against justice, Molina proceeded further, questioning whether the man withholding what he knew sinned against charity. Again it was not a sin against charity, because the act of disclosing what he knew was supererogatory. To omit a supererogatory act was never a sin. Still, we see that business ethics for Molina

[133] Marcus Tullius Cicero, *De Officiis*, trans. Walter Miller (Cambridge, MA: Harvard University Press, 1961). 318–327. The case Cicero referred to was an ethical discussion between Diogenes of Babylonia and his disciple Antipater.

[134] "... quoniam hoc contra iustitiam peccaret, ad restitutionemque tenretur, sane, qui ignorantes brevi superventuras merces, suas venderit pretio currenti, quanvis non pecarent, excussante illos ignorantia invincibili, tenerentur nihilomninus ad restitutionem, sicut ille, qui cum opposite scientia illas vendit." II. 354. 3. p. 250.

[135] II. 354. 3. p. 250.

went beyond justice. Evangelical counsels also touched on business practices,[136] in which there was also room for charity.

Molina explored the case further and questioned whether, if the information that affected the price was that of an upcoming decree, it would be just to profit from it. Here his opinion changed, because knowledge about the law should be public knowledge, and to make profit out of privileged information that should be common knowledge was unjust.

We can see that Molina distinguished between private and public knowledge; to derive profit from some knowledge that was private was acceptable. To derive profit from knowledge that should be public was not acceptable, because it was an illegitimate privilege.[137] For Molina it was clear that knowledge was money, and he discussed different uses of it. Still, he held that it was common knowledge that should determine pricing, and for this transparency was necessary. For private knowledge, disclosure was not necessary, even if it was still commendable in some cases. This discussion shows us that for Molina the discernment of business practices were not restricted to criteria of justice, but also included charity and the consideration of evangelical counsels.

3.7. *A Just Market*

For Molina it was clear that a private commercial contract was not something that affected only the two parties who participated in the contract. The introduction of money had introduced the community into this private contract, because money was created by the community. Also, since the introduction of money had somehow introduced an element of inequality, it was up to the community to guarantee the equality of the exchange.

Molina opted for the utility value theory in the problem of pricing. This meant that he favored the demand side circumstances in his theory of how a natural price was to be determined. But this was far from what we understand today as a market price. First of all, if the market was to be taken into account, the market had a very specific and not at all abstract

[136] "Dubium est, utrum, esto hic contra iustitiam non peccet, nec restituere teneatur, peccet nihilomninus lethaliter contra charitamen. Sunt qui affirment. Contrarium tamen innuit aperte Divus Thomae, dum solum ait, cumulatoris esse virtutis manifestare abundantiam futuram mercium, aut minuere de pretio: quibus verbis aperte docet esse id solum opus supererogationis, ac proinde contrarium non esse peccatum. Atque ita proculdubio est affirmandum: quipped is suo iure utatur, vendatque merces suas pretio iusto." II. 354. 4. p. 250.

[137] II. 354.5 pp. 250–251.

face. The market was first of all a physical place in which real people came together. These people possessed a moral conscience that was also part of the economic process.

Precisely because he knew about the difficulty of fixing a price, Molina allowed for haggling to reach the just price, as well as for a range for the just price. But the just price was the result of the *communis aestimatio* and also of the advice of prudent men. The *communis aestimatio* was the economic translation of the moral theology term *communis opinio*. In the market the *communis opinio* was the *communis aestimatio* and this, as happened with any case of moral reasoning, was a sure way of evaluating behavior. It was a probable opinion. As happened with moral reasoning, Molina believed that in the market there were prudent people whose experience made them understand better what would be good, in both the economic and moral senses. For Molina, unlike for contemporary analysis, it made no sense to try to separate them. Prudent merchants in the market were like the approved doctors; they were the people who were more familiar with the nature of the case—*natura rei*—and therefore were most able to find the just thing to do in those circumstances. Again, as with any other instance of moral reasoning, there was the element of uncertainty, because *recta ratio* was a probable reason. This uncertainty called in prudent people, as I have said, but also explained the range for a just price. If there were cases that not even God could know, how would even the prudent ones be able to determine a price, as mathematical models do today? In this Molina departed from Aquinas and allowed a greater degree of indeterminacy, as his theology of grace and human freedom also did.

In chapter I we saw how, according to Molina's theology of divine grace, human freedom was enhanced, resulting in some degree of indeterminism. For Molina, pricing involved both the nature of the case and the will of those coming to the market; it was a science about future contingents, a 'middle science' open only to God. Nominalists had always held some degree of skepticism about the possibility of knowing the world order. That skepticism might have moved them to opt for production cost more than for utility in order to price goods. This, however, was not acceptable to a Thomist worldview. Molinist epistemology was applied to the analysis of economic moral problems. Compared to this 'middle science' involving knowledge open only to God, human knowledge about just prices could only be a probable science, never a necessarily true one. And a probable science called for the opinion of prudent and discreet people.

We are dealing here with a different paradigm of the market and of economic activity; therefore, an outright equivalence of just price theory to modern classical market price theory would be impossible to trace. The market was not an abstract 'place' but a very concrete one. It was a place and a community, one in which the just price was reached not by competition, but through cooperation. If *negotiatio* was just when it sought to meet a social need, it was due to the organic notion of society, and to the social nature of money. In an organic conception of society, it was inconsistent to present parties as sheerly competitive in the market place; in Molina's mind buyers and sellers did seek to obtain a profit, but not at the expense of the others. Sheer competition made no sense according to this mind-set.

A just price could only be reached in situations featuring the free informed consent of both parties to the sale contract and where the equality of the exchange was respected. Without freedom there was no human act, no possible justice. But freedom required a moral ecology without which it could not flourish, and for it justice was necessary.[138] The call for restitution, which affected even the heirs of those with ill-obtained wealth, can be understood as a perpetual claim to maintain the balance that rendered that moral ecology possible. Against the uncertainty of human moral judgements, which Molina acknowledged, he proposed prudence and regard for the community, not just a merely mechanical world of causality.[139]

A just market was a free market, but a free market was a market of free people and freedom had to be preserved. This required positive actions. Free markets were one thing and freedom in the markets was something else. Without freedom in the markets there could hardly be virtuous behavior, but virtue also required the control of natural forces.

---

[138] I am using this expression that gives title to the book of Daniel Finn, *The Moral Ecology of Markets: Assessing Claims About Markets and Justice* (Cambridge: Cambridge University Press, 2006). I am indebted to the author for the expression, but I do not intend to use the expression in the technical sense the author uses it, but just in the sense it would convey in common parlance.

[139] Dealing with money exchange Molina tells us how at the time there were many noble ladies in Lisbon who possessed farm land in Castille. The land was let. To receive their rent these ladies used the services of merchants who collected the rents in Castille and paid them in Lisbon. To determine what the commission for this service should be Molina calls for the assessment of prudent merchants. "Tamentsi haec arbitrio prudentes reliquuntur, semperque consulendum mercatoribus sit, ut moderate se gerant in eiusmodi stipendiis ac lucris: praesertim cum parum laboris ac molestiae; nihilque periculi hac in re habeabt." II. 404. 8. p. 401.

Left to itself nature did not produce virtue; virtue was a second nature that required exercise and restrictions. Freedom to enter into a contract involved more than a free market understood as a completely deregulated one, but a market in which legislation allowed individuals to exercise their freedom, and where the common good was taken into account. Again, the market was not an abstract institution but a very concrete one for Molina.

Finally we should note that the problem of just prices, as presented by Molina, only made sense if there existed a shared right to the goods of Creation. If there was such a right—and I have shown in the last chapter that this was almost self-evident within the world of scholastic theology—prices could be unjust if they barred someone from access to the goods of Creation, or just, if they allowed people to access the goods of Creation. If there is no such right, then talking about just prices makes no sense, but then arises the problem of justifying private property, or any kind of property.

Within the problems of buying and selling, there was a particular type of exchange, the exchange of money. I shall deal with this in the next section.

4. Money Exchange and Credit Creation

4.1. *Introduction*

I established in the first chapter how the triumph of Aquinas in the sixteenth century as the common doctor led also to a transformation of his doctrines, especially on particular issues. In the section about usury I have shown the peculiarities of Molina's interpretation of the received tradition; in money exchange the transformation was even more dramatic, leading Noonan to affirm that the new scholastic approach was "a revolt from these theories of the past [...], a revolution in the practical judgment on exchange banking among the theologians."[140] It took both a good command of moral theology and a deep understanding of the money markets to bring about this transformation that actually became possible because, during the fifteenth and the sixteenth centuries, the best moral analysis of economic problems took place in the discussion of exchange banking.[141]

140 Noonan. 312.
141 Ibid.

The first move had been to draw up the limits between money exchange and money lending. When William of Moerbeke, O.P. translated at Aquinas's request the works of Aristotle, the translation seemed to imply that exchange should be condemned; following Aristotle, Albert the Great and Saint Thomas condemned money exchange as a way of money lending.[142] During the late Middle Ages, the contention that money exchange was not a loan but a purchase or a sale was rejected by most moral theologians.[143] Alexander the Lombard was the first to reason in favor of money exchange, against the previous common condemnation, arguing that it was a *venditio sub dubio*, a sale subject to doubt.[144] In the fifteenth century the Tübingen School built the argument that money exchange amounted to a virtual transportation of money, which provided a legitimate title for charging for the exchange; furthermore, the idea of a virtual transportation served as a construct to render acceptable the idea of a money market.[145] Cajetan helped to move the discussion further along by pointing to another difference between usury and money exchange: whereas the state fixed the legal value of money in its dominions, it could not do the same outside of them.[146]

In his study *The Exchange Contract in the Moral Theologians from the Thirteenth Century to the Mid Seventeenth Century*, Luciano dalle Molle found in Luis de Molina the author with the most comprehensive vision and the most precise judgment of his time. Molina synthesized the best argumentation up to his time; his full and thorough treatment of money exchange gives us a summary of the thought and doctrine of the sixteenth-century moralist and jurists.[147]

---

[142] "By happy, or unhappy, fault, however, William of Moerbeke in the translation of the Politics available to St. Albert and St. Thomas, rendered καπηλικῆς the term for retail trade as "campsoria," a term with the specific meaning of money changing. Thus instead of being presented with a condemnation of all retail trade, which medieval Christian theologians would not have accepted, the early scholastics found in Aristotle only a condemnation of traffic in money; and themselves already suspicious of the *campsores*, they found this highly natural." Ibid. 47.

[143] Ibid. 181.

[144] Ibid. 183.

[145] Ibid. 317.

[146] Ibid. 325.

[147] Luciano dalle Molle, *Il contratto di cambio nei moralisti dal secolo XIII alla metà del secolo XVII* (Roma: Edizioni di Storia e Letteratura, 1954). 109.

4.2. *Types of Exchange and Its Lawfulness*

As we have seen him doing previously, Molina began his discussion of money exchange with the juridical aspects of the problem. Again there was a fiscal side to the juridical discussion. Was an exchange subject to taxation? And if so, what was the tax base? Molina acknowledged that money exchange was a particular case of exchange, in which the exchanged goods were not taxable.[148] Molina realized that money was a special kind of good, and operative not only in fiscal matters; therefore, he dedicated disputations 398 to 410 to discussing the different problems that arose from money exchange.

Cambium—as money exchange was known—was nothing other than an exchange of money for money, the reason for this exchange being a difference in the material, the form or the public seal money bore, as well as a difference in the place where money was located.[149] In short it could be the exchange of the same or different currencies. The person practicing the art of exchange was the money exchanger or banker.[150]

Having defined the terms of the discussion, as a good scholastic author would always do, Molina proceeded to discuss the justice of the business. Along with Mercado, Molina thought that exchange was a dangerous trade, yet accepted that there were ways in which this profession could commendably be practiced for the advantage of the commonwealth.[151]

---

[148] "Cum in cambio presse sumpto pecunia utrique commutetur: pecunia autem privilegiata sit, ut ex illis alcavala non debeatur, ut supra dictum est; constat ex cambio presse alcavalam non deberi." II. 397. 17. p. 384.

[149] "Cambium presse, ut ex dictis dist. 396 liquet, non est aliud, quam commutationem pecuniae pro pecunia. Neque ad cambia rationem est necessarium, ut pecunia, quae commutatur, diversa ab ea sit, pro qua commutatur, vel in materia, vel in forma, sub publico signo illi impresso, qicquid Joannes Medinae q. 1 de cambiis, in contrarium asseruerit. Cambium quipped pecunia reddenda in alio, vere est cambium, esto pecunia reddenda, neque in materia, neque in signo, sit diversa, ut Sotus 6. de iust. Q. 8. art. 1. recte adnotavit." II. 397. 1. p. 384.

[150] "Atque hinc ad ipsorum distinctionem, extrema huius contractus sortiuntur diversa nomina: isque a quo cambium petitur, quique ad alterius petitionem suam operam ac industriam apponit, dicitur campsor, praesertim si publicum cambiendi munus habeat dicitur nummularius, trapazita, collybista et argentarius; tametsi quaedam horum nominum latius aliquando pateant, de qua re legandus est Covar. de collat. veter. numismat. c. 7. in princ. ad fin. num. 4. Hispaniae autem *vanquero* dicitur: is autem, qui cambium petit, a Conr. de contract. q. 99. a Med. q. 1 de camb. Et ab aliis, campsarius appellatur." II. 397. 2. p. 385.

[151] "Dicendum es, quamvis ex se periculos sit, plus adhuc, quam ea negotiatotia ars, quae emendo et permutantdo lucrum intendit; quamvis item personas aliquas, ut Ecclesiasticas, dedeceat, eisque prohibita sit; nihilominus, si modo in sequentibus exerceatur, neque ut iniust, neque ut illicita est damnanda, quin potius meritorie excerceri valet, ut

Molina's taxonomy of the exchange business followed the standard distinctions of the time: petty exchange, real exchange—performed usually through exchange bills—and dry exchange. The difference between the sum received and the sum returned in a money exchange could not be due only to the passing of time, lest it be disguised usury.[152] Molina, who defended the prohibition of dry exchange that Pius V had established in *De cambiis*,[153] had to find other grounds to explain the apparent inequality of the exchange.

Soto had talked about a fourth type of exchange—complementing the threefold standard taxonomy—in which the difference in the sums of money within the exchange was due to the different value of money in different places.[154] Molina dealt with this exchange and used Soto's explanation to justify the difference in value, but thought there was no need for a fourth category, and integrated the case into real exchange.[155]

4.2.1. *Petty or Manual Exchange*

Petty exchange, in which one type of currency was changed into another, was the least complicated type of exchange from a moral point of view. Molina dealt with it in a short disputation, disputation 400: "Whether it is licit to take more than the legally fixed commission in petty exchange."[156]

---

de arte megotiatoria circa emptiones et commutationes disput. 339 dictum ostensumque est. Esse vero utilem Reipublicae sicut et illam aliam, ex sequentibus erit manifestum." II. 398. 3. p. 385.

[152] "Universim autem in cambiis semper est attendendum, num ratione temporis aliquid ultra sortem accipiatur: quoniam quicquid ratione temporis accipitur, nisi ex capite lucri cessantis, aut ex aliquo laio, excusetur, iuste accipitur, usurasque in ea acceptione intervenit: eo quod ratione mutui formaliter, aut virtute, intervenientes accipiatur." II. 398. 4. p. 385.

[153] "Nempe, quando in cambio solum accipitur incrementum ab donationem temporis, exspectatamve solutionem, quod est usura. Diccitur autem siccum, quasi humorem carens, sterileque ad fructificandum lucrumve offerendum. Atque in hac significatione usurpantur haec vocabula in bulla Pii V de cambiis. Quia nomine, cambii sicci, intellegunt cambium, quo campsor prius dat, ut cum incremento postea accipiat, esto receptio futura sit in loco distanti. Exsistimo autem ex eadem radice habuisse ortum acceptionem hanc: eo quod eiusmodi cambium usurarium ex sui natura sit existimandum, et sterile ad licite aliquid ultra sortem accipiendum, ut multi doctores affirmant." II. 398. 6. pp. 385–386.

[154] Noonan. 336.

[155] "Arbitror tamen necesarium non esse distinguere quartam hanc speciem: quandoquidem diversitas haec ex circumstantiis locorum distantium consurgit, sed inter explicandum capita, ex quibus in cambio ob loci distantiam licitum est accipere aliquid ultra id, quod campsor dat, sufficienter id caput explicabitur." II. 398. 5. p. 385.

[156] "Utrum pro cambio minuto licitum campsori sit incrementum accipere ultra pretia monetarum lege taxata." II. 399. pp. 386–388.

The basic doctrine was that petty exchange was useful for the commonwealth, and that its practitioners should adjust to the regulations issued by the public authority, who, seeking to avoid fraud, usually fixed the commission that ought to be charged. This commission fixed by the public authority for the common good was binding in conscience, and any excess in what was charged was liable to restitution. The main question Molina discussed was whether an exchanger could practice his trade without a public license, in cities where the matter was not regulated. Where no regulation existed, different circumstances would account for setting a fair commission.[157] We should note two things. First, a conventional decision by the legitimate authority for the common good was binding in conscience, even if the case itself did not incline naturally towards one solution or another. We can see here a practical example of how natural law and positive law interact in Molina's moral theology. A decision by the legitimate authority binds in conscience; the claim upon conscience, however, comes through natural law. Where natural law was 'indifferent' positive law could determine an issue. Secondly, we should note that for the sake of the common good, public authorities could suppress the commission, which in itself was a legitimate profit.[158]

Although a simple matter for moral discussion, petty exchange was not a minor concern, because there was an ample amount of sheer fraud at the fairs of the time. The large amount of legislation about the rate that could be charged in money exchange was a sign that many abuses were being committed.[159] In Medina a special office was created to check the weight and the value of coins, in order to prevent fraud.[160]

4.2.2. *A Strange Monetary System*

The reason for the creation of an office to check the weight and value of coins was a clear desire to avoid fraud, something as old as trade. A troublesome factor in the sixteenth century, however, was the monetary system. The monetary systems of the time were not as clearly defined as those of our day, where within a territory there is only one currency subdivided into smaller units. Additionally, in our monetary systems there is no metallic value to the currency, and the parity between coins

---

[157] II. 399. 4 and 6. p. 387.

[158] II. 399. 5. p. 387.

[159] Cristobal Espejo and Julian Paz, *Las antiguas ferias de Medina del Campo. Investigación histórica acerca de ellas* (Valladolid: Imprenta La Nueva Pincia, 1908). 109.

[160] Ibid. 87. The book provides a minute description of the money exchange practices in the Medina fairs, pp. 71–128.

within one monetary system cannot be altered because of a variation of the prices of precious metals. That was not the case with the monetary systems of the sixteenth century, where within a single territory several different monetary systems might coexist. Foreign and old coins were kept in circulation, simply because of their metallic content. Gold and silver coins coexisted with an equivalence fixed by law that could, and did, change. To complicate matters further, the metal value of the coins caused the coins exchange rates to vary according to the prices of silver and gold.

In a long disputation, disputation 400,[161] Molina offered a minute account of the monetary system in force in Spain and Portugal at the end of the sixteenth century. United under the same king, the two kingdoms had different administrations, but strong commercial ties. In Spain and Portugal many different gold and silver coins circulated, but there was neither a gold nor a silver standard as we understand it in our day. In 1566, during Phillip II's reign, the legally established equivalence between the golden escudos and the silver maravedis changed from 350 maravedis per escudo—the exchange rate fixed by Charles V when he created the escudos—to 400 maravedis.[162] The gold content of the escudos, however, did not change. Old coins, such as Isabella and Ferdinand's ducat, were still in circulation.[163] Because of its gold content, a merchant would always accept a Venetian ducat, or any other hard currency, in an exchange.[164] In this complicated monetary system fraud was easy, and the resolution of problems related to money exchange became more complicated.

---

[161] "De variis aureis, atque argenteis monetis in Castella et in Lusitania temporis progressu cusis, deque earum valore tunc, et modo, atque valore massae auri, et argenti, in eisdem regnis diversis temporibus." II. 400. pp. 388–393.

[162] II. 400. 9. p. 390.

[163] A ducat was a 23 and ¼ carat gold coin minted by Isabella and Ferdinand. Molina tells us that out of half a pound of gold 65 ⅓ ducats could be minted. A coin of two ducats was called a doubloon. Later a doubloon was used to name a two-escudos coin. An escudo was a 22 carat gold coin minted in the time of Charles V. Out of half a pound of gold, 68 escudos were minted. The problem was that there were also silver coins, the maravedis and the reales, silver coins of lesser value, but with equivalence to the gold coins and among themselves. The exchange rate among these also changed with time.

[164] A good and brief account of the international rates of exchange can be found in Valentín Vázquez de Prada, "Moneda y cambios internacionales a finales del siglo XVI y comienzos del XVII," in *Aportaciones a la historia económica y social: España y Europa, siglos XVI–XVIII.*, ed. Jesús María Usunariz Gayoa (Pamplona: Eunsa, 2000). 401–407.

4.2.3. *The Difficulties of Exchange Bills*

By the second half of the century the fairs had become more like monetary clearing centers than centers in which goods were traded, making more acute the moral problem related to money exchange. Part of the scandal expressed by theologians was that financial business was so profitable that merchants would abandon productive activities in favor of financial activities.[165] A merchant could easily obtain a 12% annual profit in money exchange. It was not an exorbitant return, but it still tempted merchants away from ordinary trade. A speculative money exchange between places in which money was abundant and those in which it was scarce led to frequent bankruptcies.[166] Additionally, speculation created scarcity of money even in the fairs of Spain—something rather ironical—forcing the merchants to borrow money on a long-term basis at higher interest rates.[167] The fairs had also grown to be the places where the Crown financed the often depleted public treasury.[168]

We can see why the Spanish moralists devoted much more attention to foreign exchange than did the medieval schoolmen. Reading the theologians of the time, one is tempted to think that they had a great animosity against trade and merchants, but reading about the proposals sent by the cities to the Cortes, and the legislation approved by the Cortes, reveals that apprehension about the conduct of the merchants was not limited to theologians. City councils, the Crown, public officials, legislators and even merchants, who suffered the most from excessive interest rates or from payment in currency of lesser value, were worried about commercial and financial practices that did not seem honest, and in the long run hampered trade.[169] Banking and bankers were also under suspicion as they helped the various nations and city-states wage war.[170]

Again following Mercado, Molina distinguished two types of bankers. A first group of bankers operated in trade fairs, their main business being the management of payments in different places. A second group of bankers were situated in large cities and although they participated in the trade of virtual transportation of money, their main business was to

[165] Grice-Hutchinson, *The School of Salamanca; Readings in Spanish Monetary Theory, 1544–1605*. 10.
[166] Ibid. 17.
[167] Ibid. 7.
[168] Espejo and Paz. 129–170.
[169] About the illegal acts see Ibid. 71–128.
[170] de Roover, "The Scholastic Attitude toward Trade and Entrepeneurship." 215.

receive deposits, which they used to finance other business operations.[171] The first type of trade raised the problem of the lawfulness of an apparently unequal money exchange. The second type of trade raised the problem of credit creation. I shall analyze these two problems in the next two sections.

4.3. *Different Values of Money*

Having discussed the problems of petty exchange, Molina moved on to discuss real exchange or exchange conducted through exchange bills, *cambium per litteras*. These were of two types. In the first, the money-exchanger received money with the obligation to return it in another place, at a later date. In the second, the money exchanger gave money and would receive it later in another place at a later date.

It was clear that if in an exchange contract the only reason to receive something above the capital was the passing of time, this was a case of disguised usury. And so the theologians had to look for other legitimate titles. *Lucrum cessans* was one of the legitimate titles to justify the gain of the merchant.[172] I have previously discussed it with respect to usury; therefore I will explain, through the examples that Molina gave, the two main reasons, exclusive of money exchange, that allow for a difference in the sum exchanged.

The first legitimate reason for a difference between a sum given in, say, Medina and the sum received in, say, Antwerp was the cost of transportation. There was a cost and a risk in transporting money from one place to another. Even if the transportation of money was virtual, that is, it did not really happen, as it usually did not, the cost of virtual transportation was a legitimate title to charge for the exchange. Merchants did not transport the money, but issued exchange bills instructing their representatives in others cities to pay a certain sum. This led some theologians to question the validity of the cost of transportation title; since there was really no transportation and the merchant did not incur any travel expenses,

[171] Belda. 61–62. II. 408. 1. pp. 404–405.

[172] He reports something which reaffirms what he had said in the disputation about the lawfulness of *lucrum cessans* as a title of interest. Being in Lisbon a merchant came to him and told him that for merchants, money was their tool and that without it they ceased to be able to do business and make a profit. The merchant had said: "Scias, inquit, instrumentum, quo mercatores negotiamur, ac lucramur, esse pecuniam, et quo plus pecuniae habemus, eo nos plus negotiari ac lucrari." II. 404. 11. p. 401. He had shortly before mentioned the title of *lucrum cessans* in II, 398, 4, p. 385.

and did not run the risk of a real transportation. Still, Molina thought it legitimate to charge for this as a virtual transportation cost. In doing so he reasoned by analogy: if a man were to go on a trip, and another man wanting to transfer a horse from one place to another should ask him to take his horse to another city, although it meant no trouble for the man traveling—and could actually be an advantage—it would still be just to charge the horse owner for a service that he would have paid for anyway.[173]

There was, however, a second and greater theoretical and moral problem that experience brought to bear on the matter. When money was sent from Castille to Lisbon the agio, that is the exchange rate, was much smaller than the agio for sending money from Castille to Lisbon. Molina reports that in Castille the real was worth 34 maravedis, while in Lisbon one would get 40 maravedis for a real. If a Lisbon merchant needed to purchase merchandise in the fairs of Medina worth 10,000 reales, he would be charged in Lisbon 400,000 maravedis for an exchange bill allowing him to pay off his debt. Yet a merchant in Medina who needed to pay 10,000 reales in Lisbon, would be charged 340,000 maravedis for an exchange bill that would allow him to accomplish the same item. Transporting money from Lisbon to Medina could not be that much more expensive that transporting it from Medina to Lisbon.[174] This difference could not be explained through the virtual transportation argument.

Soto had been the first to deal with the different values of money. Azpilicueta replaced the idea of estimation with that of purchasing power, thus transforming the theory and leaving it ready for diffusion. The theory was popularized by Mercado, and Molina supported it with solid arguments.[175] Molina explained it by saying that the value of money was different in one place from another, due to two factors: law or custom and supply and demand for money. Law or custom were the first cause for a difference in the value of money; a silver real was worth 34 maravedis

[173] "Ac hoc dubium affirmanter est respondendum. Ratio est, quoniam effectus ac ministerium, quod alteri praestat, valet re vera incrementum illud: per accidens autem est, quod alia via id etiam redundet in commodus ipsisus ..." II. 405. 2. p. 403.

[174] A similar example was reported by Tomás de Mercado. According to Grice-Hutchinson Mercado says in his *Suma de tratos* that when money was sent from Flanders to Spain the agio was much smaller than the agio for sending money from Spain to Flanders. Mercado reports that in 1583 the exchange rate was 360 maravedies in Medina to 410 in Antwerp, and 360 in Antwerp to 435 in Medina. [*Suma de tratos*, 88]. Grice Hutchinson, *The School of Salamanca; Readings in Spanish Monetary Theory, 1544–1605*. 15.

[175] Pribram. 29.

in Castille and 40 in Portugal.[176] The second reason for a difference in value was the supply and demand for money. When there was an abundance of money in one place, it was worth less when it came to buying goods.[177] Today we would say that the purchasing power of that money was lower. Molina knew that the same amount of money bought fewer goods in Peru than in Spain;[178] or bought fewer goods in Molina's time than eighty years before.[179] Not even throughout Spain was the purchasing power of money stable.[180] Molina realized that demand and supply of money caused the value of money to vary, the same way as happened with other goods.[181] The justice of any exchange resided in its equality; an exchange in which the sums of money exchanged were not equal could, nevertheless, be just if the reason was the different value of money in various place.[182] To find what the right exchange

---

[176] "Uno, quia lege publica, aut consuetudine recepta, diversum valorem comparatione aliarum monetarum habet in locis diversis. Quo pacto in Lusitania ducatus valet 400 reais, et in Castella 375 maravedinos, realis argenteus valet in Castella triginta quattuor maravedinos, et in Lusitania iam hodie valet 40 ..." II. 406. 1. p. 404.

[177] "Altero modo potest pecunia aliqua habere maiorem valorem in uno loco, quam in alio; quia in uno est minor copia illius, quam alio. Caeteris einm paribus, quo maior est pecuniae copia in aliquo loco, eo minus in eo valet ad res emendas; et ad comparanda caetera, quae pecunia non sunt. Quemadmodum enim abundantia mercium facit eas decrescere in pretio, existente aequali pecunia ac mercatorum copia, sic etiam pecunia abundantia facit merces accrescere in pretio, existente eadem mercium ac meractorum copia, atque adeo in causa est, ut, pecunia ipsa in se valescat, ad res emendas ad comparandas." II. 406. 2. pp. 404–405.

[178] "Inde etiam videmus, multo minus valere pecuniam in novo Orbe, praesetim Peru, ubi maior illius est abundantia, quam in Hispanis." II. 405. 2. p. 405.

[179] "Hinc videbimus, longe minus valere hodie pecuniam in Hispaniis ad comparandas res, propter illius abundantiam, quam valeret octoginta annis antea." II. 406. 2. p. 405.

[180] "Neque hic idem pecunaiae valor est ubique aequalis in Hispaniis, sed diversus: regulariterque minus valere solet pecunia in Hispali, quo classes ex novo orbe appellant, et ubi ea ratione solet esse maior illius abundantia, quam valeat in aliis easundem Hispaniarum locis." II. 406. 2. p. 405.

[181] "Pecunia quippe unius loci, commutanda pro pecunia in alio, at negotiationem, lucraque mercatorum, et caetera quae commemorata sunt, habet se instar mercis leges minime taxatae, cuius valor modo accrescit, modo decrescit, prout illius est maior, vel minor, indigentia in uno loco, quam in alio: quare sicut abundantia aut penuria alicuius mercis, maior vel minor illius necessitas, copia maior vel minor mercatorum, eam facit in valori in aliquo loco." II. 406. 3. p. 405.

[182] "Observandum autem est, nos in hac disputatione non arguere de incremento, quod campsor rationii cambii potest licite accipere, neque de capitibus unde illud potest licite accipere; sed de commutatione ipsa(seclusis illis capitibuset secluso eo incremento) inquirimus, num sit ad aequalitatem, quando pecunia, quae in un loco minus valet comparatione pecuniarum aerearum minutarum commutatur pro alia reddenda in loco, ubi comparatione pecunairum aeraearum plus valet, an vero non sit ad aequalitatem, sed compensandum est excessus ille, ut contracttus sit ad aequalitatem." II. 407. 1. p. 406.

rate was, there was no better rule than the *communis aestimatio* of the merchants, whose practice was a superior rule than the opinion of the scholastic doctors.[183] Praxis was a better source of moral knowledge than any purely theoretical analysis. This movement was possible, because in Molina's natural law theory, *ius naturale* was what the nature of the case dictated, not what was universally equal everywhere. The legally fixed value of money did not hold a universal claim valid everywhere. What determined the *ius* was the universal claim regarding the equivalence of the exchange, along with the nature of the case. A change in the analytical natural law allowed a non-problematical change in the moral assessment of the case.

This early version of the purchasing-power theory removed the taint of usury that accompanied almost any type of money exchange, because it gave a satisfactory explanation of the movements of capital. It was the most original and noteworthy achievement in economic theory of the Spanish scholastics.[184] It also refuted the idea that a change in the value of money amounted to the debasement of currency. Up to that date there was a vague notion that the value of money depended on its rarity; the effects of debasement were also known. Copernicus had written a treatise on the debasement of money.[185] Molina dealt with this problem in disputation 312 of the second treatise,[186] but there he differentiated debasement from money exchange.

The theological discussion regarding exchange cleared up the differences between lending and money exchange, gave birth to an incipient theory of the purchasing power of money, and brought about the abandonment of the idea that money was a fixed measure, allowing the recognition of the effect of market circumstances on its value.[187]

---

183 "Non potest autem melior alia regula hac in parte tradi, quam ut attendatur ad commune pretium fori cambiorum mercatorum inter se ab aliis locis ad illum, et ab eo loco ad alia, atque pretio illi tamquam iusto, et in communi aestiamtione mercatorum inter se recepto, stetur." II. 407. 8. p. 407. "In contrarium est, et fuit semper mercatorum praxis, qui meluis norunt rerum aestimationes, quam Doctores scholastici, et quorum iudicio est potius standum circa rerum valorem; praesertim quando illo inter se utuntur in negotiationibus, quas inter se ipsos exercent, nemine eorum conquerente, aut reclamante." II. 407. 2. p. 407.

184 Grice-Hutchinson, *The School of Salamanca; Readings in Spanish Monetary Theory, 1544–1605*. 52–53.

185 Ibid. 34.

186 II. 312. 154.

187 Noonan. 340.

4.4. *The Problems of the Creation of Credit*

I have shown how exchange bills were linked to the economic problem of what we today call the parity purchasing power of money, and how the moral problem led to the development of economic theory and a new ethical assessment of the morality of exchange bills. There was yet another problem linked to exchange bills: credit creation. Money was not only being virtually taken from one place to another, 'near money' was also being created by the bankers when they lent part of the money they had received as deposits.[188] Near money affected the money supply.

Molina did not pose the question of credit creation—to expect to find this question in his writings would be anachronistic—but he did in a sense deal with the problem when he studied credit sale, lending and exchange bills.[189] Molina knew about the creation of near money when he said that the merchants used the money of depositors to trade, because it was almost impossible that they would all come at once to request their deposits. In places such as Seville, Lisbon or Antwerp, bankers took deposits free of charge and used the money deposited with them to finance the operations of other businesses. The gold and silver arriving from the Indies, as well as the reserves that any merchant would keep, served as a basis for the creation of credit and near money.[190] Molina considered the bankers as real owners of the money because when they receive deposits they agreed to give back not the same money, but an equal quantity of money. Therefore, they did not do wrong in using that money for other business purposes.[191] They would sin, however, if they ran an immoderate risk in lending it or lent too much, even if they did not

[188] Near money (quasi money) is "an asset that is immediately transferable and may be used to settle some but not all debts, although it is not as liquid as banknotes and coins." Bills of exchange are examples of near money. Near money is not included in the money supply definitions. *A Dictionary of Finance and Banking*, (Oxford University Press, 2005, accessed January 23 2007); available from ⟨http://www.oxfordreference.com/views/ENTRY.html?subview=Main&entry=t20.e2466⟩.

[189] Belda. 54–55.

[190] Grice-Hutchinson, *The School of Salamanca; Readings in Spanish Monetary Theory, 1544–1605*. 8.

[191] "Dum autem adversa non utuntur fortuna, cum multorum hominum pecunias habeant in suo deposito, ut mercatorum, et campsorum Olyssiponensium, Genuensium, Florentinorum, Venetorum, Metinensium, Toletanorum, et plurium aliorum, habeantque nonnullorum multa ducatorum millia in deposito, nunquam evenit, ut depositores omnes ita pecunia indigeant, quin semper multa ducatorum millia maneant in deposito, quipus bancarii megotiari suo comodo, ac detrimento possint. Sunt vero tam hi, quam caeteri bancarii, veri domini pecuniae, quam apud se depositam habent, in quo multum ab aliis depositariis differunt ..." II. 408. 5. p. 406.

go bankrupt. Their obligation was to be prudent, and always ready to give back to their clients the same quantity of money they had deposited.[192]

Molina was aware of other ways of creating near money.[193] When someone became a guarantor of a debt, the person benefiting from the guarantee acquired a purchasing power that was not balanced by anyone's losing it. Near money was again created, and the guarantor did not suffer any sacrifice if the person benefiting from the guarantee repaid his debt. In this case credit had been created and Molina considered that the guarantor had a just title to profit for the onerous service he rendered.[194] Another practice was that of allowing depositors to overdraft and another that of granting a credit against the deposit of some financial instruments.[195]

In all the cases he examined, Molina approved the practice of credit creation,[196] although he admitted that there could be abuses and misconduct resulting from it. His basic principles to judge the concrete case were three. The first principle was that the title to charge for the money exchange was not to be the mere passing of time. Time, however, affected the price of credit because it could change the liquidity preference, that is, the factors that determined the amount of money that merchants wanted to hold. But this was not charging for the mere passing of time.[197] The second principle was freedom of contracts; credit had to be granted freely, and not as an imposition connected to some other business operation.[198] The third principle was the prudence of those granting credit so that the deposits they had taken were safe. We could summarize these three principles saying that no exchange contract could be charged for, unless there were a justifying *titulus extrinsecus*.[199]

---

[192] "Circa bancarios, praesertim prioris generis, est observandum, illos lethaliter peccare, si pecuniam depositam in tanta quantitate ita suis negotiationibus expendant, ut inhabiles reddantur ad tempore congruo solvendum, quae depositores petierint, aut solvere iusserint, ex pecunia, quam in ipsorum deposito habent." "Nec solum tunc lethalither peccant, quando res sinistre succedit, sed etiam quando succedit prospere, idque propter periculum, cui se exponunt, nocendi deponentibus, fideiussoribus, quos pro deposito dederunt." II. 408. 7. p. 406 bis. I use bis for this page and for some others because in the edition I am using there is a pagination error and, after page 408 the next page number is again 405, until it reaches again 408. Then pagination goes back to normal.

[193] Belda. 69–70.

[194] II. 319. 1–4. pp. 167–168. This case he analyzed in the section of usury.

[195] II. 408. 9. p. 406 bis–7 bis.

[196] Belda. 69–70.

[197] II. 404. 2. p. 400.

[198] Belda. 66.

[199] Ibid. 69.

4.5. *Moral Dimensions of Money*

Money exchange practices posed a major moral problem in the sixteenth century. Pure and sheer fraud was the first dimension of the problem. A second dimension of the problem was the need to explain and justify the apparent inequality of exchange. Molina only hinted at the purchasing power theory when he talked about the different values of money in different places, and he also pointed out some of the basic factors that affected this difference in value. He offered a precise analysis of business practices, but did not quantify the way the different factors worked in determining the price of money. Neither did Molina quantify what percentage of deposits ought to be kept by the banker when creating credit, in order to be able to return money to his clients. Both the determination of the different values of money and the percentage of the deposits a banker could use to create credit were left as matters of prudence.

In Molina's time mathematical analysis had not yet reached the level of development and acceptance that it would soon have. Additionally, Molina's epistemology was not inclined to expect a perfectly precise knowledge of reality. He shared this view to some extent with all the scholastics of his time, but also his theory of the middle science helped him to move in that direction. Prudence was the virtue that brought about what today we attribute to calculus. Prudence was indeed the science of experience, but of a morally informed experience and not just of empirical data. Molina linked it to justice. Also the norm—and custom was an important kind of norm—accounted for a good share of an informed moral decision. The importance of doing, the nominalistic skew toward the law and the communal dimension of any virtuous act converged in the importance of custom.

5. Conclusion

In this chapter we have analyzed Molina's treatment of three economic practices: usury, pricing and money exchange. The three of them give us a clear picture of the main moral issues in the economic ethics of the age. The term 'economic ethics' is somehow a misnomer because what we understand today as 'economic' and 'ethics' were the same discipline in the sixteenth century. Although I have tried to demostrate as much as possible how Luis de Molina helped in the development of economic science and how that affected his moral theology, Luis de Molina did not write an economic treatise. He wrote a book on justice and law. His main concern was justice, which in the Thomistic framework in which Molina worked was a moral virtue.

Up to this point my work has been dedicated mainly to analysis. In the first chapter I presented the economic, scientific, and theological realities of the sixteenth century. In my second chapter I laid out Molina's fundamental moral theology. The third chapter addressed the theological and economic problem of private property. The chapter now concluding has dealt with three specific economic practices. All these works point to the final chapter, treating Luis de Molina's ideas about justice in an economic context, and a conclusion revealing Molina's significance for today. I have shown that Molina worked with economic theories that were incipient and sketchy compared to our contemporary analysis. The focus of my work, however, is not economic theory. What can be learned from Luis de Molina is how in his work theology, economics and issues regarding justice come together. In this we can still draw inspiration from his ideas about justice, "for justice is undying."[200]

[200] Wisdom 1:15.

CHAPTER FIVE

JUSTICE AS VIRTUE IN AN ECONOMIC CONTEXT

1. Justice a Virtue

1.1. *Transforming Paradigms*

Molina set out to write a commentary on Aquinas's *Summa* and ended up writing two independent treatises on two important and related theological matters. *De Iustitia et Iure* was the result of an initial project to write the standard commentary on the *Summa*, something that was expected of any good theologian of the time. But undertaking this task was a recent innovation in the field. The first to write an influential commentary on the *Summa* had been Cajetan at the beginning of the sixteenth century. Up to that time, the standard academic work for a professor was a commentary on Peter Lombard's *Sentences*. Molina's project nevertheless was never accomplished, because changing times were rendering it impossible. By the end of the sixteenth century the theological literary genres had been so greatly transformed that no one thought any more of producing a commentary on the *Summa* or on Lombard's *Sentences*. Molina was one of the agents of this transformation both with the *Concordia* and *De Iustitia et Iure*.

Molina's *De Iustitia et Iure* sought to provide the theologian with a comprehensive treatise that would survey everything that was vital for the usefulness of the governance of the Church and the Christian commonwealth.[1] Jean Porter rightly states that "the discussion of justice (II^a–IIae, qq. 58–122) is the longest, the most complex, and arguably the most difficult treatment of a particular virtue in the *Summa theologiae*"; its length resulted from "the complexity of the traditions which informed his own reflections."[2] Notwithstanding Aquinas' prolix treatment of the questions on justice, Molina found the Thomas's approach to be, if most

[1] "nihil viro theologo deerit, quod ad Ecclesiae gubernationem et Reipublica Christiana utilitatem necessaries fuerit iudicatum" I. Prologue. p. 1.

[2] Jean Porter, "The Virtue of Justice," in *The Ethics of Aquinas*, ed. Stephen J. Pope (Washington D.C.: Georgetown University Press, 2002). 272.

wise, actually insufficient. That is why he decided to depart from the idea of a mere commentary and opted for the literary genre that Domingo de Soto had inaugurated in 1553, a treatise on justice and law. By doing so he was able to deal with many of the new problems that were arising, while incorporating them into the Thomistic order.[3] In abandoning the Thomistic outline, the notion of justice was also transformed. Molina's notion of justice was not a mere repetition of Aquinas' but a new one, transformed by theological, historical and economic developments.

Molina began his work with treatise one, in which he gave a brief general overview of justice that followed the Thomistic tradition. Then he proceeded to analyze the particular issues of commutative justice. In the last three chapters I have analyzed Molina's doctrines of natural law, property and three specific economic topics. The work of this chapter is that of synthesizing Molina's ideas about justice. I shall present first Molina's more general overview on justice as he presented it in the first treatise; then I will highlight the elements of justice that appear in Molina's discussion of particular topics related to justice from which we can draw inspiration.

1.2. *Justice in General*

In the prologue to his work, Molina informed the reader of the outline he would follow in the treatise. The work would deal in the first treatise with justice in general, then with commutative justice for the three next treatises. The fifth treatise would be dedicated to judgment and its execution. This is the treatise in which he developed his ideas about law. The sixth and last treatise was to be dedicated to distributive justice. Molina died before completing his project, and was only able to publish the first four treatises during his lifetime. The fifth was published after his death. The sixth treatise, on distributive justice, was never written.

Had he lived longer, Molina might have had the opportunity to finish his work, yet the manner of progression in his analysis did not contribute to the possible completion. If the first treatise was a brief exposition of what justice was and of its divisions, when he began dealing with commutative justice, he analyzed thoroughly the theoretical foundation of the issues he dealt with and then he engaged in the discussion of

[3] "Hoc consilio ductus, multisque aliis gravissimus de causis permotus, ordinem D. Thomas in his 23. quaestionibus, praeter nostrum morem, relinquere, opusque hoc de iustitia in varios Tomos distributum earum loco inserere statui," I. Prologue. 1.

specific cases. This slowed down the pace of the progression of his work. We can see Molina discussing cases, after he had completed the theoretical discussion of a topic. If we compare the different contexts and elements he introduced, we see the differences between one case and the next. The method slowed the progress of the discussion, but at the same time brought the discussion closer to reality, and made it less abstract. This is one of the differences between Molina and Aquinas.

1.2.1. *Meanings of Justice*

Following Aristotle and Aquinas, Molina began by distinguishing among the various meanings of justice. Justice could mean total justice, that is, the act of any virtue, not regarded in itself as the act of an individual person, but as the act of man as part of the commonwealth; as such, justice was the virtue that ordained all acts to the common good.[4] He compared this first understanding of justice to Aristotle's exposition on prudence, where Aristotle distinguished a type of prudence that he called monastic, from a prudence that he called political. Where the former referred to the prudence that dictated the private acts of a single person, the later prescribed what each person ought to do as part of the whole community. Political prudence affected both the subjects and the prince; the latter ought to have architectonic prudence in giving the laws that determined the rights and duties of each person within the community. Political prudence, however, in the strict sense, referred to the subjects and dictated to each one of them their place in the commonwealth and what their responsibilities were in order to contribute to the common good. In a similar way justice could be compared to monastic prudence, and this was the cardinal virtue of justice.

For Molina, legal justice was a virtue analoguous to political prudence, which ordained every human action to the common good as was expected of the pact that established the way of government of the commonwealth.[5] The virtue of legal justice resided primarily in the prince,

---

[4] "Uno, pro actu cuiuscumque virtutis, non qua talis est, sed quatenus ordinatur ad commune bonum multitudinis, cuius pars est ille, qui eum excercet. Seu (et in idem redit) quatenus emanat ab homine, non ut in se singularis quaedam persona est, quae per pruentiam monasticam conformiter ad rectamrationem operatur, sed ut est pars Reipublicae; quae eo modo operando optime se habet ad suum totum, bonumque commune." I. 1. 1. p. 2.

[5] "Altero, ut qui eum elicit, bene eo sese habet ad suum totum bonumque commune, per prudentiamque politicam ab eo elicitur, quatenus pas est Reipublicae: quo pacto spectatum docet, sortiri formalem rationem iustitiae late sumptae, quae omnibus virtutibus

and it comprised not only what cohered and was in harmony with the laws, but also everything that came up to the level of the perfection and dignity of the commonwealth.[6] In his definition of legal justice Molina did not differ from Aquinas who defined it in similar terms in IIª–IIae q. 58 a. 6; however, it also bears a noteworthy parallel to prudence and the emphasis given to it. Molina drew on prudence more than Aquinas did. I have already talked about the importance of prudence in the last chapter, and I will return to it later.

Molina also considered non-moral notions of justice. He dealt first with the notion of justice inherited from the Roman legal tradition. Ulpianus had defined justice as the constant and lasting will to give each one his due. The requirements of the law (*iuris*) were to live honestly, to harm no other and to honor each according to his essential dignity.[7] Molina had studied law for a year in Salamanca before becoming a Jesuit. He had to honor his previous studies in his development of a doctrine on justice. It is especially noteworthy of this definition that he found beyond the Aristotelian-Thomistic tradition a basis for a conception of justice not merely based on law. In the Roman law tradition Molina found a notion of justice that not only required fairness in the distribution of social goods, but expected the prince to actively foster the morality of the citizens. Justice was not only granting good laws, but also establishing what fostered the virtues that the common good required.[8]

---

est communis, non quidem per essentiam, quasi sit de ratione intrinseca cuiusque earum sed quia comitatur actus omnium virtutum, in eisque invenitur modo tamen, dum sunt, in commune Reipublicae bonum eo pacto, quo explicatum est, ordinetur." I. 1. 1. p. 2. For Molina's ideas about the origin and nature of civil society and of political authority see Costello. 23–57.

[6] "Eius modo ergo virtus … postulat, adaequatur." I. 1. 4. p. 3.

[7] Digest 1.1.10 pr: "Iustitia est constans et perpetua voluntas ius suum cuique tribuendi. Iuris praecepta sunt haec: honeste vivere alterum non laedere, suum cuique tribuere."

[8] "Ex dictis infero, ad legislatores Reipublicaeque administrators, pertinere constituere, non eas solum leges, qua ad iustitiam, virtutem cardinaled, sed etiam eas, quae ad alias virtutes, fortitudinem, scilicet temperantiam, et caeteram expectant: id quo Aristoteles 5 Ethicorum capite etiam affirmavit. Munus quipped eorum est, tales susi legibus et administratione constituere cives, quales bonum commune, decusque Republicae postulat. Ad quod non satis est, si iustitita non transgrediantur, sed fortitudinem eos servare necesse est, non deserendo suum locum in bello, et temperantiam, Sodomiae vitium et alia, quae Rempublicam foedant, fugiendo, moderateque in vestitu, cultu et cibo se habendo, ne facultates inutiliter expendantur, ac molles fiant. Quo circa recte *Ulpianus l. Iustitia ff. De iustitia et iuris: Iuris,* inquit, *praecepta sunt hae, honeste vivere, alterum non laedere, suum cuique tribuere*, quibus verbis non sola iustitiae praecepta comprehenduntur." I. 1. 6. p. 3.

The theological discussion of the time moved primarily along the lines of integrating as much as one's position allowed, what had been said before on the topic being discussed. This is why Molina took a step further in presenting the idea of justice that appeared in the Bible. Molina pointed out the continuity between Aristotle and the Bible. Human justice and divine justice were intrinsically related matters. What was at stake here was the continuity between natural justice and supernatural justice, which could only be understood for Molina in the light of the Thomist maxim *natura paesuponit gratiae*. There had to be continuity between the doctrines about natural justice and those referring to divine or supernatural justice.[9] The natural doctrines about justice, according to Molina, provided an opening to talk about justice with a fully theological meaning. Justice was every act of virtue that directed human action towards God's will. The natural law had a claim on human conscience, but this claim reached its perfection through obeying the divine command.

Yet if this constituted the moment of continuity between nature and grace, Molina knew about a moment of discontinuity. He stated soon after that fulfilling the natural law was not enough to attain the supernatural end, which required grace and charity. Grace and charity were what made men and women just before God, and as much as this was so, grace and charity could be called justice in a broad sense. Regarding grace and justification he referred to *Concordia*. On the relationship between charity and justice, I will elaborate later.[10]

Molina's two main theological works were on justice. The first one in justice as justification of the sinner before God, the second one on justice as the perpetual will to give each one his due. *De Iustitia et Iure* dealt with

---

[9] "Ad primum ergo dicendum quod lex vetus distinguitur a lege naturae non tanquam ab ea omnino aliena, sed tanquam aliquid ei superaddens. Sicut enim gratia praesupponit naturam, ita oportet quod lex divina praesupponat legem naturalem." Iª–IIae q. 99 a. 2 ad 1.

[10] Charity and justice are not opposed in Molina, certainly not if charity is understood as an infused virtue. They cannot be. Nowadays, justice and charity appear as opposed or as complementary, depending on the account given and the predilection of a given author. In Molina they appear in continuity, not only in the brief and preliminary treatment of them, but also in the specific development of particular cases. They are both linked to the organic conception of society. They both work for the common good, what can help distinguishing them is the need for restitution when a sin against justice is committed, something not due in the case of sins against charity. Justice belongs to the *ius*, to what it should be because of the teleological order of reality; charity pertains to the order of grace, to things that please God, and draw man closer to him, but to things that do not pertain to the order of nature, to what we are, but to the order of the supernatural, what we are called to be by God.

the latter, but Molina made sure that the continuity and the relationship between the two were not lost by the reader; and although he reasoned most of the time in terms of the natural law, he would always leave open the door for grace, even in questions of economic justice.

There was, according to Molina, a final meaning of justice, justice as a moral virtue. It is what he focused on for the rest of the treatise. To justice in the strict sense, as that which is equal, right and fair, I shall turn my attention now.

1.2.2. *Justice as Moral Virtue*

Molina followed Aquinas closely in the definition of justice as a moral virtue. The very heading of disputation 8 in which he defined justice as a moral virtue warned the reader that he followed question 58 of the Iª–IIae. Molina reconciled the Aristotelian definition of justice (justice is the sort of habit or character that makes men apt to do what is just) with the Roman law definition (*constans et perpetua voluntas ius suum uniscuisque tribunes*), and defined justice as "the constant and perpetual will, that is, the habit that inclines one person with perseverance and steadiness to will what is just for each one."[11] As a moral virtue in the Aristotelian-Thomist tradition, it consisted in the elective habit of a moderation defined by prudence, a middle way in the case in comparison with others. Molina was not very original in the definition he gave; he was strictly following Aquinas, but the text read more smoothly and presented a synthetic definition of what Ulpianus and Aristotle had said. Aquinas presented question 58 in a more analytical way and did not actually give a synthetic definition.

Justice was divided into two major subcategories: commutative justice and distributive justice. They both referred to some duty and the establishment of some type of equality. They differed in the rule establishing that duty and that equality. Distributive justice attended to the distribution of the public goods among the different parts of the commonwealth according to a 'geometrical proportion'.[12] The idea of geometrical

[11] "Unde sensus preadicta definitioinis est, iustitia est constant et perpetua voluntas, id est, est habitus quo inclinamur cum constantia et firmitate ad volendum ius suum unicuique." I. 8. 1. p. 10.

[12] "Juxta hactenus dicta inhunc modum possumus definire iustitiam distributivam. Est iustitia particularis quae partibus Reipublicae id reddidit, quod ea ratione eis est debitum, quod bona communia si redundant, dividendaque sint partibus Reipublicae, iuxta Geometricam proportionem appropriandam. Et quia, id iuxta eam proportionem exequi, potestatibus publicis incumbit, affirmat D. Thomas 2.2. quaest. 61. art. 1 ad

proportion conveyed the idea that there was not a perfect equality among all the members of the commonwealth. In Molina's time there was no such a thing as an equality of rights among all the citizens, although basic rights, such as the rights to the goods of Creation or self-defense, were acknowledged for all.

Commutative justice was, for Molina, the type of particular justice that sought to render each one what was due in force of any other title.[13] It was in fact to this kind of justice that *De Iustita et Iure* ended up being circumscribed to, since Molina was never able to complete the sixth treatise dedicated to distributive justice.

For Molina, the division of justice was based on the division of the reality to which justice referred. The reality of the social body was what determined the taxonomy of justice. The object of justice was *ius*. The divisions of *ius* help to explain how society was conceived, as we shall see below.

1.2.3. *The Object of Justice:* Ius *and its Divisions. The Order of Reality*

I dedicated chapter two to the exposition of Molina's fundamental moral theology. Within that chapter I dedicated the largest part to the exposition of Molina's natural law theory, placing much emphasis upon the distinction between *ius* and *lex*. *Lex* could well be translated as law, but *ius* has a more problematic translation. Molina defined *ius* as the object of justice. *Ius* was actually taken by Molina in two ways. In the first way it referred to various legal bodies that regulated various aspects of life, as when we specify civil law or canon law. According to this first criterion *ius* could be divided into natural law and positive law. Positive law could, again, be divided into Divine positive law and human positive law. Human positive law was again subdivided into canon law, civil law, and *ius gentium*. This classification was the result of the conciliation of Roman law ideas with Patristic ideas about the natural law and the canonical developments of the Middle Ages.

Molina nevertheless offered another classification of *ius: ius paternum, dominativum, economicum*. This classification was not made attending to the different legislators and the constituencies that received the laws, as

tertium, virtutem hanc potissimum residere in Reipublicae rectoribus. in subditis vero solum cerni quatenus eis complacet, contentique sunt, ut in ea distributio eo modo fiat." I. 12. 5. p. 13.

[13] "Iustitiam quoque commutativam possumus etiam definire, esse iustitiam particularem, qua unicuique reddit quicquid quovis alio titulo est illi debitum." I. 12. 6. p. 13.

the previous one I have presented. *Ius paternun, dominativum* and *economicus* referred to the nature of social relations, even before the setting up of any political body and any kind of government. *Ius paternum* referred to what was just between a father and a son; *ius dominativum* to the relationship between a slave and his master; and *ius oeconomicus* to the relationship between husband and wife. In these three types of *ius*, there was actually a measure of inequality: a son was not equal to his father, nor a slave to his master nor a wife to her husband. These basic inequalities are inadmissible for us today. Yet what is important in our analysis is that justice and the just referred to the analysis of reality, not just to a human construct and pact. In offering this threefold taxonomy of *ius*, Molina was linking justice to the order of reality and to nature. There was a fundamental human sociability prior to any government and it implied rights and duties. Justice had as its object the *ius*, that is the right; but this right was determined by reality itself, not by a mere common agreement on certain rules. Justice was not primarily a matter of fair play, but of a clear and precise understanding of reality. This call for reality was not a call for rigidity, but it actually allowed for great flexibility. I have pointed out in the previous chapter how the development of the analytical natural law allowed the development of the judgments passed through the normative natural law. Also in the third chapter I established how natural law principles and the order of reality played a role in Molina's conception of private property.[14] The reality of society informed the ideas of justice; these were neither some basic conventional principles, nor a moralization of some roughly observed sociological or economic regularities of conduct.

Up to this point I have related Molina's general ideas about justice. Now I will proceed to synthesize some of the elements that emerged in the analysis of the previous chapter that can assist us in understanding better Molina's ideas about justice, and particularly those things relevant to moral economic analysis that were not explicit in the common Aristotelian-Thomist taxonomies of the time. They are not explicitly developed by Molina, and sometimes not even reflected upon, because

[14] Molina's disputations on slavery provide another example of the interplay among natural law principles (all were created free), reality (yet reality might allow slavery), and circumstances (and in the way it is conducted the Portuguese slave trade off the coasts of Africa is a mortal sin that affects the king, his ministers, and the priests and bishops that easily absolve slave traders without demanding restitution). II. 32–37. pp. 86–110.

they are part of the scientific paradigm to which he belonged. These elements are crucial for his moral analysis. By examining them closely we can detect in what way they differ from our own conceptions and draw then perhaps some inspiration from these observations.

2. The Importance of Cultural Contextualization

2.1. *The Detailed Analysis of Casuistry*

The scholastic treatment of justice came within the discussion of contracts. The Scholastics did not have a vision of an economic system in the sense we have today, although they often discussed matters of justice that pertained to society. They judged the justice of a certain contract or a certain trade practice.[15] Their discussion of certain basic issues, such as the legitimacy of private property, and the discussion of contracts offer points of departure for exploring their views on economic justice and this opens up the possibility of learning something valuable for our day.

The lengthy scholastic exploration of cases resulted in mammoth treatises, which in our mind become almost unbearable. Nevertheless these treatises bear witness to a concept of justice that was complex and that took an interest in very concrete situations, because the justice or injustice of an economic practice resided not just in certain theoretical principles, but was also affected by the very particular case. Justice was not a schematic theory projected upon reality, but something to be found in particular situations. Molina had said that the *ius* was to be sought in the concrete case.[16] This treatment offers us a very good example of the cultural embeddedness of moral reasoning, and particularly of moral reasoning on ethics and economics. It instructs us that moral rules do not exist in a vacuum. Moral rules must be applied in particular historical and cultural circumstances. Even when the moral principles were clear, as they were for Molina in his natural law theory, the applicability of the principle required the determination of how the reality being analyzed was constituted, and what principles were invoked to resolve the case. It implied the distinction between related, yet different acts, the acceptable

[15] de Roover, *La pensé économique des scolastiques. doctrines et méthodes*. 17.

[16] "Hoc est, cuius obligatio oritur ex natura ipsa rei, de qua est praeceptum ac lex naturalis, et non ex arbitrio voluntate praecipientis. Et quia res eandem naturam retinet se apud omnes, idcirco ius naturale idem est, eandemque vim apud omnes habet." V. 49. 1. p. 161.

exemptions, the legitimate extensions of some cases and the logical deductions that could be drawn from some principles.[17]

Casuistry has often been misunderstood, as Jonsen and Toulmin have shown. The cases were nothing more than generic contexts of a scientific analysis: a set of assumptions that tried to delimit the reality under examination. Today an economist has to specify the precise economic conditions that constitute a monopoly or a free market. That was what casuistry did, not in order merely to describe what happened, but to pass a moral judgment on what had been described. Molina performed a detailed economic analysis and then rendered a moral judgment on things. He was affected by the scientific trends of the time, the importance of doing and the minute description of reality, but he also in turn influenced the same scientific trends. He contributed to the development of economic analysis in the search for a better understanding of morality. For him it was clear that the investigation of reality always featured a moral dimension.

One of the results that my research offers is the certainty that the criteria of economic rationality have evolved along with history, sometimes representing a real split from the economic rationality of previous times. This forces us to perform a cultural contextualization of economic rationality, which even today is certainly influenced and based in culture—understood in a very broad sense—that includes values. Economic rationality is affected by values even if economists prefer to engage in some type of hermeneutic reduction that excludes moral considerations from the generic contexts they work with. Just as moral theology is affected by social sciences, changing patterns of social sciences influence moral reasoning. There is no such thing as pure facts that we then hold up for moral analysis. We must be reflective about the way the patterns of thought of the sciences affect our moral reasoning and how social dynamics affect moral reasoning.

When an economist describes a set of conditions in order to study a certain economic situation, he is doing what the scholastic doctors did in defining a case. Not by chance is the Latin expression *caeteris paribus* a common tag at the end of the description of an economic situation, to alert readers that the analysis is valid if all the other variables remain unaltered.[18] The study of scholastic theology, an endeavor which took

[17] Noonan. 3.

[18] The common economic term *ceteris paribus* is a term that comes from the scholastic moral analysis, a reminder of the days when ethics and economics were not estranged.

considerable interest in economic issues, has shown us the cultural, and moral, embeddedness of economic reasoning.

2.2. *Cultural Embeddedness of Economic Practices*

There is always a development in what a term means according to its social use. This cannot be ignored when thinking about moral theology and economics. In the case of usury, we can see how at a certain moment it became clear that money was not used anymore as a consumer good, but had become a 'tool' to create wealth. It took theologians some time to appreciate this social development. There was somehow an attachment of certain value judgments to certain acts, but as society changed, these acts acquired a different meaning, a different social significance. In a loan to a poor person for the sake of consumption, interest would endanger the person's life, especially if the interest was as high as 35 percent, and would be, therefore, immoral. But when the case became that of a merchant lending to another merchant for the sake of profit, the situation was transformed in nature.

Cajetan, and later Soto, opposed the *montes pietatis*, regarding them as institutionalized usury. There were, indeed, features of the *montes* that matched the basic elements of the definition of usury. Yet Cajetan had not been a rigorist regarding usury, and although he displayed some suspicion regarding the triple contract, he did not plainly reject it, but was willing to accept that it could be just in certain cases. Similarly we

---

Alfred Marshall in his *Principles of Economics* said about the notion of ceteris paribus: "The element of time is a chief cause of those difficulties in economic investigations which make it necessary for man with his limited powers to go step by step; breaking up a complex question, studying one bit at a time, and at last combining his partial solutions into a more or less complete solution of the whole riddle. In breaking it up, he segregates those disturbing causes, whose wanderings happen to be inconvenient, for the time in a pound called Ceteris Paribus. The study of some group of tendencies is isolated by the assumption other things being equal: the existence of other tendencies is not denied, but their disturbing effect is neglected for a time. The more the issue is thus narrowed, the more exactly can it be handled: but also the less closely does it correspond to real life. Each exact and firm handling of a narrow issue, however, helps towards treating broader issues, in which that narrow issue is contained, more exactly than would otherwise have been possible. With each step more things can be let out of the pound; exact discussions can be made less abstract, realistic discussions can be made less inexact than was possible at an earlier stage." Alfred Marshall, *Principles of Economics*, 9th ed. (London, New York: Macmillan for the Royal Economic Society, 1961). Book V. Chapter V. in paragraph V. V. 10. Anyone familiar with casuistry will recognize the origin of such a notion.

have seen Soto developing the idea that money held different value in different places, which accounted for the apparent inequality of money exchange. This notion built on Cajetan's observation that the state could fix the legal value of money in its territory, but lacked that power outside national boundaries. We observe here two men who were willing to accept differentiations in matters of usury, and yet were inflexible about a practice that helped the poor and had been approved by an ecumenical council. We cannot question Cajetan's and Soto's intellectual reasons against the *montes*, but we certainly can infer that part of their opposition, consciously or unconsciously, arose from the Franciscan origin of the idea. Franciscans and Dominicans had been at odds theologically since the almost simultaneous foundation of both orders. The example shows us that *odium theologicum* was sometimes a weighty reason. According to Bertrand Russell the antidote to *odium theologicum* was science,[19] however, we can see analogous phenomena in economic science. The theological discussion was not influenced by merely theological aspects, but also by a power struggle and non-scientific friendships or enmities.

Another example of the cultural embeddedness of economic reasoning and its consequent moral dimension can be found in language, a basic tool for any science and especially for a social science such as economics. Although some authors revile the scholastic theologians for their naiveté in the analysis of usury, a linguistic approach to the problem shows us that even if the scholastic theories might be long forgotten, part of their legacy still endures. The major European languages attach to the word 'usury' a negative connotation. *Usura* in classical Latin was merely what we would understand today as interest, the sum above the capital paid in a loan. Usury today is not lending money at interest, but lending money with an abusive interest. Employing the word 'interest' to refer to the payment above the principal is a scholastic development, coming out of Roman legal sources. The scholastics certainly bequeathed us the idea that there were unconscionable or exorbitant interest rates, an idea still present in modern legal bodies. The idea commonly accepted today that there exist exorbitant interest rates is the result of a long ethical and economic discussion that belongs to our cultural matrix, a doctrine with a moral valence.

---

[19] Bertrand Russell, "An Outline of Intellectual Rubish," in *Unpopular Essays* (London: Routledge, 1995). 116.

2.3. *The Moral A Prioris of Case Building*

There is a cultural and therefore moral embeddedness of any kind of economic analysis that cannot be avoided. In his monumental *History of Economic Analysis*, Karl Pribram reports that at the beginning of the 1930's, while teaching at the University of Frankfurt, widely divergent economic doctrines were represented in the schools of economics throughout Germany. As he points out, some of the divergences, which made the different schools incompatible, were rooted in factors that were not, strictly speaking, economic. These factors were to be found in the history of Western reasoning, and

> the irreconcilable antagonisms between different schools of economics could thus be related to deep-seated divergences in forming fundamental economic concepts; the methods used in defining the objectives and problems of economic research could be regarded as the primary determinants in shaping the history of economic reasoning.[20]

The case studies in economics featured by each school leaves certain elements out and includes others. The definition of a case is not merely scientific; it includes moral appreciations that define the case. This is one of the dimensions in which ethics can enter into dialogue with economics, a dialogue that was natural for Molina. Economics professes to prescind from any moral judgment; if this might be true once the case has been constructed, it is questionable whether the construction of the case has no moral dimension to it. The rhetoric of globalization is an example of this. By choosing which elements of globalization are taken into account in the narrative of globalization, a moral choice is implicitly being made in what is being left out. It is not the goal of this book to propose a model through which economics can take into account its moral dimension, that task belongs to economists. However, part of the goal of this work is to foster the dialogue between economics and ethics, by pointing out in the field of economics its moral dimension, a dimension also sometimes forgotten by ethicists who tend to adopt the economic theory that best suits their interest and who then portray it as a pure fact devoid of value judgment.

There is a further moral significance of case building. Against what Jonsen and Toulmin hold in their book *The Abuse of Casusitry*,[21] case building is based in common moral assumptions. If in their experience

---

[20] Pribram. xvi–xvii.

[21] Jonsen and Toulmin. 16–20.

casuistry was helpful in solving bioethics cases in the 1970's, I think there is a strong case to be made that this might have happened partly because the members of the committee shared, even with different religious backgrounds, a great deal of common morality. They were all Americans, which meant sharing many core values. Beyond that, most likely they were all members of academia, which represents much more than a specialized knowledge about certain topics. When one reaches the higher ranks in academia, it is because one has committed oneself to many values regarding what is scientific research and the values that guide it. Academia, as any other human community, involves socialization and socialization means the assumption of certain values. To go through a doctoral program implies adherence to a certain ethos. This commonality was discounted by Jonsen and Toulmin, when they argued that casuistry was an able method to explore ethical issues in groups of people of different religious and philosophical backgrounds. Against Jonsen and Toulmin, James Keenan affirms that "casuistry's insistence on the concrete is an insistence on the pretheoretical. In fact, because it is concrete and pretheoretical it is context dependent."[22] Jonsen and Toulmin discounted the importance of the context.

Even behind the veil of ignorance, the reasoning that leads to any theory of justice carries with it some moral presuppositions. A similar case can be made for economics, even if different schools of thought offer different solutions and alternatives. In these, modern schools of economics do not differ from their scholastic predecessors. Although they all agree on the point regarding leaving morality out of economic discourse, and although they commit themselves to analyzing society and the economy devoid of any moral concern, they end up with diametrically opposed solutions.

3. The Basic Metaphor Regarding Society: The Body

Molina had no doubt that justice was a virtue, and although he accepted other meanings of it, in *De Iustitia et Iure* he fastened upon the notion of justice as virtue. A general pattern can be observed in his development of the conceptions of justice. Both in the more theoretical developments and in the cases he explored, we find the idea that merchants who engaged

[22] James F. Keenan, "The Return of Casuistry," *Theological Studies*, no. 57 (1996). 137.

in lending money, buying and selling or in money exchange practices belonged to the same body; it is thus not surprising that some type of fraternity bounded them, an idea that appeared already in the Digest.[23] We find the conviction that the good of the others was the responsibility of each one, an honest and virtuous merchant could not be indifferent to the good of the commonwealth. This idea had a long history.

3.1. *The Origins of the Idea and the* Respublica Christiana

The ideas regarding property showed us that humankind was conceived as having a common origin based on the Biblical accounts of creation. Humankind's common origin implied that fraternity was more that just an inspiring idea. Beyond the power of common origin binding all humankind in one family, God originally intended the common destination of goods. Although the Fall had affected the first mode in which this original intention was carried out, the common destination of all goods was a basic context for any economic and moral analysis, and a litmus test for any economic measure. We saw Molina reject fixed legal prices for wheat because they actually did not help the poor, but ended up harming them. A second reason he gave against fixed legal prices was that it burdened the grain owner with the weight of helping the poor without involving other people in this task. The common good, and helping the poor was one dimension of it, could not pertain only to those who owned wheat. Rather, the common good touched everyone, because the image Molina had of society was that of a body, in which all organs attended to each other according to their ability and function.

The idea of society as a body is rooted in both the writings of the ancient philosophers and in Scripture. The pagan idea of society as a body was matched in the New Testament by the ecclesiological ideas of Paul who frequently portrayed the Church as a body in which each person or group of persons constituted a member of that body, for whose integral well-being all were obliged to provide.[24]

The antecedent of ancient philosophy and Christian dogmas resulted in the notion of the *Respublica Christiana*, a notion that, if in the Middle Ages it was used to refer to Christendom, in Molina's time was applied to each of the nascent national states. Society was conceived

[23] Digest 17. 2. 63. pr.

[24] Rm 12:3–8; 1Cor 12:12–31; Ep 4:11–16; Col. 1:28.

by Molina as a body, a living organism that was both a political body and a Christian body.[25]

We have seen in the third chapter how the idea of the common good was a *quasi servitutem* to any law, and certainly on the regulation of private property. Again in the fourth chapter we have seen the importance of the commonwealth in moral reasoning in matters of just price and money exchange; even in regard to usury, some of the arguments against it emphasized the evil consequences it brought to the commonwealth, more than its intrinsic injustice.

In discussing how different political regimes constituted different ways of exercising the supreme political power belonging to the commonwealth, Molina defined monarchy as the way of ruling by which the commonwealth was ruled by one head.[26] This precise trait, that the body was governed by one head, laid the foundation for the preference of this way of government over all others. Monarchy represented the most perfect way of government because in it art, the art of politics, imitated better nature, in which one head moved and governed all the limbs.[27] Each political body was better ruled by one person who acted as head. Nature knew no cases of polycephalous beings. Each commonwealth was a body to whose common good the different 'limbs' of society ought to contribute. The responsibilities were different, as has been shown in what Molina said about distributive justice, because the different members of a body were different. The idea that the commonwealth was a body had great moral impact.

3.2. *Economic and Moral Implications of the Organic Model*

3.2.1. *Economics of a Body*

The idea of society as a body was a basic metaphor that affected economic and moral reasoning. For many centuries all intellectual life was

[25] Salaverry highlights the influence of Pauline ecclesiological ideas in the ecclesiology of Luis de Molina. Joaquín Salaverri, "La noción de Iglesia del Padre Luis de Molina," *Revista española de teología* 20 (1960). 204–205.

[26] "Etenim respublica aut regitur per unum commune caput ac principem, cui Reipubl. Potestas est demandata, et tunc dicitur Monarchia seu regnum, principisque ipse rex ac Monarcha nuncupatur." II. 23. 1. p. 64.

[27] "Ars praeterrea eo perfectior est, quo plus naturam imitatur: in rebus autem naturalibus regimen unum reducitur, ut uno corde membra omnia moventur et gubernatntur, et unica ratione potentiae reliquae, una apes caeteris praeest, et regimen totius universi ad unum supremum rectorem et moderatorem Deum reducitur. Quo fit ut monarchia caeteris regiminibus sit praestantior." II. 23. 14. p. 66. Molina develops his political ideas in the discussion.

in the hands of the Church, and although the Church felt the pressure of the feudal powers it was able to remain independent. As Schumpeter puts it, the men who performed economic analysis, all clerics, "acknowledged the supreme authority of the pope, which was essentially international: their country was Christendom, their state was the Church,"[28] the basic social structure to which they referred any idea of economic analysis.

Adrien de Roover pointed out that the scholastic discussion did not have a vision of an economic system in the sense we have today. Discussion regarding justice came in the discussion of contracts. They did not possess the concept of the economy as a whole in which one action unleashes a number of reactions. They rendered judgments regarding the justice of a certain contract or a certain trade practice. Their point of view was that of a jurist or of a moralist, never that of an economist.[29] The scholastics, nevertheless, did have an idea of economics beyond mere legalism. According to Aquinas division of labor was necessary, and divine providence had endowed different people with different aptitudes. No one was able to provide everything for him or herself; the division of labor, and the necessary cooperation it implied, were precepts of natural law.[30] This idea was complemented by Aquinas's teacher, Albert the Great, who stated that countries, like people, were not self-sufficient.[31] Richard of Middletown gave the example of how two countries A and B could benefit from trade if each one was able to give what it had in surplus in exchange for what it needs.[32]

Molina continued this line of thought. We saw in chapter IV his appraisal of negotiation, how he considered it beneficial when it was entered into with the right intention, and was undertaken to meet a social need. The juridical twist of the discussion that led to dealing with this matter under the heading of justice was more than mere legalism. Exchange, if on an equitable basis, was bound to benefit both parties.[33] If trade was analogous to the exchanges that occurred in a living organism, it was suitable that some measure of equivalence be always sought.

---

[28] Schumpeter and Schumpeter. 75.

[29] de Roover. *La pensé économique des scolastiques: doctrines et méthodes*. 17.

[30] *Quodlibet VII*, q. 7 a. 1 co.

[31] Albert Magnus, *In IV libros sententiarum*, dist. 16, art. 46.

[32] Ricardus Media Villa, *Quodlibeta*, Venice, 1509. Quodlibet II, q. 23, art. 1. quoted in de Roover, "The Scholastic Attitude toward Trade and Entrepeneurship." 338.

[33] IIª–IIae q. 77 a. 1 co.

Molina's basic metaphor of society as a body allowed him to discuss matters of justice in a way that went beyond the mere commutative justice of a contract. I have shown how this worked in the matter of pricing. Prices were certainly established in the market through the interaction of buyers and sellers, but the just price was always the result of the *communis aestimatio*, and took into consideration the entire commonwealth, at least the community formed by the people who came to the market. Part of the lawfulness of *negotiatio* was based in its ability to meet social needs, as a result of which we saw that the idea of market competition made no sense in Molina's mindset, because different organs of a body cannot compete against each other if the body is to stay alive.

It is important to underline the basic metaphor regarding society, because it predetermined the results in the discussion on justice. In our day, inadvertently following the maxim that it is more perfect for a discipline to follow nature more closely, the basic metaphor of the social body is that of atoms. This mechanization of economics helped to consign to oblivion the idea of moral duty in economics. This oblivion cannot be attributed to Adam Smith, who in the idea of the impartial spectator reflected the moral demands of economics.[34] According to Oscar de Juan and Fabio Monsalve, it was Bentham's utilitarianism that introduced the idea of man "conceived as a machine prepared to compute and achieve for himself the "maximum net pleasure." Ethical considerations had no place, either in individual behavior, or in the new economics that struggled to be acknowledged as a positive science."[35] This led, in Amartya Sen's words, to the displacement of the "ethical approach" by the "engineering approach."[36]

This paradigm shift was partly possible because the new scientific paradigm, the one the scientific revolution brought about, opted for the principle of the uniformity of nature. If nature is uniform, and the art of politics, even political economy, imitate nature, it makes no sense to hold

[34] "No man during, either the whole of his life, or that of any considerable part of it, ever trod steadly and uniformly in the path of … justice … whose conduct was not principally directed by a regard to the sentiments of the supposed impartial spectator of the great inmate of the breast, the great judge and arbitrer of conduct." Adam Smith, *An Inquiry into the Nature and Causes of the Wealth of Nations*, R.H. Campbell and A.S. Skinner ed. (Oxford: Oxford Clarendon Press, 1976). 357, quoted in Oscar de Juan and Fabio Monsalve, "Morally Ruled Behaviour: The Neglected Contribution of Scholasticism," *The European Journal of the History of Economic Thought* 13, no. 1 (2006). 102.

[35] de Juan and Monsalve. 103.

[36] Amartya Sen, *On Ethics and Economics* (Oxford: Blackwell, 1987). 2–7.

qualitative differences among the different members of a social body, and this is the basic idea of scholastic social theory. The change in the basic metaphor of society entailed an immense impact in economics, as well as its ethical dimension.

3.2.2. *The Economic Common Good*

It is the different paradigm that renders impossible for many of our contemporaries the idea of the common good, especially in an economic context. An atomic system is a zero-sum game in which energy is neither created nor destroyed, and the energy gained by one particle comes as a result of some other's loss. Those who hold this basic metaphor of society have serious difficulty understanding how individual rights and the common good can be reconciled,[37] and in the conflict they usually opt for the former and jettison the latter. If the individual experiences a gain, the common good cannot also advance and vice versa. But for the scholastics individual rights and common good were not at odds, because of the organic metaphor of society as a body. If a member of society becomes worse off, this would ultimately affect negatively the entire commonwealth. In an organic metaphor it makes no sense that the eye can benefit at the expense of the foot. As Saint Paul points out "if (one) part suffers, all the parts suffer with it."[38]

For this same reason, the notion of social justice was foreign to the scholastics. Social justice and social reform would be ideas of a much later age. Scholastics also abstained partly because it would have been foolish to reform a body. A body was what nature had made of it; of course it could be healthy or unhealthy, and the mission of virtue was to keep a body strong. We cannot forget that the root word *virtus* has the meaning of virtue in the moral sense, but it also means strength. For the scholastics wealth should be distributed according to rank, merit, and abilities, in the same way that some parts of the body receive more energy than others. Because the criteria of distribution changed from one place to another, the scholastics would wisely abstain from formulating universal rules about it.[39] But we have seen in Molina's discussion of monopolies

---

[37] "The first natural rights theories were not based on an apotheosis of simple greed or self-serving egotism; rather they derived from a view of individual human persons as free, endowed with reason, capable of moral discernment, and from a consideration of the ties of justice and charity that bound individuals to one another." Tierney. 77. The same idea is defended in Höpfl. 283–313.

[38] 1 Corinthians 12: 26.

[39] de Roover, *La pensè èconomique des scolastiques: doctrines et mèthodes*. 43.

and fixed legal prices that, beyond the basic social inequalities which he took for granted, he proposed measures to ensure that no one lacked the essentials for a decent life. For Molina the pivotal concept of applied economics was the idea of the common good, conceived, in Schumpeter's words, "with reference to the satisfaction of the economic wants of individuals as discerned by the observer's reason or *recta ratio*." Schumpeter found that this method was "exactly the same thing as the welfare concept of modern Welfare Economics."[40]

3.2.3. *Taxes and the Common Good*

As I have said, Molina never wrote the final treatise of his original project on distributive justice, something he was aware might happen because in the prologue to the disputations on taxes he said that he would deal with tithes "if God would grant him life" to do it.[41] It is noteworthy that we have his disputation on taxes in the treatise on commutative justice. Taxes, according to our paradigm, would fit best in a section about distributive justice. Molina explained the placing of taxes in this part of his treatise about commutative justice by saying that, after having dealt with *dominium*, the titles that justify the transference of *dominium*, and the special kind of *dominium* that the institution of primogeniture and entailed estates represented, he would deal with what referred to the public authorities and what was due to them because of the *dominium iurisdictionis* and the common good of the commonwealth.[42] What Molina seems to imply is that taxation was not an infringement on the rights of private property, but truly part of the comprehensive regulation of *dominium*, in its two major manifestations, political power and private property. Additionally, he seemed to imply that what was due to the common good was a demand of commutative justice, not of distributive justice. As part of a body, people received many things from the commonwealth; taxes, in themselves, were a just return in that exchange.

Relying on the authority of Varro, Molina explained that the name *tributum* (taxes) came from *tribus*, the tribes into which the Roman people were originally divided. The *tributum* was the money or personal

[40] Schumpeter and Schumpeter. 97.

[41] "De sustentatione vero, quae Ecclesiasticis potestatibus debetur, inferius in materia de religione, si deus vitam concesserit, est dicendum." II. De Tributis. p. 270.

[42] "Nuc autem disserendum consequenter nobis est de tributis, quae laicis potestatibus ratione dominii iurisdictionis, quaeque in commune reipublicae bonum debentur." Ibid.

service that for war or the help of the commonwealth the tribes were instructed to pay.[43] There was also the authority of Festus whose *De verbu significatu* was discovered in the early Renaissance. According to Festus *tributum* came from *tribuendo*, that is to divide, assign, allot. Independently of arguments regarding the origin of the word Molina stated that its signification had extended from the payment itself, to the authority to estimate the value of what each one had to contribute, an authority that resided in the government. What is noteworthy about these etymological disquisitions is that, whatever the actual etymology of *tibutum* was, the idea carried a very communal notion. Taxes were the result of social division, and had been originally a communally performed task. Taxes were asked not of singular individuals, although of course individuals bear the burden of taxes, but taxes were demanded of tribes, different associations within the larger social body. Taxes were an expression of the contribution to the life of the commonwealth that became especially evident in the tribal and, later regional, nature of the contributions to the army. Tribes or regions would contribute a legion or a regiment to the defense of the commonwealth. This is what he called the personal aspect of taxes. There was a contribution due to the commonwealth, simply by virtue of belonging to it.

Molina knew also about schemas of taxation that depended on the wealth of the person. It is what he called the real part of the tax, the obligation that arose, not from being part of the social body, but the tax that was to be determined on account of the assets a person held. He called it real because it was a burden bestowed not upon the person but upon the goods themselves that the owner had to fulfill. To own goods carried with it the obligation to pay taxes for some of them. It was part of the conception of *dominium*.

Molina knew that taxes could be, and many times were excessive, to the point of forcing people to sell part of their assets to pay the taxes. But for Molina, taxes in themselves were an expression of membership in the community, a membership that was expressed by the sharing of the burden of taxes both on persons and goods.

[43] "dicitur a tributis, quod ea pecunia, quae ad bella, in subsidiumque reipublicae solvi praecipiebatur, tributim, hoc est per singulas tribus, iuxta censum, facultative cuiusque a singulis solvebatur." II. 549. 1. p. 270.

3.2.4. *Economics: A Probable Science*

Another corollary of the basic metaphor of society as a body that affected economic thought was that it made of economics a probable science, not an exact one. In an atomic world the idea of intention makes no sense, and an economic science modeled after Newtonian physics is a necessary science that reaches universal and necessary conclusions. But the science that seeks to invigorate a living organism can only be a probable science, or even a mere art, as medicine is an art, which relies on scientific knowledge, yet depends on prudent, and, therefore, probable judgments. The economic analysis of Molina depended on his epistemology. As we have seen, probabilism was a moral system, but also an epistemological statement. Molina had concluded in *Concordia* that the 'middle science' was not accessible to human beings, only God had super-comprehension. The science of future contingents could only be infallibly known with certitude by a cognitively perfect being. Pricing, as I pointed out, was a case of 'middle science'. Prices depended on certain natural factors that responded to a natural knowledge, but also of human will, which made it free knowledge. Knowledge about prices was knowledge about future contingents. For Molina it was reasonable to observe and discuss some laws that were observed in experience, but these laws were flexible laws that offered some indication, but not a necessary knowledge. Prudence and *communis aestimatio* were necessary for the justice of prices. About prudence I shall say more later; let me return now to the importance of the metaphor of the body. The basic metaphor of the body allowed Molina not only to talk about justice in relation to economics; it also allowed him to deal with another Christian virtue, namely charity, in relation to economics, as I shall demonstrate in the next section.

4. Church and State: The Role of Charity

4.1. *Church and State*

Blending the Christian and pagan legacies that referred to society as a body had been partly possible because of the admiration of the cultural legacies of Greece and Rome, an admiration that the rebirth of classical studies in the fifteenth and sixteenth-century had reinvigorated. But what ultimately made the blending of ideas possible was the alliance for many centuries of the throne and the altar. The idea of Christendom as a body in which the pope took care of spiritual matters and the Emperor looked after the worldly ones, passed to the nascent nation-states of the sixteenth century, in which the perimeter of the Church and of the state coincided. Molina appreciated the difference between Church and state. His discussion of the different types of *dominium* and the competencies of each type, which we saw in chapter IV, demonstrate this awareness. We cannot ignore, however, how the coincidence of Church and state made irrelevant the distinction in the discussion of justice of what belonged to the state and what belonged to the Church; on the contrary what applied to the Church applied to the *Respublica Christiana*.

One meaning of justice coincided for Molina with charity and grace. These two made a man just before God, which allowed conceptualizing charity and grace as justice. We have seen in chapter III how economic matters were not merely relegated to the realm of justice, but were also constitutive of the realm of charity. For Molina a sin was not committed against a precept or a norm, but against a virtue; therefore, a given economic practice could be determined not to constitute a sin against justice yet it could constitute a sin against charity.[44] Moreover, I have offered some examples of how evangelical counsels, which referred to grace, could also be part of economic reasoning and the business world. In the first chapter I presented an example regarding a merchant who lived by these standards, Gonzalo de la Palma. The ideas that Molina developed were not the theoretical lucubrations of a university professor, but the rational reflection of lived faith. For Molina, and for a merchant such as Gonzalo de la Palma, it was easy to move from charity to justice, from evangelical counsels to market operations, because of the coincidence between the commonwealth and the Church.

4.2. *Ecclesiology and Moral Theology*

Molina followed the common distinction of the time between the Church militant and the Church triumphant, the latter constituted by the angels and all the just who were already in heaven, the former constituted by all those who were pilgrims on this earth. Molina dedicated most of his attention to the Church militant.[45] In the Church militant Molina

---

[44] II. 354 4. p. 250.

[45] "Bajo este aspecto [that of the Church formed by men not considering the angels] nos la define en la Concordia diciendo, 'que la Iglesia universal es un Cuerpo Místico formado por los hombres desde la caida de nuestros primeros Padres hasta el fin del mundo, y que tiene por Cabeza a Cristo en cuanto hombre'." Salaverri. 206–207.

differentiated three states: the Church of the natural law, the Church of the Mosaic law and the Church of the law of grace.[46] The two former portrayals of the Church were united into one with the coming of Christ. For Molina only through baptism is one incorporated into the Body of Christ and able to begin to live in the Christian Church, which confers saving grace. I do not intend to present Molina's ecclesiology as a helpful instrument for ecumenical dialogue or, least of all, for inter-religious dialogue, although according to him the just of the Churches of the natural law and the Synagogue were really sons and daughters of God and obtained eternal grace.[47] My purpose is to point to the parallel he established between ecclesiology and moral theology, particularly in matters of justice. The same way that the natural law Church and the Synagogue were assumed and elevated in the Church of the law of grace, Molina held that the precepts of natural law and the moral precepts of the Old Law (not the ceremonial ones) had been assumed and elevated in the law of grace.[48] If a natural law precept was binding in conscience in itself, through divine command it reached its fullness. There was continuity between natural law and grace, justice and charity, Church and politics. In defending these views Molina was holding a Catholic position against such figures as Wycliffe, Huss, or Luther, who had stressed the invisibility of the Church to such an extent that they had almost renounced the Church's involvement with any secular institutions in matters of politics, and in general, matters of justice; this position led, in those places where the teaching of these reformers were accepted, to the subjugation of the Church by the state.[49] Potentially, there is a similar danger if we separate too sharply charity and economics.

---

[46] He also referred to the three states as the natural law, the Old or Written Law and the New law, or as the Church of the Primitives, the Sinagoge and the Christian Church. Ibid. 210.

[47] II. 5. 1–4.

[48] II. 5. 65. 1. and II. 5. 66. 5.

[49] Bellarmine, in defending the Catholic position would go to the other extreme holding that: "The one and true Church is the community of men brought together by the profession of the same Christian faith and participation in the same sacraments under the authority of legitimate pastors and especially of the one Vicar of Christ on earth, the Roman Pontiff … The one true Church is as visible and palpable as the Kingdom of France or the republic of Venice." Robert Bellarmine, *De Controversiis*, II, 3.2, as quoted by Avery Dulles, *Models of the Church* (Garden City: Doubleday, 1974). 14.

4.3. *Justice and Charity*

In our day the mere mention of such concepts as grace or evangelical counsels in relation to economics would make any person in business scoff, even a pious Catholic. Charity has, since the separation of Church and state, become a word that certainly does not seem applicable to the economic world. Charity tends to evoke the blandness of some actions that try to remedy what justice is unable to resolve. The relationship between justice and charity has become problematic, even within ecclesiastical discourse.

The economic world also exhibits difficulties in coming to grips with the idea of charity in its realm. Odd Langholm points out that "it is no less than remarkable how the most ardent upholders of the libertarian ethic fall back on individual liberality or magnanimity (if not Christian charity) to counteract the ill effects of supra-personal market forces running wild."[50] What emerges as a mere concession in a libertarian economic analysis, was part of the intellectual and social framework for the scholastics.

The relationship of charity and justice did not seem adversarial or conflicting in Molina. We have seen Molina conceding the existence of monopolies for the promotion of the common good, recommending the forced sale of grain, and pressing the need of restitution for every ill-gained profit. Although it is impractical to return to that age, and certainly not commendable, we cannot fail to observe that this discourse exerted great influence upon society.

The importance of grace and charity in moral discussions regarding economics is something that we cannot overlook. Molina was able to bring in these two elements without a problem because in his time ecclesiology and social ethics were close to each other. Today they have drifted apart, but Christian social ethics can only bring together grace and charity, two major factors of Christian life, if it reflects on its ecclesial dimension. To crassly equate social ethics with ecclesiology is to go too far, but a door is nevertheless, open to the study of the ecclesial dimension of Catholic social ethics, as well as the ethical implications of certain ecclesiological truths. Charity needs to be a social virtue.

---

[50] Odd Langholm, "Scholastic Economics," in *Pre Classical Economic Thought: From the Greeks to the Scottish Enlightenment. Recent Economic Thought Series*, ed. S. Todd Lowry (Boston: Kluwer-Nijhoff Pub., 1987). 134.

5. Money, Metaphysics and Society

According to Marc Bloch, "of all the tools that can reveal to the historian the deep movements of the economy, monetary phenomena are without doubt those more efficient."[51] Our analysis of usury, just prices and money exchange has revealed the neural centers of the economics of the sixteenth century and the way a theologian reacted to them, offering moral advice. Additionally, in this chapter I have probed the internal relationships that unite social theory to theology, ecclesiology to social ethics, epistemology to economics. Ultimately this has been possible because money expresses a global relationship between the individual and society, especially regarding the trust of the former in the latter.[52] Money is without a doubt an eminently material thing, yet it also reveals many invisible, but nevertheless real dimensions of the person and of society.

Aristotle had dismissed usury because a life of money-making contradicted the means that guide us towards the *telos* of a good life.[53] Christianity had from its very beginning a strand of suspicion towards money. The medieval scholastics took great care in analyzing the ways in which money was used. They knew that money was a social creation and were perceptive regarding the social meaning of money and the problem it presents with respect to justice. Money was for them a measure to value things, a means of payment and a guarantor of future necessities. Aquinas' analysis of money had concentrated on its legal aspects, which led him to condemn any type of money-lending at a profit. Nicholas of Oresme, bishop of Lisieux, wrote a treatise *On the Origin, Nature, Juridical Status and Variations of Coinage*, in which he concentrated on the problem of debasement of money, a practice that undermined the trust of individuals in the government and in money as an apt means for social transactions, an opinion that became the common opinion of the doctors.[54]

Molina followed the general Christian warnings against greed, but was able to perceive the changing social meaning of money, drawing from Aquinas, but also from the nominalists who had written extensively

[51] "De todos los instrumentos capaces de revelar al historiador los movimientos profundos de la economía, los fenómenos monetarios son, sin duda, los más eficaces." Quoted in Vilar. 19.

[52] Ibid. 30.

[53] Alasdair C. MacIntyre. 111.

[54] Schumpeter and Schumpeter. 94–99.

on usury, prices and money exchange. Molina was able to pass moral judgments on the justice of many social situations that had seemed unjust to many of his predecessors. He was able to overcome two illusions: the realist illusion that gold and silver were things with an immutable essence and an immutable social meaning that were thrown upon men without them controlling it; and the nominalist illusion that the sign that coins bore established by the positive law made their value inalterable lest there be money alteration. The old dispute between realists and nominalists regarding universals had turned up in monetary theory. Molina was able to offer a realist ground on the *ius* of the case studied, and a flexible nominalist approach on the concrete study of the situation, this combination of solid principles and specific analysis was unprecedented.

According to Vilar, the voyages of Columbus were not an extra-economic phenomenon, but the coronation of a long internal process of the European economy in search of gold, as well as other products such as spices or silk.[55] Gold was important, but not more than other goods and actually less than silver, yet both metals expressed social relations of the larger economy. Gold and silver tended to depart America, not just on account of the conquistadors' greed, but because it had higher value in Europe and Asia than in America. By merely escaping America, the precious metals gained value.[56] Molina knew this when he said that in Peru gold bought fewer goods than in Spain. Molina had realized that the social value given to a good, whether it was rusty things for the Japanese, cheap jewelry for the Ethiopians or gold for the Europeans, depended on its social valuation, *aestimatio*. Money expressed social values and social trends, and was also in turn affected by them.

As a measure to value things money depended on its metallic content, but also on social values. As a means of payment, money depended on the financial preferences of the merchants. As a guarantor of future needs, it begged the question of the common good and justice, because of the need to guarantee everyone's necessities, whether present or future, and because of the element of inequality that the introduction of money established. The call for restitution was a constant call for the justice of economic transactions, a justice that found a model in the original common property of the goods of Creation, in which no one lacked for anything.

---

55 Vilar. 85.

56 Ibid. 187.

Molina realized the various uses of money, and the inequality that money had introduced in society. He, therefore, had no problem in explaining that a certain equity in the transaction was maintained, even though apparently there seemed to be inequality in it. We can observe in what ways money worked, and the reactions of society in relation to it were heavily dependent upon economic conditions, but also on social and mental habits.[57] Money was a creation of the community, not a neutral instrument, and therefore it begged for communal control. Money was a social creation to the extent that it was even a 'tool' for wealth creation. This introduced another question, one regarding the relationship between risk incurred and profit earned, a question that directly affected the distribution of wealth. To this question I shall devote the next section.

6. Risk, Profit, and the Distribution of Wealth

6.1. *Business, Risk and Gambling*

In economic practices, as in many other areas of human life, the problem of risk is ubiquitous. Lending money, buying on credit or exchange bills create uncertainty regarding outcomes. The scholastic analysis of risk was especially developed in maritime insurance. According to James Franklin, when in the twelfth century widespread commerce resumed, "the maritime loan was almost the only way of creating large-scale credit ... The partnership as such encountered no problem from canon law, but the implicit charge of interest did, because of the prohibition on usury."[58] The basic scholastic principle concerning risk was that the owner could run a risk on his goods and derive legitimate compensation for that, but to gain from the risk of goods belonging to other people was usury. What is noteworthy is that the analysis of the risk of maritime insurance was often conceptualized through the analogy of betting, which is very revelatory of how economic risk was understood at the time.[59] It is always difficult to appreciate the fullness of a given metaphor for eco-

---

[57] Ibid. 190.

[58] James Franklin, *The Science of Conjecture. Evidence and Probability before Pascal* (Baltimore: The Johns Hopkins University Press, 2001). 262–263.

[59] Mair was an exception, but as Vereecke shows it was a common conceptualization in the sixteenth century. "La insistenza dei teologi nel paragoare l'assicurazione con la scomessa si piega, l'abbiamo visto, con la moda delle scommesse nel XVI secolo." Vereecke. 485.

nomic risk, but it is important to take into account the metaphor being used because it certainly predetermines or at least greatly influences the outcome.

In the fifteenth century, for both Saint Bernardine of Siena and Saint Antoninus of Florence, any riskless investment was considered usury,[60] yet risk was accepted as a measure for profit when it was incurred by the owner of the money at risk. Part of the scholastic problem was that of determining how assuming risk entitled one to a profit. The estimation of a risk, and the consequent economic reward for it, was a matter intimately related to probability, to which development the scholastic contribution is generally underrated. Franklin greatly values the scholastic contribution to the development of probability, especially the contribution of those who came after Ockhan and Scotus.[61] Although the late scholastics were attacked by every major thinker from Descartes on, as they represented an alternative model of science, and are reviled nowadays by many Thomists as decadent, these men made contributions "to every aspect of probability—evidence in law and moral theology (and 'probabilism' and 'moral certainty') and to understanding of aleatory contracts."[62] Probability referred to more than a moral system about which we have already spoken; it also referred directly to the evaluation of aleatory contracts, and was therefore directly related to the appraisal of risk and its economic estimation.

As commerce moved west to cities like Antwerp, Seville and Lisbon, both by medieval and modern standards markets operated free of regulation, as we have seen in the cases of the wool trade in Cuenca or the system of money exchange between countries, or with the bourse in Antwerp. The lack of regulation led to an intense atmosphere of speculation. Merchants used exchange bills to profit from the different agios between Antwerp and Seville, Lisbon or Medina. There were also futures markets, such as the wool trade of Cuenca; but along with these economic activities, there was outright betting. In the bourse of Antwerp wagers were placed regarding the timing of the next trip of Phillip II to the Netherlands.[63] Molina gave the example of betting on when the fleet from the Indies would arrive.[64] The association bewteeen wagering and

60 Noonan. 70–80.

61 Franklin. xii.

62 Ibid. 344.

63 Ibid. 279.

64 "Et quiddem, quando sponsio sit circa futurum aliquod contingens, quod proinde in utramvis partem evenire potest, ut quod tali die, aut intra tantum tempus, pluet, quod

merchants was clear, and theologians insisted on associating the insurance contract with betting, partly because of the widespread practice of betting in the sixteenth century.[65] A future on spices was a risky investment, one that depended on the arrival of the fleet. Between a future on spices and a mere bet there was apparently little difference, both in the risk incurred and on the possible result.

By the sixteenth century Spain had become the first insurance market.[66] Molina analyzed the insurance contract in disputation 507 of the second treatise.[67] After some theoretical discussion regarding the insurance contract, he analyzed the usual insurance contract practiced in Seville at the time, and concluded that it was reprehensible.[68] It is noteworthy that immediately after treating the insurance contract, Molina dealt with the wagering contract,[69] the contract of drawing lots,[70] and the gambling contract.[71] Molina dedicated eleven disputations solely to gambling; to insurance he had dedicated only one.

Sponsio, that is wagering, was for Molina a contract in which one person on one side and another person on another side bet money or some other thing on the truth of some event. It was a contract lawful in itself. The amount of risk run accounted for a greater or smaller gain. As an example of bets on future events he mentioned the future arrival of the ships from the Indies, but also questions of when it would rain and the gender of an expected child. He was also aware that there existed wagers in which the industry of the betting parties counted, as in a bet on who would arrive first to a certain place.[72] What he described was remarkably similar to certain economic practices. Although he concluded that

---

naves Indicae intra tantum tempus pervinient, quod gravida masculum pariet, etc. nullus dubitat, sponsionem esse iustam, eo quod uterque se exponent incommode et lucro." II. 508. 1. p. 663.

[65] Vereecke. 485.

[66] Ibid. 457.

[67] II. 507. pp. 658–663.

[68] "Paucis dicam, quod sentio. Contractus hic omnino est dissuadendus, et condemnandus iniustitiae, cum onere restituendi: quoniam spectatis circumstantiis omnibus concurrentibus, est omnino inaequalis." II. 507. 14. p. 662.

[69] II. 508. p. 663.

[70] II. 509. pp. 663–665.

[71] II. 511–521. pp. 665–684.

[72] "Sponsi, seu vadiatio(Hispane a puesta) est contractus, quo in re dubia unus pro una parte, et alius pro alia, spondent, sive pecunia, sive quodvis aliud ut is lucretur, qui eventum reive veritatem attingerit. Est que contractus iustus, ac licitus, nisi circumstantia aliqua maculetur." II. 508. 1. p. 663.

gambling was not against the natural law, he offered after discussing it many human laws, both civil and ecclesiastical, that forbade it. In the scholastic paradigm the insurance contract, and with it the idea of economic risk, belonged to the same category as gambling. Casuistry worked by using proven cases as a model to explore new cases, which meant that the decision regarding what case fitted a new occurrence was an important one, for it tainted morally the case to be studied.[73] In the language of Thomas Kuhn we could say that the paradigm employed to address a case greatly conditioned not only its solution but the general moral dye of it. The paradigm of risk was gambling, and this affected significantly any judgment that might be reached regarding it.

6.2. *Risk and Indetermination*

Molina had placed immense importance upon indetermination in the *Concordia*. Human freedom was some type of indetermination that only God's 'middle science' could penetrate. We saw him willing to admit the pricing of a future gain that had been forgone for the reason of a loan, his justification of *lucrum cessans*. He concluded, in direct contradiction of Soto, that the future gain could be estimated. He also was ready to admit a profit in credit sales, on account of the variability of the future price, which again was unknown. Despite the connection between risk in trade and gambling, and despite the connection between gambling and superstition and between rationality and not gambling,[74] Molina was willing to accept an economic gain on account of risk.

The determination of the present value of future goods always requires a good deal of thought. The most difficult question is precisely what to calculate.[75] Molina offered a solution that allowed for it; in order to do so he resorted to prudence and custom, as expressed in *communis aestimation*, as ways to determine it. The field of mathematical probability had not yet been developed, but Molina entrusted to prudence and custom the estimation of risk. The idea of the *communis doctoris sententia* is of great importance not only for understanding the fundamental moral theology of the time, but also for understanding the elaboration of doctrines regarding justice. The way the doctrine was elaborated was a communal one. The pricing of goods was actually left to the economic

[73] Jonsen and Toulmin. 304 332.
[74] Franklin. 337.
[75] Ibid. 258.

equivalent of the *communis docotoris sententiam*. It was the community of merchants, especially of prudent merchants, that was relied upon for pricing goods. We can attribute this to 'the market' as long as we think of it as a community, but certainly not if we think of it as an abstract idea governed by blind forces.

His views about future contingents and about human freedom allowed Molina to go where other scholastics, as Soto, in the case of *lucrum cessans*, could not consistently go. Molina is among those scholastics, who, according to Franklin, "were the last link in the chain joining the pricing of hopes and perils of Roman law with the problem of the just division of stakes in an interrupted game of change, the problem that led directly to the mathematical theory of probability."[76] We cannot forget that the development of modern mathematical probability was fostered by the question the Chevalier de Méré proposed to Pascal, the great enemy of Jesuit probabilism, and Fermat on the division of the stake between two players whose game was interrupted before its close.[77] We can see how the question of risk begs the question of distribution of wealth.

6.3. *Wealth Creation and Distribution*

In his *Sentences* Peter Lombard said that soldiers or merchants who were not willing to give up their professions could not be received as penitents.[78] This view was not received by the common doctrine, but the suspicion of trade remained. In commenting on Lombard's *Sentences*, Aquinas said that both soldiers and merchants were necessary for the commonweal of the city, and therefore these two professions could be exercised without necessarily sinning. Still he thought that in most cases that rarely happened.[79] As de Roover puts it, it happened with merchants as it happened with knights who "could be irreproachable heroes, but they rarely were, except in romances of chivalry."[80]

---

[76] Ibid. 228.

[77] Ian Hacking, *The Emergence of Probability. A Philosophical Study of Early Ideas About Probability, Induction and Statistical Inference*, 2nd ed. (Cambridge, UK: Cambridge University Press, 2006). 57.

[78] *Sententiarum*, IV, dist 16, qu 4, art. 2, quaestiuncula 2.

[79] In X libros, lib I, lectio 1; Summa Contra Gentiles, lib III, cap117.3, 129. 4 and 131. II^a–IIae q. 109, art. 3, ad 1 and q. 129, art. 6, ad 1. Opusculum XVI (De regimine principium) lib I, cap 1.

[80] de Roover, "The Scholastic Attitude toward Trade and Entrepeneurship". 337.

A merchant was one who bought to sell for profit; those who sold the produce of their own land were not considered merchants. Most people lived on agriculture in the fifteenth and sixteenth centuries,[81] and trade was restricted to a small number of people. The merchant was the intermediary between the farmer and the consumer. In his discussion on negotiation we saw Molina praising the advantages of the mediation of the merchants, but, according to de Roover, there were also those who thought that "the ideal was to eliminate trade altogether by bringing consumers directly into contact with producers. In most towns, markets were introduced for this purpose, but these markets were merely local."[82] If we look at it through this lens, perhaps many modern movements such as fair trade and local production resemble the scholastic quest. The remaining ethical problem was to determine who obtained what part of the final price.

Another concern was the problem of wealth accumulation. The scholastics favored a political system in which royal power was checked by countervailing forces. The king had no more authority that what had been bestowed upon him by the commonwealth, and any usurpation of power transformed the monarchy into a tyranny.[83] In a similar way, an excessive accumulation of wealth was also objectionable. Both property and political authority were a result of the original Fall and should always be controlled. Today the rhetoric against big government is a popular one, yet the concomitant suspicion against an excessive accumulation of wealth is accorded less voice. Scholastic theology displayed a more balanced rhetoric that looked with suspicion on both. Certainly within a notion of society as a living organism, an excessive accumulation of wealth by some organs would amount to elephantiasis, and the idea of restitution provided a balance to an excess of wealth accumulation.

For Molina it was clear that the dutiful activity of the merchants benefitted the commonwealth, and as long as the practices sought to meet a social need they should be encouraged. Nevertheless, he knew that not all trade activities sought to meet a social end. The cases of true usury, not lawful money lending, clearly show his awareness that wealth obtained without wealth creation was an unlawful gain subject to restitution. One of the causes that worried theologians regarding speculation in the

[81] Höffner. 14.
[82] de Roover, "The Scholastic Attitude toward Trade and Entrepeneurship." 339.
[83] II. 23. 15. p. 66.

financial markets was unlawful gain, but also the concern that the large profits that could be made in financial operations would draw merchants away from productive activities.[84]

For Molina, intention was the key determinant for judging the justice of any exchange and its consequent profit. Gain for the sake of gain was in itself evil, but gain for a just cause was not. If the merchant entered *negotiatio* to provide for his family or to help others, it was a good act; but the same act with only the raw intention of selfish gain, was greed. That is what frequently makes the scholastic discussion seem like mere formalities, but for scholastic moral theology an act had to be good in its beginning, means, and ends. The change in the end pursued could constitute the key difference between the same external act performed by two persons. What was apparently the same might not be if intention was taken seriously.

Intentions are, however, always difficult to appraise. If probability developed the analysis of risk, it also developed the notion of presumption that sharpened the appraisal of intention in moral and juridical matters. I shall now turn to the importance of law, and prudence, in Molina's ideas about justice.

7. Law and Prudence: Its Importance for Justice

In the absence of certitude, prudence and law became especially relevant. The abundance of legal quotations, both from civil and canon law, in the work of Molina can easily be dismissed as sheer legalism alien to moral theology. This is nevertheless anachronistic and projects on a sixteenth-century author a problem of moral theology in the twentieth century. The abundance of legal quotations was partly the result of an epistemology that was entirely aware of the uncertainty of the world in which it lived, and preferred to regulate that uncertainty by referring it to prudence and law, both of which originated within the community, rather than to fate, which certainly no one could control.

The abundance of legal quotations reflected the importance of institutions for a life of virtue. Since the times of Aristotle, it had been clearly established that a virtuous life could not be lived in isolation. A life of

[84] Grice-Hutchinson, *The School of Salamanca; Readings in Spanish Monetary Theory, 1544–1605*. 17.

virtue could only be lived in society. Crucial to the structure of a society were its institutions, a set of norms and practices to which individuals committed and contributed and in which they participated. But because institutions were formed by practices, the quest for virtue, and—in our case the quest for justice—could not take place without just institutions. This is what led the scholastic analysis to drink deeply of legal analysis. The *mons pietatis* are an example of how they realized that mere moral condemnation of wrongdoing was not enough; institutional alternatives to evil social practices had to be proposed, so that where moral theology condemned structures of sin, institutional structures of grace were set in place as an alternative. Just institutions helped form just people and vice versa.

Molina's analysis was often formal, but we cannot forget that in Thomistic thought form was what conferred its entity to things, more so than the material. That is why we observe that actions with similar effects are, nevertheless, judged differently, if the contracts were formally different. As Noonan notes, "an identity of effect [did] not necessarily imply an identity of contract."[85] We cannot forget that money is a social creation regulated by law, and as Franklin notes, even today "many of the more abstract entities considered in finance are in reality contracts (of sale on conditions, options, insurance, and the like); that is, they are legal entities. The interface between finance and law is especially apt to generate subtle concepts."[86] The same subtlety led Diego Laynez to complain about the great complexity of finance, because "the least change of circumstance makes it necessary to revise one's judgment."[87]

There was another element that rendered positive law important, for it could change the circumstances making natural law applicable or inapplicable or calling for the application of one principle or another. As we saw with prescription of property, although this is merely one example, natural law and positive law were intimately related. Positive law could change the circumstances of a case, making natural law applicable or inapplicable.

Law, however, was not able to foresee everything, and even if it was capable, it would always need an explanation regarding how it needed to be applied. This is what leads Alasdair McIntire to say:

---

85 Noonan. 167.
86 Franklin. 262.
87 Quoted in Ibid. 287.

> "What can never be done is to reduce what has had to be learned in order to excel at such a type of activity to the application of rules. There will of course at any particular stage in the historical development of such a form of activity be a stock of maxims which are used to characterize what is taken at a stage to be the best practice so far. But knowing how to apply these maxims is itself a capacity which cannot be specified by further rules, and the greatest achievements in each area at each stage always exhibit a freedom to violate present established maxims, so that achievement proceeds both by rule-keeping and by rule breaking. And there are never any rules to prescribe when it is the one rather than the other that we must do if we are to pursue excellence."[88]

The flexibility of laws could only be exercised as a communal task. Justice was a communal task; that is why the *communis doctoris opinio* translated into the importance of the merchant's opinion. Even for prices, Molina thought that the truth about them was reached by guesswork. In the scientific paradigm of the time, the opinion of prudent merchants fulfilled the role that in contemporary economic paradigms is fulfilled by the Smithian invisible hand of abstract market forces. That is why it makes sense for the scholastics to talk about just prices, and why it does not make sense in the liberal economic paradigm.

Prudence was not a minor element in the public ethical discourse, but was recognized as a virtue of great importance, to which exercise many problems were referred as a final arbitrer. Behind it was the conviction that law could not foresee everything, that the justice of a business practice could be determined better by an honest and prudent merchant than by any scholastic doctor uninformed about the specific context in question. There was also the conviction that to make a good judgment more was required than adequate knowledge of the business world; also necessary would be a proven moral character to allow for sound judgment, because scientific knowledge and moral character were two necessary dimensions of a good moral decision. *Recta ratio* did not involve just a correct knowledge of the situation. *Recta ratio* was fallible, practical, situated, but it was less fallible in the case of an honest and prudent merchant. That is why Keenan says that "those interested in using casuistry must ask the key question about virtue—about who they are and who they ought to be—questions about self understanding and goals."[89] All these elements were present in Molina's moral analysis of economic practices.

---

[88] MacIntyre. 31.
[89] Keenan, "The Return of Casuistry," 138–139.

CONCLUSION

The goal of a historical study is not just the recreation of a certain time period or author. History is usually pursued with the intent of knowing who we are and how we got here. This is done, generally, with the purpose of knowing how to proceed from now on. The contact with great minds of the past is always a help to walk into the future.

To conclude the journey through Molina's conception of justice as virtue in an economic context I would like to offer a reflection on the significance of Molina and his moral theology for our days, and how what he wrote is still relevant for our time. To do so I will highlight some of the topics to which I have referred along the way. I will try to render explicit some of the questions and lessons that are implicit in this book, and I will offer some suggestions on how they might apply to our troubled economic landscape. I will concentrate on four topics: Molina's contribution to economics and ethics, his contribution to natural law, his contribution to methodology—particularly his understanding of how circumstances shape the case—, and the way he conceives the relation of justice and the common good.

1. Molina on Economics and Ethics

It is a rather common axiom that ethics and religion hinder the development of science. To proof-text this sentence the Galileo case is the standard example. This is just an oversimplification of history, and of the relationship between ethics, religion and science. Molina's work is a good example of a serious commitment to the study of moral theology that not only does not hinder the development of science—in this case of economic science—but rather it stimulates it.

We have seen that Molina was the first scholastic doctor to allow for a legitimate life dedicated to money lending. It is worth noting that he was never criticize for it by other scholastics. We cannot think that this happened because no one paid any attention to what he wrote. We know that even before the publication of the *Concordia*, Molina's works were not just being read, but scrutinized. If he was able to make such a move, we should think that this can only be attributed to the solidity—

the internal probability as a scholastic doctor would say—of his case. Molina was able to make this move without contradicting a longstanding teaching of the Church, because by deepening the understanding of economics, he was able to realize that the scope of the traditional teaching applied to some cases but left out others. He realized that a more nuanced scientific knowledge of the economic practices of the time could only lead to a more nuanced moral judgment of them. He avoided the extremes of wide and indiscriminate moral condemnations, and of just suspending any judgment because of the complexity of the cases. He was aware that moral pronouncements about economics were necessary, but only possible after long and serious studies. These studies were partly to be conducted in dialogue and direct contact with businessmen and trade people. Doing this, he received solid and real information from those on the field, but he also offered a precious service. He was able to lend his brilliant analytic mind to conceptualize and formulate a solid presentation of economic theory. The capacity for abstract thought and theoretical formulation was a good complement to a detailed field work. This is what lead Schumpeter to say: "... with their systems of moral theology and law ... economics gained definite if not separate existence, and it is they who come nearer than does any other group to having been the 'founders' of scientific economics ... I am positive that [Lessius, Molina and Lugo] must be included in any history of economics."[1] As we have seen, for Schumpeter it was the system of moral theology and law that gave economics a definite existence, although not a separate one. The moral quest was an impetus for scientific development. The articulated concept of an analytical natural law—describing how things are—and a normative natural law—formulating how things ought to be—is key to this synergic working of ethics and economics. This articulation could still be applicable to the concepts we confront today. This leads us to another way in which Molina contributed, and still could contribute, to economics and ethics, the question of declared values.

Being a theologian Molina was unashamed of declaring his values. He did not exactly use the language of values when writing about moral theology. The language of values, as we know it today in ethical reasoning, is due to Max Scheler. Molina declared his values through the ends he assumed as obvious for any human person. A person's ultimate end was God and the happiness of the beatific vision. More proximate

[1] Schumpeter and Schumpeter. 97.

ends were the acquisition of virtue within the commonwealth: fortitude, temperance, justice and prudence.

Let us take two examples: the defense of liberty and private property. It is not uncommon that economists will defend the importance of freedom, and especially of free markets. The basic argument for it is economic efficiency, so that a basic axiom of economics—its detachment from any ethical judgment—is preserved. This is however a deceit. Some economists of our time claim to present a value-free economic thought, those who Amartya Sen calls engineering economists. This is, though, a false claim. There is not such a thing as value-free economics. There is economic thought that declares its values and economic thought that does not. The defense of free markets and of freedom in general is not at all value free, and it is also dependent on what each author understands under the name of freedom. It is not always exactly the same, and it is tied to a certain moral vision. Economics is always culturally embedded and therefore has always—even when it is not conscious or acknowledged—an ethical valence.

A second example of declared values that we can find in Molina is the question of private property. I think a second reflection on the discussion shows us that the foundation and the justification of private property is ultimately a theological question. Theological not because it should exclusively be discussed by professional theologians or in a theology school. Private property is a theological question because—whatever the legal formulations or particularities of it in the different legal systems—it is an assertion of human ends on this earth. For scholastic theology it was clear that private property was based in what is called nowadays the common destination of the good, that is, that what there is on the face of the earth is for the sake of all men and women. In scholastic theology, private property is understood to have been instituted to regulate and guarantee everyone's access to the goods of the earth. John Locke also agrees that God gave the goods of the earth in common. According to Locke it was labor that justified the private appropriation of these common goods. Economists have built on this Lockean idea of the justification of private property through labor. They reflect little, however, on its ultimate—that is theological—foundation, and how it might affect the way this institution should be regulated. If hard-working people stay poor—think of the so called 'working poor'—that is propertyless, there is something in the regulation of private property that is not working. Even if we can discount the Catholic principle of the universal destination of goods, labor should be a standard way of access to property.

In his 1920 *The Economics of Welfare* Charles C. Pigou elaborated on Alfred Marshal's concept of externalities. Externalities—or economic spillovers—are costs or benefits that are not transmitted through prices, but incurred by a certain party that has not agreed to the action which causes the cost or benefit. To compensate in the case of an externality which was a cost, Pigou advocated the introduction of a tax. This type of tax came to be known as pigovian taxes. The idea became almost common doctrine until in 1960 Ronald Coase—Nobel Price in 1991—in his article *The Problem of Social Cost* challenged the rationality of pigouvian taxes. He did it with a case study that showed that an agreement between a rancher—whose cattle destroy crops—and a farmer—whose crops were destroyed—would be better than the intervention of the state. Since then pigouvian taxes are a discussed topic in economics, although in some cases—such as air pollution—there is major consensus in favor of them.

The idea of externalities shows that economists agree on having blind spots. Prices cannot transmit all the cost of a certain economic action. I would venture to say that there is a case to speak of moral externalities, moral spillovers of any economic agent that should be at least acknowledged by economic analysis. A refusal to engage in this interdisciplinary dialogue in the name of this value free economics would be in itself a moral pronouncement with ethical value.

2. Molina on the Natural Law

For Molina *ius naturale* is that which has the same validity everywhere and does not depend upon our acceptance. That means that *ius naturale* is an objective ethical instance whose validity is not subject to human whim or caprice. The nature of the thing is what determines the obligation, and it is expressed by the *lex naturalis* applicable to the case. The natural law tradition is certainly much older than Molina. I have shown how it stemmed out of Greek and Roman philosophy blended with Biblical wisdom. The idea that morality is bound to objective principles, to something that goes beyond the subjectivity of the moral agent is part of this natural law tradition. In Aquinas this is formulated saying that natural law is a participation in eternal law, which is in God, and therefore not subject to be altered by human will.[2] In this same tradition, however, there is a conviction that this objectivity of the moral principles and

[2] II^a–IIae, q. 91, a. 2.

the *ius*—the right thing to do—of the case, does not relinquish the responsibility of the moral agent to discover what that *ius* is and what moral norms—*leges naturales*—should inform the action. In Aquinas this is expressed by saying that natural law is not a written law.[3] Aquinas along these lines makes the distinction of first principles of natural law, its necessary conclusions and more remote conclusions that are not necessarily drawn from the first principles. In Scotus the idea of being in harmony or consistent—*congruuus*—with strict natural law also renders the idea of the need of the intellectual and moral effort the agent should make before acting.

This tension between the objective good of the concrete case—and the objective norm applicable to it—and the subjective intellectual effort and free appropriation of it, is kept in Molina's concept of the natural law tradition in a way that can still today offer some help to our ways of reasoning. It would be of help in order to avoid either a legalistic or a subjectivistic position. Natural law—taken as a collective noun not as a single norm—provides us with a number of moral principles that can inform our action: do good, avoid evil, thou shall not steel, a deposit should be returned. These principles, as we can see in the examples, have a different degree of concretion. There are first principles. There are the necessary conclusions linked to these first principles. There are the more remote conclusions deduced from the two just mentioned. All these constitute prescriptive natural law, which is intrinsically connected with analytical natural law.

Analytical natural law is based on the study of the reality of things, and certainly presupposes that there is in nature a certain order of things. This order can be investigated. This order can be known at least to a certain extent. This natural order that we can know has a normative value because of its intrinsic connection with prescriptive natural law. The Humean objection of the natural fallacy would be immediately adduced against this type of reasoning. I would argue that Molina's way of reasoning is not an 'is' that impinges on the 'ought', but that the 'ought' has claims on what the 'is' should arrive to be. In order to do so we have to investigate what the 'is' really is, so that we can determine what 'ought' has a claim on it. An investigation of the objective order of reality of things allows us to allocate better claims of the human condition on any human action.

---

[3] IIa–IIae, q. 94.

It is this way of moral reasoning in the tradition of natural law and the brilliant articulation of *ius naturale* and *lex naturalis* what allowed Molina to accept as legitimate a living dedicated to money lending. He was able to take this step without breaking away from the teachings of the Church. He was able to do this by better explaining the reality of money, the way it worked and in which cases money lending should be reputed as usury.

In this respect it is important to recall the theological status of natural law according to Molina. Natural law was a participation in God's providence, understood as self-providence. Any human being was called to it. The precepts of natural law were immutable, and the *ius* of a certain case was also immutable as long as its circumstances did not change it. However, natural law understood as self-providence—personal and communal—was subject to change. The *ius naturalis* was necessarily mutable in the sense of unfolding. Divine providence was immutable in its determination to save human kind, but it unfolds itself in changing ways in order to rightly achieve this immutable determination.

This way of moral reasoning can help moral theology today, and serve to explain development in moral teaching. Let me give an example. When in the 1920's organ transplantation became a field of research and experimentation in medicine, the first reaction of Catholic moral theologians was to condemn it on the grounds of mutilation. Eighty years later, August 29th 2000 John Paul II addressing the 18th International Congress of the Transplantation Society declared that "transplants [were] a great step forward in science's service of man", and that "one way of nurturing a culture of life is the donation of organs, performed in an acceptable ethical manner."[4]

One way of—cynically—interpreting this move would be to judge it an opportunistic accommodation of Catholic moral theology. It would be a better interpretation to acknowledge how the moral quest is a difficult one, in which—especially in front of new realities—it is not easy to quickly pass a moral judgment. In the case of organ transplantation the first reaction was negative because the category that was being used to read this new phenomenon was mutilation. Any new reality tends to be assimilated to some pre-existing one for the sake of moral assessment. The first assessment is always influenced by the pre-existing category that has been chosen. Further research and study allows us to delineate better

[4] John Paul II, *Insegnamenti di Giovanni Paolo II. XXIII, 2*. (Stato Città del Vaticano: Libreria Editrici Vaticana, 2000). 281.

the similarities and the dissimilarities between the pre-existing case and the new phenomenon. This can lead to a change in the moral assessment of the emerging realities. A better understanding of the reality of things can lead to change the verdict upon the morality of a certain action. This is not a renounce to moral principles, but a better application of them. For Molina—and in this he was following Aquinas—the more remote the conclusions drawn from the first principles of the natural law, the easier the possibility of an error. There was also the possibility of having to change one's own judgment when some circumstance changed, because the circumstances would alter the case itself and the *lex* applicable to it. This brings us to the third contribution we can still draw from Molina: his methodology and specially how circumstances shape the case.

3. Molina and Methodology

One of Molina's more remarkable contributions is that of methodology for moral reasoning. As I have said natural law and casuistry are not for him opposed moral methods, but rather two sides of the same methodology that is both faithful to principles and attentive to particularity. This is based on his conception of *ius naturale* as we have already specified. *Ius naturalis* is that which "has the same validity, and does not depend on our accepting it or not."[5] The *ius* is given by the nature of the thing, but this can change when a certain circumstance accrues; if the nature changes, so does the *ius*. In saying this Molina was following the Council of Trent. In Chapter 5 of Session XIV, the Council had stated that the penitent had to confess the sin with the circumstances that would or could mutate the species of the sin. Circumstances were vital to determine what was right or wrong in a certain situation.

Molina gave different examples of the kind of circumstances that could shape the case. One type of circumstance was human law. In its interaction with natural law human law could change the obligations arising from a certain situation. The case of prescription was an example of this. According to natural law what belonged to a person could not lawfully pass to another by the mere way of fact. Legal prescription is a way to deal with the insecurity to which this could lead. Prescription states that property that has come in to some others' hands belongs to

[5] V. 7. 1. p. 113.

this person after a number of year and certain conditions. Prescription creates a legal circumstance for the sake of legal security that makes the obligations of the situation different than those which would have arisen from mere natural law.

Another circumstance could be based just on the will of a single person. When Peter promised to pay Paul a certain amount of money, he was bound by his promise. There was an obligation to pay based on a natural law principle: *pacta sunt servanda*. Paul could not dispense the promise. He could, however, condone the debt. Peter would be no longer bound to pay. The *ius* arising from the situation had changed from an obligation to pay to no obligation to pay at all. This was not due to a dispensation of the *lex naturalis* or a change in it, but a change in the *ius* arising from the nature of the case. This change was due to a circumstance based on human will.

There were also circumstances based in a fact. The case of the depositary of a sword is paradigmatic in this sense. One is bound by natural law to return a thing given as a deposit when the depositary claims it. About this nobody had a doubt. Scholastics also agreed that it was not right to return a sword to the depositary when one was aware that the person was about to do something wrong with it. Molina's explanation was that the factual 'deficiency' in the depositary claiming his sword changed the situation, to the extent that the precept on the obligation to return the deposit was not applicable any more. He did not deny the precept. He just denied its pertinence because a factual circumstance had reshaped the case.

We have two examples of how a fact affects the moral judgment on realities that—although similar—deserve different assessment. It is interesting to note that in both cases, what makes the difference is a certain deficiency that it is not present in the original case. We could conclude that there is an ideal mode of things, and a second one that is certainly non-ideal but acceptable, given a certain deficiency. In moral theology the greatest deficiency is sin. This mode of reasoning—the ideal and the acceptable—is also witnessed by the use that Molina makes of evangelical counsels, not just referring to vowed religious life, but to many other human realities, in our case usury and other business practices. This mode of reasoning offers a greater space for moral growth.

This method of moral reasoning could be of help even today to overcome certain aporias. There are principles, norms or values that if accepted as belonging to natural law are certainly non-negotiable. Negotiation is based on human will, the *ius naturale* on the objectivity of the nature of the thing. Yet there are cases in which the standard natural law principle or norm seems impossible to follow, and it is hard to attribute moral guilt to the presumed trespassers. Molina's methodology seems to be a way of upholding the soundness and goodness of the principle, while also allowing the subject to act in good conscience, thus leaving an space for moral growth. It seems to be a virtuous mean between the extremes of relativism and legalism.

Molina makes a wide use of Scotus' notion of harmony with natural law. It is most likely this that allows him not to fall into legalism in spite of the wide use he makes of human laws in his moral reasoning. Natural law did not just bind morally through the precepts that strictly speaking belonged to it, leaving the rest to the free decision of the agent as if there were in this free field a moral vacuum. One of the ways of using the term law was as a common noun referring to a number of norms grouped by a common end. All the norms, all the ways of conduct referring to the human person's natural end were natural law. Most of them belonged to it by its harmony with the first principles of natural law. To ascertain whether these ways of conduct were in harmony with the first principles of the natural law was the task of the moral agent. This Scotistic approach to the natural law coincided with Aquinas when he established that no human act was indifferent. Our exposition on the topics of usury, just price and money exchange has shown a practical case of how this works in justice in the market.

4. Molina on Justice and the Common Good

Molina did not dedicate a disputation or a set of them to the notion of the common good. He dealt with it as he thought necessary according to the issue he was discussing. The idea of the common good was to some extent taken for granted as part of the reasoning on justice. The closest Molina comes to a definition of the common good is when he refers to it as "peace, security and justice among men."[6] Hardly anyone would not find this desirable for the commonwealth. The common good appears in his moral analysis as an end regulating many economic institutions. Private property, money, monopolies, and fixed legal prices in certain cases are examples we have seen of this.

[6] II. 22.9. p. 63.

According to Molina the common good after the Fall, the imperative that all should be able to take part in the goods of Creation postulated the establishment of private property. If things were still held in common after the Fall most people would not work enough, and fights would break over the use of goods. In this situation the strongest would prevail and the weakest would be the worst hit. The common good and *recta ratio* after the Fall recommended private property. Precisely because of this the common good would demand and allow restrictions and modifications in the legal system of private property. First of all the end should dictate the norms of the legal institution. The legal system should facilitate access to property for all, or at least to the greatest part. When this does not happen the regulatory system of private property should be changed or rearranged. Prescription is another example we have cited related to private property and the common good. Private property was not of *ius naturale*, but it is certainly very commendable for the common good. Prescription was possible because private property was not of *ius naturale* and because the common good required legal security as to whom a certain good belonged.

Money was also a case of justice and common good. Before the creation of money, exchange was done by barter on an equal basis between the two parties involved in the exchange. The creation of money as a measure by which to value things, a means of payment and a guarantor for future necessities by the community had created an inequality in the exchange. The introduction of money differentiated buyer and seller. This had been done by the introduction of money, whose legal value was guaranteed by the community. The problem of justice, once money had been introduced, went beyond commutative justice. Prices, buying and selling had become questions of the common good. This is what allowed Molina to consider a monopoly or a fixed legal price for basic goods in certain cases. Molina was not very much in favor of restricting freedom, but would allow for it in some cases. The Austrian School of Economics saw in Molina and other scholastics the forerunners of their theories, largely because of the idea of indeterminism in pricing. There appears to be an error though, because where the Austrian School called for detachment from any moral judgment in economic affairs as a result of indeterminism, Molina called for *communis aestimatio* and the assessment of prudent merchants.

It is telling that Molina's dismissal of a fixed legal price for wheat was not made on the grounds that it burdened the owners of wheat, but on the grounds that it burdened only them. The entire community should collaborate in helping those in need, not just the wheat owners. His solution relied not on the idea of respecting someone's property, but on the idea that everyone was called in matters of common good.

5. Conclusion

Justice was for Molina the virtue that ordained all action to the common good. This virtue was not realized only by good private actions, by making good laws and by following just norms. Justice was also served by fostering the virtues that the common good required and could be done in the community of merchants, especially among the prudent ones. Merchants were bound by certain ties forming a community. This idea that merchants formed a community is what allowed Molina to think of justice and charity not as concurring virtues, but as synergic virtues. From charity's perfection depended justice's perfection, because only he who is bound by the ties of love can fully give to the other his or her own due.

What we learn from Molina is not a set of solutions, but dynamics regarding how to use the tradition while being at the same time faithful and creative. In his magisterial work *Sources of the Self*,[7] Charles Taylor shows how the modern idea of self is the result of what we could call a "historical development." In a similar way, we can see how the multi-layered analysis found in Molina witnesses to the fact that views regarding justice are the result of a long evolution. Four hundred years later, Molina's insights continue to instruct us that we can hardly present a theory of justice that disregards history and contemporary experience. Justice cannot be a theory or a thought experiment, but must always remain a living quest.

---

[7] Charles Taylor, *The Sources of the Self: The Making of Modern Identity* (Cambridge, Mass: Harvard University Press, 1989).

BIBLIOGRAPHY

Adams, Marilyn Mc Cord. "The Structure of Ockham's Moral Theory." in *The Context of Casuistry*, ed. James F. Keenan and Thomas A. Shannon, xxiii, 231 p. Washington, D.C.: Georgetown University Press, 1995.

Aldama, José Antonio. "Luis de Molina: de Spe, II, qq. 17–22." *Archivo Teológico Granadino* I (1938): 111 ff.

Andrés Martín, Melquíades. *La teología española en el siglo XVI*. Madrid: BAC, 1977.

Aristotle. *The Nichomachean Ethics* Loebb Classical Library. Cambridge, MA: Harvard University Press, 1999.

——. *Politics*. Translated by H. Rackham The Loeb Classical Library. Cambridge, MA: Harvard University Press, 1959.

Azevedo Alves, André and Moreira, José Manuel. *The Salamanca School*. New York-London: Continuum, 2010.

Azpilcueta, Martín de. *Manuale De'Confessori Et Penitenti*. In Vinetia: Appresso Gabriel Giolito di Ferrari, 1569.

Belda, Francisco. "Ética de la creación de créditos según la doctrina de Molina, Lesio y Lugo." *Pensamiento* I (1963): 53–92.

Beltrán de Heredia, Vicente. "La enseñanza de santo Tomás en la Compañía de Jesús, durante el primer siglo de su existencia. La legislación." *La Ciencia Tomista* XII (1915): 388 ff.

——. "La enseñanza de santo Tomás en la Compañía de Jesús, durante el primer siglo de su existencia. La práctica." *La Ciencia Tomista* XII (1915): 34 ff.

Benson, Robert L. "Medieval Canonistic Origins of the Debate on the Lawfulness of the Spanish Conquest." in *First Images of America: The Impact of the New World on the Old*, ed. Fredi Chiappelli, I. Berkeley: University of California Press, 1976.

Berman, Harold Joseph. *Law and Revolution: The Formation of the Western Legal Tradition*. Cambridge, Mass.: Harvard University Press, 1983.

Biel, Gabriel. *Treatise on the Power and Utility of Moneys*, ed. Robert Belle Burke. Philadelphia, London: University of Pennsylvania Press Oxford University Press, 1930.

Braudel, Fernand. *The Mediterranean and the Mediterranean World in the Time of Phillipp II*. Vol. II. New York: Harper and Row, 1976.

——. *Carlos V y Felipe II*. Madrid: Alianza Editorial, 1999.

Brodrick, James. *Robert Bellarmine, Saint and Scholar*. Westminster, Md.: Newman Press, 1961.

——. *The Progress of the Jesuits 1556–1579*. New York: Longmans, Green & Co., 1947.

Broglio, Paolo. *La teologia e la politica. Controversie dottrinali, Curia romana e Monarchia spagnola tra Cinque e Seicento*. Firenze: Leo S. Olschki Editore, 2009.

Cajetan, Tommaso de Vio. *Perquam Docta, Resoluta Ac Compediosa De Peccatis Summula*. Lugduni: apud V. de Portonariis, 1538.

Canning, Joseph. "Introduction: politics, institutions and ideas," in *The Cambridge Companion to History of Medieval Thought*, ed. J.H. Burns. Cambridge, U.K.: Cambridge University Press, 1991.

Carande, Ramón. *Carlos V y sus banqueros. Edición Abreviada*. Barcelona: Crítica, 2000.

Caro Baroja, Julio. *Las formas complejas de la vida religiosa: religión, sociedad y carácter en la España de los siglos XVI y XVII*. Madrid: Akal, 1978.

Carpintero Benitez, Francisco. "En torno al método de los juristas medievales." *Anuario de Historia del Derecho Español* LII (1982).

Carter, C.H. "The New World as a Factor in Interantional Relations 1492–1793," in *First Images of America: The Impact of the New World on the Old*, ed. Fredi Chiappelli, Michael J.B. Allen and Robert Louis Benson. Berkeley: University of California Press, 1976.

Cassel's Latin Dictionary. New York: Wiley Publishing, 1977.

Caycedo, José. *Ideas jurídicas de Luis de Molina sobre la propiedad privada*. Excerpta Ex Disertatione in Pontificia Universitas Gregoriana. Pontificia Universitas Gregoriana, 1957.

Chafuen, Alejandro Antonio. *Christians for Freedom: Late-Scholastic Economics*. San Francisco: Ignatius Press, 1986.

——. *Faith and Liberty: The Economic Thought of the Late Scholastics* Studies in Ethics and Economics. Lanham, Md.: Lexington Books, 2003.

Lewis, Charlton T. *A Latin Dictionary Founded on Andrew's Edition of Freund's Latin Dictionary*. Oxford: Oxford Univesity Press, 1998.

Cicero, Marcus Tullius. *De Officiis*. Translated by Walter Miller. Cambridge, MA: Harvard University Press, 1961.

Cipolla, Carlo M. "Introducción." in *Historia económica de Europa*, ed. Carlo M. Cipolla, 2. Barcelona: Ariel, 1979.

Codina Mir, Gabriel. *Aux sources de la pédagogie des jésuites, Le "Modus Parisiensis."* Roma: Institutum Historicum S.I., 1968.

The Concise Oxford Dictionary of Current English. Oxford: Claredon Press, 1979.

Congar, Yves M-J. "Quod omnes tangit, ab omnibus tractari et aprobari debet." *Revue de Histoire du Droit Français et Etranger* (1956).

Consobrinus, Johannes, and Francesco Medici. *Tractatus P[Er] Utilimus De Iusticia [Com]Mutatiua*. Imp[re]ssus vero Parisii: [Louis Martineau], 1483.

Copleston S.J., Frederick. *A History of Philosophy*. Vol. V. Modern Philosophy: The British Philosophers. Garden City, NY: Image Books, 1964.

Costello, Frank Bartholomew. *The Political Philosophy of Luis de Molina, S.J. (1535–1600)*. Roma Spokane: Institutum Historicum S.I.; Gonzaga University Press, 1974.

Crombie, A.C. *Science, Art, and Nature in Medieval and Modern Thought*. London; Rio Grande, Ohio: Hambledon Press, 1996.

Dekker, Eef. *Middle Knowledge*. Leuven: Peeters, 2000.

Deman, Thomas. "Probabilisme." in *Dictionaire de Théologie Catholique*, ed. Eugène Mangeot, Alfred Vacant, Emile Amann. Paris: Librairie Letonzey et Ané, 1936.

Dempsey, Bernard William. *Interest and Usury*. Washington, D.C.: American Council on Public Affairs, 1943.

A Dictionary of Economics Oxford University Press, 2002; Available from ⟨http://www.oxfordreference.com/views/ENTRY.html?subview=Main&entry=t19.e2421⟩.

A Dictionary of Finance and Banking Oxford University Press, 2005; Available from ⟨http://www.oxfordreference.com/views/ENTRY.html?subview=Main&entry=t20.e2466⟩.

Díez-Alegría, José María. *El desarrollo de la doctrina de la ley natural en Luis de Molina y en los maestros de la Universidad de Evora de 1565 a 1591. Estudio histórico y textos inéditos*. Barcelonna, 1951.

Donnelly, Phillip J. "Discussions on the Supernatural Order." *Theological Studies* IX, no. 2 (1948).

Dorato, Mauro. *The Software of the Universe: An Introduction to the History and Philosophy of the Laws of Nature* Ashgate New Critical Thinking in Philosophy and Index. Aldershot, England; Burlington, VT: Ashgate, 2005.

Dulles, Avery. *Models of the Church*. Garden City: Doubleday, 1974.

Duns Scotus, John, and Allan Bernard Wolter. *Duns Scotus on the Will and Morality*. Washington, D.C.: Catholic University of America Press, 1986.

Espejo, Cristobal, and Julian Paz. *Las antiguas ferias de Medina del Campo. Investigación histórica acerca de ellas*. Valladolid: Imprenta La Nueva Pincia, 1908.

Finn, Daniel. *The Moral Ecology of Markets: Assessing Claims About Markets and Justice*. Cambridge: Cambridge University Press, 2006.

Folgado, Avelino. "Los tratados *De Legibus* y *De Iustita et Iure* en los autores españoles del siglo XVI y primera mitad del XVII." *La Ciudad de Dios* CLXXII (1959).

Franklin, James. *The Science of Conjecture. Evidence and Probability before Pascal*. Baltimore: The Johns Hopkins University Press, 2001.

Gallager, John A. *Time Past, Time Future*. Mahawh, NJ: Paulist Press, 1990.

García Villoslada, Ricardo. *La Universidad de Paris durante los estudios de Francisco de Vitoria (1507–1522)*. Rome: apud aedes Universitatis Gregorianae, 1938.

Gómez Camacho, Francisco. "En torno a unos textos de Luis de Molina sobre la propiedad privada," *Revista española de teología* (1977).

———. "La 'estimación común' en la teoría molinista del precio justo," *Revista española de teología* (1978).

———. "Luis de Molina y la metodología de la ley natural," *Miscelánea Comillas* 43, no. 83 (1985).

———. *Orígenes del pensamiento económico en La Mancha: Luis de Molina, 1° Congreso de Historia de Castilla La Mancha*, vol. VII. La Mancha: Junta de Comunidades de Castilla-La Mancha, 1988.

———. *Economía y filosofía moral: la formación del pensamiento económico europeo en la escolástica española*. Madrid: Síntesis, 1998.

———. "Later Scholastic: Spanish Economic Thought." in *Ancient and Medieval Economic Ideas and Concepts of Social Justice*, ed. S. Todd Lowry and Barry Gordon. Leiden; New York: Brill, 1998.

———. "Introduction," in *Sourcebook in Late-Scholastic Monetary Theory. Contributions of Martin de Azpilicueta, Luis de Molina S.J. and Juan de Mariana, S.J.*, ed. Stephen J. Grabill. Lanham: Lexington Books, 2007.

González Fabre, Raúl. *Justicia en el mercado. Fundamentación de la ética del mercado según Francisco de Vitoria*. Caracas: CONICIT-UCAB, 1998.

Gordon, Barry. *Economic Analysis before Adam Smith: Hesiod to Lessius*. London: Macmillan, 1975.

Grice-Hutchinson, Marjorie. *The School of Salamanca; Readings in Spanish Monetary Theory, 1544–1605*. Oxford: Clarendon Press, 1952.

——. *Early Economic Thought in Spain, 1177–1740*. London; Boston: Allen & Unwin, 1978.

Grice-Hutchinson, Marjorie, Moss, Laurence S. and Ryan, Christopher K. *Economic Thought in Spain: Selected Essays*. Brookfield, Vt.: E. Elgar, 1993.

Grisel, Etienne. "The Beginning of International Law and General Public Law Doctrine: Francisco de Vitoria's De Indiis Prior." in *First Images of America: The Impact of the New World on the Old*, ed. Fredi Chiappelli, I. Berkeley: University of California Press, 1976.

Gundlach, Gustav. *Zur Soziologie der Katholischen Ideenwelt und des Jesuitenordens. Inaug.-Diss*. Berlin: E. Ebering, 1927.

Hacking, Ian. *The Emergence of Probability. A Philosophical Study of Early Ideas About Probability, Induction and Statistical Inference*. 2nd ed. Cambridge, UK: Cambridge University Press, 2006.

Hamilton, Earl J. *American Treasure and the Price Revolution in Spain, 1501–1650* Harvard Economic Studies, V. 43. New York: Octagon Books, 1965.

Hanke, Lewis. "The Theological Significance of the Discovery of America." in *First Images of America: The Impact of the New World on the Old*, ed. Fredi Chiappelli, Michael J.B. Allen and Robert Louis Benson. Berkeley: University of California Press, 1976.

Höffner, Joseph. *Wirtschaftsethik und Monopole im fünfzehnten und sechzehnten Jahrhundert* Freiburger Staatswissenschaftliche Schriften, Heft 2. Jena: G. Fischer, 1941.

Höpfl, Harro. *Jesuit Political Thought. The Society of Jesus and the State, C. 1540–1630*. Cambridge, UK: Cambridge University Press, 2004.

Hoyningen-Huene, Paul. "Kuhn, Thomas Samuel." in *Routledge Encyclopedia of Philosophy*, ed. Craig Edward, 5. London: Routledge, 1998.

Jeanrond, Werner G. *Theological Hermeneutics. Development and Significance*. New York: Crossroad, 1991.

The Jesuit Ratio Studiorum of 1599. Translated by S.J. Farrell, Allan P., ed. S.J. Farrell, Allan P. Washington D.C.: Conference of Major Superior of Jesuits, 1970.

Jonsen, Albert R. "Foreword." in *The Context of Casuistry*, ed. James F. Keenan and Thomas A. Shannon, xxiii, 231 p. Washington, D.C.: Georgetown University Press, 1995.

Jonsen, Albert R., and Stephen Edelston Toulmin. *The Abuse of Casuistry: A History of Moral Reasoning*. Berkeley: University of California Press, 1988.

John Paul II. *Insegnamenti di Giovanni Paolo II. XXIII, 2*. Stato Città del Vaticano: Libreria Editrici Vaticana, 2000.

Juan, Oscar de and Monsalve, Fabio. "Morally Ruled Behaviour: The Neglected Contribution of Scholasticism." *The European Journal of the History of Economic Thought* 13, no. 1 (2006): 99–112.

Keenan, James F. "The Casuistry of John Mair, Nominalist Professor of Paris." in *The Context of Casuistry*, ed. James F. Keenan and Thomas A. Shannon, xxiii, 231 p. Washington, D.C.: Georgetown University Press, 1995.

———. "The Return of Casuistry." *Theological Studies*, no. 57 (1996).

———. "Moral Theology." in *From Trent to Vatican II*, ed. Raymon F. Bulman and Frederick J. Parrella. Oxford, New York: Oxford University Press, 2006.

Keenan, James F., and Thomas A. Shannon. "Introduction." in *The Context of Casuistry*, ed. James F. Keenan and Thomas A. Shannon, xxiii, 231 p. Washington, D.C.: Georgetown University Press, 1995.

Kellenbenz, Hernann. "La técnica en la época de la Revolución Científica (1500–1700)." in *Historia económica de Europa*, ed. Carlo M. Cipolla, 2. Barcelona: Ariel, 1979.

Kent, Bonnie. "Habits and Virtues." in *The Ethics of Aquinas*, ed. Stephen J. Pope. Washington D.C.: Georgetown University Press, 2002.

Keynes, John Maynard. *A Treatise on Probability*. London: MacMillan and Co. Ltd, 1921.

Kleinhappl, Johann. "Die Eignentumslehre Ludwig Molinas." *Zeitschrift für katholische Theologie* 56 (1932): 46–66.

Kuhn, Thomas. *The Structure of Scientific Revolutions*. 2nd ed. Chicago: University of Chicago Press, 1970.

Langholm, Odd. "Scholastic Economics." in *Pre-Classical Economic Thought: From the Greeks to the Scottish Enlightenment. Recent Economic Thought Series*, ed. S. Todd Lowry. Boston: Kluwer-Nijhoff Pub., 1987.

Lamadrid, Rafael Sánchez de. "Luis de Molina: De Bello, Comentario a la II–II, q. 40." *Archivo Teológico Granadino* (1939): 155 ff.

Lexicon Latinitatis Medii Aevi, Praesertim Ad Res Ecclesiasticas Investigandas Pertinens. Thurnholti: Typographi Brepols Editores Pontificii, 1975.

Lima, Luís Correa. *Teologia de Mercado. Uma visao da economia mundial no tempo em que os economistas eram teologos*. Bauru, Sao Paulo: Editora da Universidade do Sagrado Coracao, 2001.

Lisson, E.L., Moore, E., Bretske, J.T. "Teología: V. Moral." in *Diccionario histórico de la Compañía de Jesús. Biográfico—Temático*, ed. Charles E. O'Neill S.J. and Joaquín María Domiínguez S.J., IV. Roma-Madrid: Institutum Historicum S.J.-Universidad Pontificia Comillas, 2001.

Locke, John. *Two Treatises of Government* Everyman's Library. London: Dent, 1975.

Lubac, Henri de. *Surnaturel. Études Historiques*. Paris: Éditions Montaigne, 1956.

MacIntyre, Alasdair C. *Whose Justice? Which Rationality?* Notre Dame, Ind: University of Notre Dame Press, 1988.

Mahoney, John. *The Making of Moral Theology. A Study of the Roman Catholic Tradition*. Oxford: Claredon Press, 1987.

Mair, John. *In Secundum Librum Sententiarum*. Paris, 1519.

Mancioni, Gianpiero. "Il "dominium altum" nella dottrina di Soto, Molina, Suarez: studio per un ridimensionamento della dottrina scolastica sulla proprietà privata." Pontificia Università Gregoriana, 1966.

Margolis, Howard. *It Started with Copernicus. How Turning the World inside out Led to the Scientific Revolution*. New York: McGraw-Hill, 2002.

Marshall, Alfred. *Principles of Economics*. 9th ed. London, New York: Macmillan for the Royal Economic Society, 1961.

McGrath, Alister E. *Iustitia Dei. A History of the Christian Doctrine of Justification*. 3rd ed. Cambridge: Cambridge university Press, 2005.

Mercado, Tomás de. *Summa de tratos y contratos*. Sevilla: Hernando Díaz, 1571.

Minchinton, Walter. "Tipos y estructura de la demanda (1500–1700)." in *Historia económica de Europa*, ed. Carlo M. Cipolla, 2. Barcelona: Ariel, 1979.

Molina, Luis de. *De justitia et jure: opera omnia, tractatibus quinque, tomisque totidem comprehensa*. Coloniae Allobrogum: Sumptibus fratrum de Tournes, 1759.

——. *Los seis libros de la justicia y el derecho*, ed. Manuel Fraga Iribarne. Madrid: Impr. de J.L. Cosano, 1941.

——. "Luis De Molina, S.J., De Caritate, Comentario a La II–II, qq 23–25." *Archivo Teológico Granadino* (1965): 199 ff.

——. "Luis De Molina, S.J., De Caritate, Comentario a la II–II, qq 26–29." *Archivo Teológico Granadino* (1966): 181 ff.

——. "Luis De Molina, S.J., De Fide, Comentario a la II–II, qq 1–16." *Archivo Teológico Granadino* (1976): 207 ff.

——. *La teoría del justo precio*, ed. Francisco Gómez Camacho. Madrid: Editora Nacional, 1981.

——. *On Divine Foreknowledge: Part IV of the Concordia*. Translated by Alfred J. Freddoso, ed. Alfred J. Freddoso. Ithaca: Cornell University Press, 1988.

——. *Concordia del libre arbitrio*, trad. Juan Antonio Hevia Echevarria. Oviedo: Fundación Gustavo Bueno, 2007.

Molle, Luciano dalle. *Il contratto di cambio nei moralisti dal secolo XIII alla metà del secolo XVII*. Roma: Edizioni di Storia e Letteratura, 1954.

Moore, Eduardo. *La moral en el siglo XVI y primera mitad del XVI*. Granada, 1956.

Musto, Roland G. *Catholic Peacemakers. A Documentary History*. Vol. II. From the Renaissance to the Twentieth Century, Part I. New York and London: Garland Publishing, 1996.

Nadal, Gerónimo. *Epistolae P. Hieronumi Nadal Societatis Jesu, Ab Anno 1546 Ad 1577*. Matriti: Typis Augustini Avrial, 1898.

Noonan, John Thomas. *The Scholastic Analysis of Usury*. Cambridge: Harvard University Press, 1957.

Novak, Michael. *The Catholic Ethic and the Spirit of Capitalism*. Toronto: Free Press, 1993.

Ocaña García, Marcelino. *Luis de Molina (1535–1600)*. 1. ed. Biblioteca Filosófica. Colección filósofos y textos. Madrid: Ediciones del Orto, 1995.

Oliveira Dias, José de. "Ainda a controvertida paternidade da chamada ciência média." *Verbum* 11 (1951): 367–382.

——. "Em tôrno do duelo Fonseca-Molina. Uma argumentaçâo suicida." *Verbum* 11 (1954): 37–63.

——. "Fonseca e Molina. Os ultimos ecos dum litígio plurissecular." *Revista portuguesa de filosofia* II (1955): 64–77.

O'Malley, John W. *The First Jesuits*. Cambridge: Harvard University Press, 2002.

——. *Four Cultures of the West*. Cambridge, Massachusetts: Harvard University Press, 2004.
Panaccio, Claude. "William of Ockham." in *Routledge Encyclopedia of Philosophy*, ed. Craig Edward, 9. London: Routledge, 1998.
Parker, Geoffrey. "El surgimiento de las finanzas modernas en Europa (1500–1700)." in *Historia económica de Europa*, ed. Carlo M. Cipolla, 2. Barcelona: Ariel, 1979.
Porter, Jean. *Natural and Divine Law. Reclaiming the Tradition for Christian Ethics* Series in Ethics. Grand Rapids, Michigan: Saint Paul University, 1999.
——. "The Virtue of Justice." In *The Ethics of Aquinas*, ed. Stephen J. Pope. Washington D.C.: Georgetown University Press, 2002.
Pribram, Karl. *A History of Economic Reasoning*. Baltimore: Johns Hopkins University Press, 1983.
Queralt, Antonio. "El fin último natural en Luis de Molina." *Estudios eclesiásticos* 34 (1960): 177.
Quilliet, Bernard. *L'acharnement théologique. Histoire de la grâce en Occident—IIIe–XXIe siècles*, Paris: Fayard, 2007.
Rabeneck, Ioannes. "*De vita et scriptis Ludovici Molina*." *Archivium Storicum Societatis Iesu* (1950): 75–145.
de Roover, Raymond Adrien, *Monopoly Theory Prior to Adam Smith. A Revision* Cambridge, Mass.: Harvard University Press, 1951.
——. *L'evolution de la lettre de change, XIVe–XVIIIe siecles*, Affaires et Gens d'Affaires 4, Paris: A. Colin, 1953.
——. *La pensè èconomique des scolastiques: doctrines et mèthodes*. Montreal: Inst. d'Études Mèdiévales, 1971.
——. "The Scholastic Attitude toward Trade and Entrepeneurship." in *Business, Banking, and Economic Thought in Late Medieval and Early Modern Europe*, ed. Julius Kirschner. Chicago: University of Chicago Press, 1974.
Rossi, Paolo. *La nascita della scienza moderna in Europa*. Roma: Laterza, 1997.
Russell, Bertrand. "An Outline of Intellectual Rubish." in *Unpopular Essays*. London: Routledge, 1995.
Salaverri, Joaquín. "La noción de Iglesia del Padre Luis de Molina." *Revista española de teología* 20 (1960): 199–230.
Salvat, Ignasi. *Servir en misión universal*. Vol. 27 Manresa. Bilbao Santander: Mensajero-Sal Terrae, 2001.
Schumpeter, Joseph Alois, and Schumpeter, Elizabeth Boody. *History of Economic Analysis*. New York: Oxford University Press, 1954.
Sella, Domenico. "Las industrias europeas (1500–1700)." in *Historia económica de Europa*, ed. Carlo M. Cipolla, 2. Barcelona: Ariel, 1979.
Sen, Amartya. *On Ethics and Economics*. Oxford: Blackwell, 1987.
Seneca, Lucio Anneo. *Lettere morali a Lucilio*. vol. 2. Milano: Oscar Mondadori, 1995.
Shannon, Thomas A. "Method in Ethics: A Scotistic Contribution." in *The Context of Casuistry*, ed. James F. Keenan and Thomas A. Shannon, xxiii, 231 p. Washington, D.C.: Georgetown University Press, 1995.
Skarvad, Jaroslaw. *De Iure Proprietatis Privatae Apud Ludovicum Molinam* Dissertatio in Pontificia Universitas Lateranensi. Roma, 1950.

Sosa Morato, Beatriz Eugenia. *La noción de derecho en "Los seis libros de la justicia y el derecho" de Luis de Molina.* Pamplona: Ediciones Universidad de Navarra, 1985.

Soto, Domingo de. *Libri Decem De Iustitia Et Iure.* Lugduni: Apud heredes Iacobi Iuntae, 1569.

Stegmüller, Friedrich. *Geschichte des Molinismus.* Münster i. W.: Aschendorff, 1935.

Stone, Martin W.F. "Scrupulosity and Conscience: Probabilism in Early Modern Scholastic Ethics." in *Contexts of Conscience in Early Modern Europe, 1500–1700*, ed. Edward Vallance and Harald Braun. Houndmills, Basingstoke, Hampshire; New York: Palgrave Macmillan, 2004.

Tavares, Severiano. "A Questáo Fonseca-Molina. Respost a Uma Crítica." *Revista portuguesa de filosofia* II (1955): 78–88.

Taylor, Charles. *The Sources of the Self: The Making of Modern Identity.* Cambridge, Mass: Harvard University Press, 1989.

Tierney, Brian. *The Idea of Natural Rights: Studies on Natural Rights, Natural Law, and Church Law, 1150–1625* Emory University Studies in Law and Religion; No. 5. Atlanta, Ga.: Scholars Press, 1997.

Turrini, Miriam. *La coscienza e le leggi: morale e diritto nei testi per la confessione della prima età moderna.* Bologna: Il Mulino, 1991.

Vázquez de Prada, Valentín. "Moneda y cambios internacionales a finales del siglo XVI y comienzos del XVII." in *Aportaciones a la historia económica y social: España y Europa, siglos XVI–XVII.*, ed. Jesús María Usunariz Gayoa, II. Las actividades industriales. Moneda y crédito: el mundo de las finanzas. Pamplona: Eunsa, 2000.

Vereecke, Louis. *Da Guglielmo d'Ockham a sant'Alfonso de Liguori. Saggi di storia della teologia morale moderna. 1300–1787.* Cisinello Balsamo: Edizioni Paoline, 1990.

Vigo, Abelardo del. *Economía y ética en el siglo XVI.* Madrid: BAC, 2006.

Vilar, Pierre. *Oro y moneda en la historia. 1450–1920.* Barcelona: Ariel, 1969.

Vitoria, Francisco de. *Obras*, ed. Teofílo Urdanoz. Madrid: BAC, 1960.

Vitoria, Francisco de. *Relectio De Indis.*, ed. L. Pereña y J.M. Pérez Prendes. Madrid: CSIC, 1967.

Vives, Juan Luis. *De Subuentione Pauperum. Siue De Humanis Necessitatib[Us] Libri.Ii.* Bruges, 1526.

Weber, Wilhelm. *Wirschaftsethik am Vorabend des Liberalismus: Höhepunkt und Abschluss der Scholastischen Wirtschaftsbetrachtung durch Ludwig Molina, S.J. (1535–1600).* Münster: Aschendorffsche Verlagsbuchhandlung, 1959.

INDEX

Studies in the History of Christian Traditions

(formerly Studies in the History of Christian Thought)

Edited by Robert J. Bast

1. McNeill, J. J. *The Blondelian Synthesis.* 1966. Out of print
2. Goertz, H.-J. *Innere und äussere Ordnung in der Theologie Thomas Müntzers.* 1967
3. Bauman, Cl. *Gewaltlosigkeit im Täufertum.* 1968
4. Roldanus, J. *Le Christ et l'Homme dans la Théologie d'Athanase d'Alexandrie.* 2nd ed. 1977
5. Milner, Jr., B. Ch. *Calvin's Doctrine of the Church.* 1970. Out of print
6. Tierney, B. *Origins of Papal Infallibility, 1150-1350.* 2nd ed. 1988
7. Oldfield, J. J. *Tolerance in the Writings of Félicité Lamennais 1809-1831.* 1973
8. Oberman, H. A. (ed.). *Luther and the Dawn of the Modern Era.* 1974. Out of print
9. Holeczek, H. *Humanistische Bibelphilologie bei Erasmus, Thomas More und William Tyndale.* 1975
10. Farr, W. *John Wyclif as Legal Reformer.* 1974
11. Purcell, M. *Papal Crusading Policy 1244-1291.* 1975
12. Ball, B. W. *A Great Expectation.* Eschatological Thought in English Protestantism. 1975
13. Stieber, J. W. *Pope Eugenius IV, the Council of Basel, and the Empire.* 1978. Out of print
14. Partee, Ch. *Calvin and Classical Philosophy.* 1977
15. Misner, P. *Papacy and Development.* Newman and the Primacy of the Pope. 1976
16. Tavard, G. H. *The Seventeenth-Century Tradition.* A Study in Recusant Thought. 1978
17. Quinn, A. *The Confidence of British Philosophers.* An Essay in Historical Narrative. 1977
18. Beck, J. *Le Concil de Basle (1434).* 1979
19. Church, F. F. and George, T. (ed.). *Continuity and Discontinuity in Church History.* 1979
20. Gray, P. T. R. *The Defense of Chalcedon in the East (451-553).* 1979
21. Nijenhuis, W. *Adrianus Saravia (c. 1532-1613).* Dutch Calvinist. 1980
22. Parker, T. H. L. (ed.). *Iohannis Calvini Commentarius in Epistolam Pauli ad Romanos.* 1981
23. Ellis, I. *Seven Against Christ.* A Study of 'Essays and Reviews'. 1980
24. Brann, N. L. *The Abbot Trithemius (1462-1516).* 1981
25. Locher, G. W. *Zwingli's Thought.* New Perspectives. 1981
26. Gogan, B. *The Common Corps of Christendom.* Ecclesiological Themes in Thomas More. 1982
27. Stock, U. *Die Bedeutung der Sakramente in Luthers Sermonen von 1519.* 1982
28. Yardeni, M. (ed.). *Modernité et nonconformisme en France à travers les âges.* 1983
29. Platt, J. *Reformed Thought and Scholasticism.* 1982
30. Watts, P. M. *Nicolaus Cusanus.* A Fifteenth-Century Vision of Man. 1982
31. Sprunger, K. L. *Dutch Puritanism.* 1982
32. Meijering, E. P. *Melanchthon and Patristic Thought.* 1983
33. Stroup, J. *The Struggle for Identity in the Clerical Estate.* 1984
34. 35. Colish, M. L. *The Stoic Tradition from Antiquity to the Early Middle Ages.* 1.2. 2nd ed. 1990
36. Guy, B. *Domestic Correspondence of Dominique-Marie Varlet, Bishop of Babylon, 1678-1742.* 1986
37. 38. Clark, F. *The Pseudo-Gregorian Dialogues.* I. II. 1987
39. Parente, Jr. J. A. *Religious Drama and the Humanist Tradition.* 1987
40. Posthumus Meyjes, G. H. M. *Hugo Grotius, Meletius.* 1988
41. Feld, H. *Der Ikonoklasmus des Westens.* 1990
42. Reeve, A. and Screech, M. A. (eds.). *Erasmus' Annotations on the New Testament.* Acts — Romans — I and II Corinthians. 1990
43. Kirby, W. J. T. *Richard Hooker's Doctrine of the Royal Supremacy.* 1990
44. Gerstner, J. N. *The Thousand Generation Covenant.* Reformed Covenant Theology. 1990
45. Christianson, G. and Izbicki, T. M. (eds.). *Nicholas of Cusa.* 1991
46. Garstein, O. *Rome and the Counter-Reformation in Scandinavia.* 1553-1622. 1992
47. Garstein, O. *Rome and the Counter-Reformation in Scandinavia.* 1622-1656. 1992
48. Perrone Compagni, V. (ed.). *Cornelius Agrippa, De occulta philosophia Libri tres.* 1992

49. Martin, D. D. *Fifteenth-Century Carthusian Reform.* The World of Nicholas Kempf. 1992
50. Hoenen, M. J. F. M. *Marsilius of Inghen.* Divine Knowledge in Late Medieval Thought. 1993
51. O'Malley, J. W., Izbicki, T. M. and Christianson, G. (eds.). *Humanity and Divinity in Renaissance and Reformation.* Essays in Honor of Charles Trinkaus. 1993
52. Reeve, A. (ed.) and Screech, M. A. (introd.). *Erasmus' Annotations on the New Testament.* Galatians to the Apocalypse. 1993
53. Stump, Ph. H. *The Reforms of the Council of Constance (1414-1418).* 1994
54. Giakalis, A. *Images of the Divine.* The Theology of Icons at the Seventh Ecumenical Council. With a Foreword by Henry Chadwick. 1994
55. Nellen, H. J. M. and Rabbie, E. (eds.). *Hugo Grotius – Theologian.* Essays in Honour of G. H. M. Posthumus Meyjes. 1994
56. Trigg, J. D. *Baptism in the Theology of Martin Luther.* 1994
57. Janse, W. *Albert Hardenberg als Theologe.* Profil eines Bucer-Schülers. 1994
59. Schoor, R. J. M. van de. *The Irenical Theology of Théophile Brachet de La Milletière (1588-1665).* 1995
60. Strehle, S. *The Catholic Roots of the Protestant Gospel.* Encounter between the Middle Ages and the Reformation. 1995
61. Brown, M. L. *Donne and the Politics of Conscience in Early Modern England.* 1995
62. Screech, M. A. (ed.). *Richard Mocket, Warden of All Souls College, Oxford, Doctrina et Politia Ecclesiae Anglicanae.* An Anglican Summa. Facsimile with Variants of the Text of 1617. Edited with an Intro duction. 1995
63. Snoek, G. J. C. *Medieval Piety from Relics to the Eucharist.* A Process of Mutual Interaction. 1995
64. Pixton, P. B. *The German Episcopacy and the Implementation of the Decrees of the Fourth Lateran Council, 1216-1245.* Watchmen on the Tower. 1995
65. Dolnikowski, E. W. *Thomas Bradwardine: A View of Time and a Vision of Eternity in Fourteenth-Century Thought.* 1995
66. Rabbie, E. (ed.). *Hugo Grotius, Ordinum Hollandiae ac Westfrisiae Pietas (1613).* Critical Edition with Translation and Commentary. 1995
67. Hirsh, J. C. *The Boundaries of Faith.* The Development and Transmission of Medieval Spirituality. 1996
68. Burnett, S. G. *From Christian Hebraism to Jewish Studies.* Johannes Buxtorf (1564-1629) and Hebrew Learning in the Seventeenth Century. 1996
69. Boland O.P., V. *Ideas in God according to Saint Thomas Aquinas.* Sources and Synthesis. 1996
70. Lange, M.E. *Telling Tears in the English Renaissance.* 1996
71. Christianson, G. and Izbicki, T.M. (eds.). *Nicholas of Cusa on Christ and the Church.* Essays in Memory of Chandler McCuskey Brooks for the American Cusanus Society. 1996
72. Mali, A. *Mystic in the New World.* Marie de l'Incarnation (1599-1672). 1996
73. Visser, D. *Apocalypse as Utopian Expectation (800-1500).* The Apocalypse Commentary of Beren gaudus of Ferrières and the Relationship between Exegesis, Liturgy and Iconography. 1996
74. O'Rourke Boyle, M. *Divine Domesticity.* Augustine of Thagaste to Teresa of Avila. 1997
75. Pfizenmaier, T. C. *The Trinitarian Theology of Dr. Samuel Clarke (1675-1729).* Context, Sources, and Controversy. 1997
76. Berkvens-Stevelinck, C., Israel, J. and Posthumus Meyjes, G. H. M. (eds.). *The Emergence of Tolerance in the Dutch Republic.* 1997
77. Haykin, M. A. G. (ed.). *The Life and Thought of John Gill (1697-1771).* A Tercentennial Appreciation. 1997
78. Kaiser, C. B. *Creational Theology and the History of Physical Science.* The Creationist Tradition from Basil to Bohr. 1997
79. Lees, J. T. *Anselm of Havelberg.* Deeds into Words in the Twelfth Century. 1997
80. Winter, J. M. van. *Sources Concerning the Hospitallers of St John in the Netherlands, 14th-18th Centuries.* 1998
81. Tierney, B. *Foundations of the Conciliar Theory.* The Contribution of the Medieval Canonists from Gratian to the Great Schism. Enlarged New Edition. 1998
82. Miernowski, J. *Le Dieu Néant.* Théologies négatives à l'aube des temps modernes. 1998
83. Halverson, J. L. *Peter Aureol on Predestination.*A Challenge to Late Medieval Thought. 1998.
84. Houliston, V. (ed.). *Robert Persons, S.J.: The Christian Directory (1582).* The First Booke of the Christian Exercise, appertayning to Resolution. 1998
85. Grell, O. P. (ed.). *Paracelsus.* The Man and His Reputation, His Ideas and Their Transformation. 1998
86. Mazzola, E. *The Pathology of the English Renaissance.* Sacred Remains and Holy Ghosts. 1998.
87. 88. Marsilius von Inghen. *Quaestiones super quattuor libros sententiarum.* Super Primum. Bearbeitet von M. Santos Noya. 2 Bände. I. Quaestiones 1-7. II. Quaestiones 8-21. 2000

89. Faupel-Drevs, K. *Vom rechten Gebrauch der Bilder im liturgischen Raum.* Mittelalterliche Funktionsbestimmungen bildender Kunst im *Rationale divinorum officiorum* des Durandus von Mende (1230/11296). 1999
90. Krey, P. D. W. and Smith, L. (eds.). *Nicholas of Lyra.* the Senses of Scripture. 2000
92. Oakley, F. *Politics and Eternity.* Studies in the History of Medieval and Early-Modern Political Thought. 1999
93. Pryds, D. *The Politics of Preaching.* Robert of Naples (1309-1343) and his Sermons. 2000
94. Posthumus Meyjes, G. H. M. *Jean Gerson – Apostle of Unity.* His Church Politics and Ecclesiology. Translated by J. C. Grayson. 1999
95. Berg, J. van den. *Religious Currents and Cross-Currents.* Essays on Early Modern Protestantism and the Protestant Enlightenment. Edited by J. de Bruijn, P. Holtrop, and E. van der Wall. 1999
96. Izbicki, T. M. and Bellitto, C. M. (eds.). *Reform and Renewal in the Middle Ages and the Renaissance.* Studies in Honor of Louis Pascoe, S. J. 2000
97. Kelly, D. *The Conspiracy of Allusion.* Description, Rewriting, and Authorship from Macrobius to Medieval Romance. 1999
98. Marrone, S. P. *The Light of Thy Countenance.* Science and Knowledge of God in the Thirteenth Century. 2 volumes. 1. A Doctrine of Divine Illumination. 2. God at the Core of Cognition. 2001
99. Howson, B. H. *Erroneous and Schismatical Opinions.* The Question of Orthodoxy regarding the Theology of Hanserd Knollys (c. 1599-169)). 2001
100. Asselt, W. J. van. *The Federal Theology of Johannes Cocceius (1603-1669).* 2001
101. Celenza, C.S. *Piety and Pythagoras in Renaissance Florence the* Symbolum Nesianum. 2001
102. Dam, H.- J. van (ed.), *Hugo Grotius, De imperio summarum potestatum circa sacra.* Critical Edition with Introduction, English translation and Commentary. 2 volumes. 2001
103. Bagge, S. *Kings, Politics, and the Right Order of the World in German Historiography c. 950-1150.* 2002
104. Steiger, J. A. *Fünf Zentralthemen der Theologie Luthers und seiner Erben.* Communicatio – Imago – Figura – Maria – Exempla. Mit Edition zweier christologischer Frühschriften Johann Gerhards. 2002
105. Izbicki, T. M. and Bellitto, C. M. (eds.). *Nicholas of Cusa and his Age: Intellect and Spirituality.* Essays Dedicated to the Memory of F. Edward Cranz, Thomas P. McTighe and Charles Trinkaus. 2002
106. Hascher-Burger, U. *Gesungene Innigkeit.* Studien zu einer Musikhandschrift der Devotio moderna (Utrecht, Universiteitsbibliotheek, MS 16 H 94, olim B 113). Mit einer Edition der Gesänge. 2002
107. Bolliger, D. *Infiniti Contemplatio.* Grundzüge der Scotus- und Scotismusrezeption im Werk Huldrych Zwinglis. 2003
108. Clark, F. *The 'Gregorian'* Dialogues *and the Origins of Benedictine Monasticism.* 2002
109. Elm, E. *Die Macht der Weisheit.* Das Bild des Bischofs in der *Vita Augustini* des Possidius und andere spätantiken und frühmittelalterlichen Bischofsviten. 2003
110. Bast, R. J. (ed.). *The Reformation of Faith in the Context of Late Medieval Theology and Piety.* Essays by Berndt Hamm. 2004.
111. Heering, J. P. *Hugo Grotius as Apologist for the Christian Religion.* A Study of his Work *De Veritate Religionis Christianae* (1640). Translated by J.C. Grayson. 2004.
112. Lim, P. C.- H. *In Pursuit of Purity, Unity, and Liberty.* Richard Baxter's Puritan Eccle siology in its Seventeenth-Century Context. 2004.
113. Connors, R. and Gow, A. C. (eds.). *Anglo-American Millennialism, from Milton to the Millerites.* 2004.
114. Zinguer, I. and Yardeni, M. (eds.). *Les Deux Réformes Chrétiennes.* Propagation et Diffusion. 2004.
115. James, F. A. III (ed.). *Peter Martyr Vermigli and the European Reformations*: Semper Reformanda. 2004.
116. Stroll, M. *Calixtus II (1119-1124).* A Pope Born to Rule. 2004.
117. Roest, B. *Franciscan Literature of Religious Instruction before the Council of Trent.* 2004.
118. Wannenmacher, J. E. *Hermeneutik der Heilsgeschichte. De septem sigillis* und die sieben Siegel im Werk Joachims von Fiore. 2004.
119. Thompson, N. *Eucharistic Sacrifice and Patristic Tradition in the Theology of Martin Bucer, 1534-1546.* 2005 .
120. Van der Kooi, C. *As in a Mirror. John Calvin and Karl Barth on Knowing God.* A Diptych. 2005.
121. Steiger, J. A. *Medizinische Theologie.* Christus medicus und theologia medicinalis bei Martin Luther und im Luthertum der Barockzeit. 2005.
122. Giakalis, A. *Images of the Divine.* The Theology of Icons at the Seventh Ecumenical Council – Revised Edition. With a Foreword by Henry Chadwick. 2005.
123. Heffernan, T. J. and Burman, T. E. (eds.). *Scripture and Pluralism.* Reading the Bible in the Religiously Plural Worlds of the Middle Ages and Renaissance. Papers Presented at the First Annual Symposium of the Marco Institute for Medieval and Renaissance Studies at the University of Tennessee, Knoxville, February 21-22, 2002. 2005.

124. Litz, G., Munzert, H. and Liebenberg, R. (eds.). *Frömmigkeit – Theologie – Frömmigkeitstheologie – Contributions to European Church History.*
125. Ferreiro, A. *Simon Magus in Patristic, Medieval and Early Modern Traditions.* 2005.
126. Goodwin, D. L. *"Take Hold of the Robe of a Jew".* Herbert of Bosham's Christian Hebraism. 2006.
127. Holder, R. W. *John Calvin and the Grounding of Interpretation.* Calvin's First Commentaries. 2006.
128. Reilly, D. J. *The Art of Reform in Eleventh-Century Flanders.* Gerard of Cambrai, Richard of Saint-Vanne and the Saint-Vaast Bible. 2006.
129. Frassetto, M. (ed.). *Heresy and the Persecuting Society in the Middle Ages.* Essays on the Work of R.I. Moore. 2006.
130. Walters Adams, G. *Visions in Late Medieval England.* Lay Spirituality and Sacred Glimpses of the Hidden Worlds of Faith. 2007.
131. Kirby, T. *The Zurich Connection and Tudor Political Theology.* 2007.
132. Mackay, C.S. *Narrative of the Anabaptist Madness.* The Overthrow of Münster, the Famous Metropolis of Westphalia (2 vols.). 2007.
133. Leroux, N.R. *Martin Luther as Comforter.* Writings on Death. 2007.
134. Tavuzzi, M. *Renaissance Inquisitors.* Dominican Inquisitors and Inquisitorial Districts in Northern Italy, 1474-1527. 2007.
135. Baschera, L. and C. Moser (eds.). *Girolamo Zanchi,* De religione christiana fides – Confession of Christian Religion (2 vols.). 2007.
136. Hurth, E. *Between Faith and Unbelief.* American Transcendentalists and the Challenge of Atheism. 2007.
137. Wilkinson R.J. *Orientalism, Aramaic and Kabbalah in the Catholic Reformation.* The First Printing of the Syriac New Testament. 2007.
138. Wilkinson R.J. *The Kabbalistic Scholars of the Antwerp Polyglot Bible.* 2007.
139. Boreczky E. *John Wyclif's Discourse On Dominion in Community.* 2007.
140. Dowd C. *Rome in Australia: The Papacy and Conflict in the Australian Catholic Missions, 1834-1884* (2 vols.). 2008.
141. Perrone S.T. *Charles V and the Castilian Assembly of the Clergy.* Negotiations for the Ecclesiastical Subsidy. 2008.
142. Smith, K.A. and S. Wells (eds.). *Negotiating Community and Difference in Medieval Europe.* Gender, Power, Patronage and the Authority of Religion in Latin Christendom. 2009.
143. Mixson, J.D. *Poverty's Proprietors.* Ownership and Mortal Sin at the Origins of the Observant Movement. 2009.
144. Moser, C. and P. Opitz (eds.). *Bewegung und Beharrung.* Aspekte des reformierten Protestantismus, 1520-1650. 2009.
145. Henriksen, E. *Milton and the Reformation Aesthetics of the Passion.* 2010.
146. Martínez, H.S. *Alfonso X, the Learned.* Translated by O. Cisneros. 2010.
147. Biller, P., Bruschi, C. and S. Sneddon(eds.). *Inquisitors and Heretics in Thirteenth-Century Languedoc.* Edition and Translation of Toulouse Inquisition Depositions, 1273-1282. 2010.
148. Dahl, G. *Book Collections of Clerics in Norway, 1650–1750.* 2010.
149. Travassos Valdez, M.A. *Historical Interpretations of the "Fifth Empire".* The Dynamics of Periodization from Daniel to António Vieira, S.J. 2010.
150. Roldán-Figueroa, R. *The Ascetic Spirituality of Juan de Ávila (1499-1569).* 2010.
151. Abé, T. *The Jesuit Mission in New France.* A New Interpretation in the Light of the Earlier Jesuit Experience in Japan. 2010.
152. Alonso-Lasheras, D. *Luis de Molina's* De Iustitia et Iure. Justice as Virtue in an Economic Context. 2011.

brill.nl/shct

www.ingramcontent.com/pod-product-compliance
Lightning Source LLC
LaVergne TN
LVHW021545021026
849161LV00005BA/1148